Infrastructure Leader's Guide to Google Cloud

Lead Your Organization's Google Cloud Adoption, Migration and Modernization Journey

Jeremy Lloyd

Foreword by Nirav Mehta
Senior Director of Product Management,
Google Cloud

Apress®

Infrastructure Leader's Guide to Google Cloud: Lead Your Organization's Google Cloud Adoption, Migration and Modernization Journey

Jeremy Lloyd
Guildford, UK

ISBN-13 (pbk): 978-1-4842-8819-1
https://doi.org/10.1007/978-1-4842-8820-7

ISBN-13 (electronic): 978-1-4842-8820-7

Managing Director, Apress Media LLC: Welmoed Spahr
Acquisitions Editor: Celestin Suresh John
Development Editor: Laura Berendson
Coordinating Editor: Mark Powers

Cover designed by eStudioCalamar

Cover image by Alp Duran on Unsplash (http://www.unsplash.com)

Distributed to the book trade worldwide by Apress Media, LLC, 1 New York Plaza, New York, NY 10004, U.S.A. Phone 1-800-SPRINGER, fax (201) 348-4505, e-mail orders-ny@springer-sbm.com, or visit www.springeronline.com. Apress Media, LLC is a California LLC and the sole member (owner) is Springer Science + Business Media Finance Inc (SSBM Finance Inc). SSBM Finance Inc is a **Delaware** corporation.

For information on translations, please e-mail booktranslations@springernature.com; for reprint, paperback, or audio rights, please e-mail bookpermissions@springernature.com.

Apress titles may be purchased in bulk for academic, corporate, or promotional use. eBook versions and licenses are also available for most titles. For more information, reference our Print and eBook Bulk Sales web page at http://www.apress.com/bulk-sales.

Any source code or other supplementary material referenced by the author in this book is available to readers on GitHub (https://github.com/Apress/). For more detailed information, please visit http://www.apress.com/source-code.

Printed on acid-free paper

For my wife and parents, thank you for your encouragement and support during the writing of this book.

And for my daughter, thank you for the distractions, laughter, and joy you bring.

Table of Contents

About the Author

Jeremy Lloyd has over 20 years of experience in IT. He has spent the last eight years helping organizations worldwide adopt and migrate to the cloud. During this time, he's guided and advised technology leaders from some of the world's most well-known companies on their cloud adoption, migration, and modernization strategies. In addition, he is a mentor to technology leaders and a speaker at numerous events across the United Kingdom and internationally.

About the Technical Reviewer

Raymond Blum leads a global team of Google engineers that develops tools to support emerging platforms and architectures. Based in New York, he was previously a Site Reliability Engineer at Google, helping to ensure that Gmail, Ads, and other Google services were always available and safe. A passionate champion of dependable infrastructure, Raymond has contributed to Data Integrity best practices published by Google and by the Association for Computing Machinery.

In previous lives, Raymond developed software for media and financial companies and ran an Internet service hosting company. In what spare time exists, he reads everything that he can and makes friends with robots.

Acknowledgments

Writing a book on technology is rarely a solo endeavor, which is true of this book. In no particular order, I'd like to thank Andy MacInnes for encouraging me to openly discuss the book with others. I'd also like to thank Elvin Turner for his passion toward this project and for his wisdom and experience in helping me navigate the writing process. Paul Ingram for his attention to detail. Mike Smith for guidance around Google Cloud security. Bogdan Alecu for his experience around CI/CD and infrastructure as code. Michael Lerperger for his insights and early access into Google's Hybrid Subnets. I'd like to thank Mike Conner, whose decision to allow remote working gave me the much-needed time to complete this book. And Raymond Blum, the technical reviewer of the book, for his insights and comments that helped put shape to it.

To the many Googlers out there who have been so supportive, Brendan Hills, Dan Perry, Attila Szabo, Sanjay Jacob, Nirav Mehta, Pete Barlow, Mehran Alavi, and so many others, you know who you are; thank you all!

Foreword

Google Cloud has been the fastest-growing "hyperscaler" for some time now with high feature velocity and a rapidly multiplying customer base. As a product leader within Google Cloud, I am always looking for ways to help our customers stay abreast with this pace of innovation and to gain familiarity with the platform. This is why when Jeremy shared his book with me, I was intrigued.

The book is an effective and comprehensive introduction to Google Cloud infrastructure but goes beyond it to provide strategic perspective for infrastructure leaders who are considering adoption of Google Cloud.

The structured information and thoughtful advice in this book will be helpful to anyone looking to gain a basic understanding of Google Cloud and to get oriented to using Google Cloud for traditional applications, cloud-native applications, and everything in between.

Nirav Mehta
Sr. Director of Product Management, Google Cloud

Introduction

Cloud computing is often referred to as one of, if not the most significant, technological advancements in our lifetimes to date. There is no question that cloud computing offers the capabilities and scale required to satisfy the most demanding use cases. There are numerous case studies of organizations that have undergone a successful migration or transformation with a cloud provider, and of course, there are the consumer-facing giants who have only been able to scale and grow at speed thanks to cloud providers. I'm talking about the likes of Spotify, Airbnb, Uber, and so many more.

In a world where the only constant is change and with every industry facing disruption from startups who think and operate differently, it leaves many organizations across the world at risk of becoming left behind. Add to this disruption the increasing external pressures from industry governing bodies and governments to reduce carbon emissions by certain timelines.

And yet the same technology and ways of working that the disruptors use exist for traditional organizations to take advantage of. And this technology also helps to run infrastructure in a more environmentally friendly way than you can possibly create yourselves. The challenges for traditional organizations lie in successfully navigating the journey from the old world to this new cloud world to harness the capabilities cloud can provide.

Cloud introduces new terms to understand, approaches and frameworks to decipher, and a continuous stream of new capabilities through products and services to land workloads into and modernize with. It can require a considerable amount of time and effort to learn and get up to speed. Once you reach a level of proficiency, something new will come along that needs to be implemented. The process of keeping your knowledge and skills current is known as continuous learning and is discussed in Part 3.

Cloud adoption has far-reaching implications, beyond just technology. It affects core ways of working and the surrounding processes that organizations have become used to over the past few decades. As IT's role in an organization has traditionally been the maintainers of the status quo, the gatekeepers to prevent change and innovation of key workloads, it has meant a rise in people outside of IT making or influencing decisions that relate to an organization's IT infrastructure. In fact, that is why I've purposely used the term *Infrastructure Leader* in the title of this book, as the number of people in an organization who now have the ability to make or influence decisions that directly affect the IT landscape has massively increased over the last decade or two. I'm talking about those decisions made outside of IT to purchase a product or service from a vendor that needs to be deployed somewhere, or if it's Software-as-a-Service (SaaS), then it needs single sign-on capability and suddenly it's an IT issue. Gartner's research says, "on average, 41% of employees outside of IT - or business technologists - customize or build data or technology solutions" (Gartner, 2021).

Who Is This Book For

This book should serve as a guide for IT directors and managers or heads of operations, engineering, and infrastructure. It should also be relevant to the numerous roles within organizations that are focused on business outcomes and reducing time to value. Typically in those latter roles, the underlying infrastructure and governance isn't something they want to think about let alone manage, but by making decisions to use a specific product or service, they are directly altering the organization's IT landscape, whether the IT function is aware of it or not! This is commonly referred to as Stealth or Shadow IT. If you fit in this category, then my aim is for you to understand the wider considerations that should be in place to ensure your organization's data and workloads remain safe and operational.

So, this book is aimed at anyone who has the ability to influence or make decisions relating to IT infrastructure. Prior understanding of basic cloud computing concepts is helpful but not critical. This book aims to guide navigating Google Cloud (formerly known as Google Cloud Platform or GCP) adoption and set you up for success in the cultural changes needed, migration strategies, and your cloud operating model, giving clarity and direction to current and aspiring infrastructure leaders. The focus is on the hosting platform side, not Google Workspace. However, I will briefly cover Google Workspace in Part 7.

Why I Wrote This Book

After speaking with many customers at various stages of Google Cloud adoption, from those weighing up Google Cloud against other clouds, or are partway or fully migrated into Google Cloud, to those who've found they've inherited a Google Cloud estate after a particular business units have started using it as shadow IT. It was clear that a common theme was a lack of knowledge and insights into where and how to get started with Google Cloud, the migration strategies and processes, and general cloud adoption guidance.

Another reason was to encourage others to follow a career journey that cloud can offer them. I'm sure you'll have read articles or watched videos that talked about IT infrastructure roles being redundant with the emergence of cloud ten+ years ago. Well they got that wrong, didn't they! While cloud has fundamentally changed the skills required and the day-to-day activities, as I will cover within the book, the demand for the core skills is high. This book will help you understand what cloud skills you require and how you and your team can learn them.

Also when I look introspectively, what is the impact I can have on the biggest challenges facing the world today? If I can help hundreds more customers move tens of thousands of servers to Google Cloud data centers, running on carbon-free energy or, at a minimum, having a carbon-neutral footprint, enabling them to shut down their on-prem, then it's the minimum I can do to make a difference.

How This Book Is Organized

I've broken down this book into seven logical parts that take you through the cloud adoption journey:

- Part 1, Understanding Why Google Cloud Is Used

- Part 2, Business and Cloud Strategies

- Part 3, Organizational Readiness and Change

- Part 4, Migration Journey

- Part 5, Cloud-Native

- Part 6, Day 2 Operations

- Part 7, Productivity and Collaboration

PART I

Understanding Why Google Cloud Is Used

In Part 1, I explain what, and who, an infrastructure leader is. I'll cover the challenges facing IT/infrastructure leaders today. I will then cover a brief history of Google and Google Cloud before going deeper into why you should use Google Cloud.

CHAPTER 1

Introduction

Let's start with covering who the infrastructure leader is and the types of varied challenges they face.

The Infrastructure Leader

What Does an Infrastructure Leader Do? Who Is an Infrastructure Leader?

An infrastructure leader or a leader in infrastructure isn't a term bound by a particular job title or responsibility. However, it is noted that certain roles I've mentioned earlier have traditionally been directly linked to IT infrastructure roles and responsibilities. And if your organization owns and maintains physical assets, then it is likely you'll associate infrastructure leaders with those traditional IT roles. After all, someone has to manage the costs related to keeping the hardware operational and up-to-date. So to understand who an infrastructure leader is, let's first look at the origins of the two words.

The word leader has origins stemming from an Anglo-Saxon Old English word for *lead* which was *loedan*, the casual form of *lithan* - to travel. Around 800 years ago, the definition of *lead* was "to guide with reference to action and opinion."

The origin of the word infrastructure comes from the Latin *infra* meaning "below, underneath" and *structura* meaning "a fitting together, adjustment; a building, mode of building" and figuratively, "arrangement, order." It was the French in 1887 who joined the words to form *infrastructure*, defined as "the installations that form the basis for any operation or system. Originally in a military sense."

So based on that, the role of the infrastructure leader is "to guide with reference to action and opinion how to fit together the underlying installations for any operation or system."

© Jeremy Lloyd 2023
J. Lloyd, *Infrastructure Leader's Guide to Google Cloud*, https://doi.org/10.1007/978-1-4842-8820-7_1

The ability to guide others with action and opinion doesn't mean you have to be a senior leader telling a team that you directly manage what to do. Being a leader doesn't mean you have to have line management responsibilities. As research has shown, it's about inspiring and motivating those around you (Forsgren et al., 2018).

How does this align to the traditional IT function?

Rather well as it turns out. With traditional on-prem IT infrastructure, the infrastructure leaders typically guide/manage or are directly involved in building, deploying, testing, and maintaining the assets that enable workloads/applications to run and serve the business needs.

How does it fit in the context of Google Cloud?

Well, with Google Cloud democratizing IT infrastructure for anyone and potentially everyone to consume, it means that in today's world, so many different roles within an organization can now make or influence IT infrastructure decisions. However, whether it's someone from within IT or outside of it, the infrastructure leader will still be a person who is guiding others on how to get a workload operational on Google Cloud to fulfill a business need.

What Are the Characteristics and Softer Skills of an Infrastructure Leader

- Can communicate messages clearly and concisely for nontechnical audiences

- Can collaborate as part of a team, treat other people's opinions with respect, and gain followers through an ability to respectfully challenge peers and leaders while maintaining integrity

- Has a passion for what the organization does and the part they play in it

- Has persistence in the face of closed doors and rejection

- Can tell a story that inspires and influences others

Types of Infrastructure Leaders

While working with organizations across different industries and of all types of sizes, I found common recurring patterns among the people I was engaged with and in turn the organization they work for. The patterns would show distinct eras of IT capability and how people and organizations generally followed the same evolutionary path when it came to the cloud.

This led me to classify the infrastructure leaders and their respective organizations into four generations as shown in Figure 1-1. With the delineation done by where your IT infrastructure currently exists and what your IT operating model is. With first generation at the top and with fourth generation at the bottom:

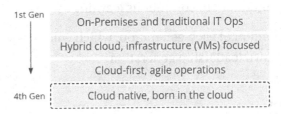

Figure 1-1. *The evolution of the generations*

Decoupling the two is important for several reasons. An organization that is currently first or second generation and has objectives to become a third generation will require experienced cloud leaders. In doing so, it has proven to increase the chances of successful adoption and migration initiatives and deliver them on-time or faster than expected. This is because those leaders can foresee the typical challenges as they've experienced them before.

Understanding which generation of infrastructure leader you are, or your organization is, can depend on several factors. The generation alignment to your organization is based on where your IT infrastructure currently resides, which can be identified by answering these questions:

- Where is your IT infrastructure now?

- How did it get there?

If it's on-prem with no cloud infrastructure, then you are first gen. If you have some on-prem and some cloud, then you are hybrid, so a second gen. If you are all-in on cloud but in order to get there you undertook a migration, then you are third gen. And finally if you are all-in on cloud but had no migration, then you are a 4th gen.

To classify your current leadership generation depends on several factors:

- The time when you first got involved in IT

- The age of the organization you currently work in (do they have technical debt on-prem)

- The pace at which that organization evolves (Waterfall approach, project mindset vs. Agile and Product mindset)

- Your own persistence and determination to affect change within your organization

- Your own commitment to continuous learning

Let's look at the definition of each generation, which will help you align your organizations and your own leadership generation.

First Generation

As a first generation, your organization existed before cloud computing did. Your physical infrastructure will most likely have evolved from mainframes (though they may still exist!) to physical servers and then hypervisors and virtual machines. It's likely your on-prem estate is now a mix of physical and virtual servers. Your IT operations will have also evolved from perhaps following the IT Infrastructure Library (ITIL) v1 to running parts of the ITIL v3 framework. As your infrastructure and applications have grown in usage and complexity, you probably find making changes to your IT operating model to say ITIL v4 a stretch goal.

As a first generation leader, the focus has been on stability, from both the physical infrastructure and application layer. And the common perspectives of change equals business disruption, and that could mean revenue loss, reputational damage, and more. Of course when changes can be made outside of the change control process and when application testing is performed in an environment that differs from production, it's no wonder that updates and releases strike fear among the teams involved.

Yet you don't have to look far to find a cloud provider showcasing a global organization that was on-prem and has made the move to the cloud. These case studies cover all industries from the ones with low compliance and regulatory standards to those in highly regulated industries such as financial services.

They've made the move fully or partly to adopting cloud. They've assessed their risks of change leading to service interruption and potential revenue loss vs. the risk of being left behind by not embracing the opportunities cloud enables. There are sadly too many examples of organizations who didn't embrace change fast enough, from Blockbuster to Blackberry: their fated history is well known.

How did other first generation organizations progress?

They reached a level of awareness, internally or by bringing in a partner, where they chose to define a cloud adoption strategy. It's what I call the strategic adoption phase. Some organizations have taken that a step further and gone to the organization transformation phase. We'll discuss these concepts in more detail in a later chapter.

As an infrastructure leader, taking a first generation organization to a second or hopefully third generation is a career-high point. It's a journey not for the faint-hearted, and that could last several years for larger organizations.

Ask yourself why you are still first generation in your current role? Is it the organization's aversion to risk? Or is it your own personal factors such as not having the awareness and knowledge to guide your organization from one generation to the next?

Whether it's you, your organization, or both who are currently first generation, I hope this book can give you the knowledge on how to progress on your Google Cloud journey and reach second and third generations.

Second Generation

Second generation infrastructure leaders will often have a cloud-first principle. Again the organizations in this generation have existed since before the cloud. To be a second generation, you'll have extended your network to the cloud. And you'll either have migrated some workloads or built some cloud-first workloads.

However, second generation organizations still have to deal with technical debt such as network connectivity between offices and customers and telephony systems that use private branch exchange (PBX) technology that requires physical kit on-prem or a mainframe that still serves mission-critical workloads/applications. These challenges can leave an inexperienced second gen leader in a paused state, unwilling or unable to get the backing to replace and modernize the challenges into cloud-based solutions.

Second generation leaders still have a focus more aligned to traditional IT operations. Stability is still prioritized, and IT objectives aren't always aligned with the organizations. IT operations revolve around hypervisor hosts, VMs, networks, and storage arrays on-prem. In the cloud environment it's mostly virtual machines, virtual private clouds (networks), and storage. Some experimentation with cloud managed services and writing infrastructure and policies with code takes place.

Solving exactly these challenges is what separates a second gen from a third gen. To remove the remaining on-prem challenges, you'll need the following abilities:

- Navigate a path to the right stakeholders and have them aligned on the business benefits.

- Have a clear cloud adoption strategy and the first draft of a cloud operating model.

- Take people on a journey and implement the required cultural changes.

- Secure a budget.

- Select the right partners and tools to accelerate the journey.

- Build in-house skills and capabilities.

Third Generation

A third generation organization has undergone a migration to cloud. Their ways of working are more aligned with a cloud operating model. IT is seen by the organization as value creation and is aligned with the organization's objectives.

The workload landscape has been rationalized, and workloads have been migrated, modernized, transformed, retired, or replaced. Often the noncompetitively differentiating workloads have been outsourced to a managed service provider (MSP) who'll provide the stability that these static or slow to change workloads require.

Third generation leaders have taken an organization from second or even firstgeneration through to operating fully in the cloud; they've surmounted the challenges using various techniques.

They have steered their organization through a cultural transformation, tackling areas like changing the mindset from project-based to product-based. They've ensured that the organization has the right skills in-house to perform cloud-native development.

The in-house team's focus is on reducing time-to-market through operational efficiencies and innovation and the freedom to operate using Agile methodologies and Site Reliability Engineer (SRE). It's this focus on cloud-native development that positions the organization ahead of the competition in their respective industry.

Fourth Generation

Slightly outside of the evolutionary model that defines the previous generations. However, there are absolutely a fast-growing number of fourth gen organizations, unburdened by on-prem technical debt or a cost structure and operating model that were designed to fit the needs of companies 20 years ago.

However, it should be noted that seemingly small and simple decisions made in the architecture early on can become painful and expensive once the organization has grown. Commonly referred to as growing pains, they are still a form of technical debt and will need investment in time, money, and skills to resolve, for example, where you decide to physically host your workloads or the products and tools you use to perform build, release, and deployment processes. Other more complex examples would be how you handle application state or how you can support database sharding.

The fourth gen is born in the cloud. They are organizations that never needed to consider the purchase of physical kit to operate their own infrastructure, upon which to build and run their workloads. They lead with a Software-as-a-Service (SaaS) first approach when it comes to purchasing business applications to fulfill needs of the organization, such as customer relationship management (CRM) products.

Fourth gen leaders operate with a product mindset (I will discuss more on this later). There are clearly defined guiding principles that drive the teams to have the mindset to see the importance of their role and the value they can bring, which means they are looking for improvements and innovation. Fourth gen leaders understand the shift-left concept and have or are trying to implement that across multiple areas such as security, financial operations, and compliance.

Moving Organizations Forward

By knowing which generation you currently align with, it helps you frame the sort of likely challenges you will face during adoption and migration to Google Cloud. It also helps you use the information in this book to your best advantage to overcome those challenges and set some direction. You are the leader who can start your organization's Google Cloud adoption momentum. Remember that it's the people within an organization that enable change and progress. And that will ultimately move your organization from one generation to the next.

Of course, you personally may find yourself in a role within an organization that you could identify as a second or third generation, but with another cloud provider. You might then challenge your current organization to adopt a multicloud strategy and go about building the business case for Google Cloud.

Or, you might find the experience you've gained could be put to use in moving a different organization forward with their Google Cloud adoption. In which case, look for roles within a first generation organization as this is where an experienced cloud leader can have maximum impact. However, given this is my classification system, you won't find it written within a job description.

So, when looking for new roles, I'd suggest you read between the lines on what a potential employer isn't asking for help with. In turn this will help you understand their current maturity and thinking. For example, if the infrastructure role (and similar IT engineering and operations roles) has no mention that they require skills in cloud technologies, this could mean the team advertising the role is focused on on-prem infrastructure, or it could mean there is no cloud usage within the organization at all. You'll need to do your research: review the organization's blogs and social media avenues they broadcast on to get a feel for what their focus is. Then be sure to ask the right questions during any interview stages to get a feel on if you could affect real change there and turn a first gen into a third gen organization.

If you are reading this book because you've just taken a new role in an organization that is looking to adopt Google Cloud or partway through a move then, in the conversations you are having, look for what is not being talked about. Assess where the gaps are in their strategies, as this helps to show the maturity and thinking of the infrastructure team and gives you a chance to make an impact with your experience.

Challenges

The challenges for an infrastructure leader are vast and varied. In my experience consulting with infrastructure leaders across a large number of organizations, I've found the following challenges come up time and time again:

- The effort and cost of dealing with legacy workloads and applications (technical debt).

- Shadow IT; it'll exist, how much do you know about it, how much can you control.

- Attitudes, having a team who fears change.

- Stale and outdated business processes such as change management.

- Accessibility issues with users requiring access from anywhere.

- Skills shortage.

- Talent retention.

- Security threats, data security, and securing the edge.

- Availability requirements of workloads, keeping the lights on 24/7/365.

- Pressure by governments to meet sustainability targets.

- Not being a blocker to progress and innovation.

With all of these challenges, how can you look to mitigate or solve them?

Use this book to help guide you in the people, process, and technology changes required to reduce or solve your current challenges by moving to Google Cloud. Your challenges might be different to those in the above list; if so, I'd love to hear what your current challenges are, so please do drop me an email.

Adopting Google Cloud is easy to say, but like adopting any cloud providers technology, it isn't without its own challenges. This book should act as your guide to ensure your move to Google Cloud has known and understood goals and business benefits, a solid migration plan, and a clear organizational readiness strategy. Staying where you are now doesn't move you or your organization forward. And the pace of change is only accelerating since the start of the COVID-19 pandemic. McKinsey has the "need for speed" as the number 4 in their top 5 CEO priorities (Hatami & Segel, 2021).

So on the journey to adopting and migrating workloads to Google Cloud, you as the infrastructure leader, the Google Cloud champion, and the person to guide with actions and opinions on how to undertake the journey, you may well find yourself out of your comfort zone. This book has been written to help orient your thoughts and direction, to help you enact lasting change within your organization.

Becoming a Profit Center

Another challenge of a different kind that I often encounter is the perception of the IT function from within the organization. How does your organization currently view the IT function? Are you classified as a cost center? Typically in most organizations, IT is, as it's not directly generating revenue, but what if it could? Or at a minimum what if you could become cost neutral, as in not make profit but also not generate a loss.

In order to make this change, you need to provide visibility into infrastructure costs and the effort to complete tasks. You'll also need to align the business and IT strategies so the workloads you are managing are known to be directly supporting business functions that serve the organization's objectives and goals.

Using Google Cloud opens up options that can help make this transition, but how?

- You can improve visibility into the infrastructure that a business unit's workloads consume by using Google Cloud project and labels.

- The above leads into accurate cost reporting which can enable cross-charging.

- Use the skills of your team to provide insights and guidance on the workload's use of technology.

- With Google Cloud, the activities and tasks you perform are against Google Cloud's APIs; therefore, they are repeatable and can be automated. This should lead you to being able to categorize the activities and tasks into a well-defined service catalog, with metrics such as the time it takes to complete and therefore the cost. Again this makes cross-charging simpler.

Summary

Cloud computing is here to stay; the benefits it offers are vast. To get you started, you should first understand the current generation of infrastructure leader you are. And you should be able to answer, what is the reason you are in that generation?

Whether you feel it's the organization that is defining your generation or it's your own factors such as lack of experience or knowledge with cloud, it is absolutely possible to move from one generation to the next through a process of continual learning for yourself and being a cloud advocate within your organization. The exception to that is a fourth generation, who don't have the limitations of having to deal with legacy applications or on-prem infrastructure.

Today's infrastructure leader faces huge pressure and a growing number of challenges. Coupled with navigating the complexity and challenges of adoption and migration to Google Cloud, it can leave you overwhelmed. That's why this book exists to guide you through it. Start with the aim of turning IT from a cost center into a profit center. Let that drive the conversations you have with your team and senior management.

CHAPTER 2

About Google and Google Cloud

Before I go into details about Google, please note how I am using the terms throughout this chapter and the rest of the book. I use "Google" to describe the search, ads, and YouTube organization. I use "Google Cloud" to describe the organization that oversees the productivity and collaboration tools and the hosting platform. Understanding these potentially subtle differences is key to avoiding any confusion further on.

Google was officially incorporated by Larry Page and Sergey Brin in 1998 as an internet search engine after the pair met at Stanford University in 1995. A couple of years after their official incorporation, they added AdWords to provide adverts to the search engine users.

Google's name is a play on the word Googol which is a mathematical term used to express a number 1 followed by 100 zeros. It's been said that this was a reflection of Larry and Sergey's mission which is "Our company mission is to organize the world's information and make it universally accessible and useful." (*How Google Search Works, Our Mission*)

Other notable product launches are as follows. Between 2002 and 2004, Google launched into news and email services. In 2005, Google Maps launched, and then in 2006 Google acquired YouTube. In 2008, Google launched the Chrome browser and the first Android powered phone and, most notably, Google App Engine. App Engine went on to form the basis on Google's entry into hyper-scale cloud computing. In 2010, Google started research into producing self-driving cars. In 2011, the Chrome Operating System launched. In 2011, Google+ launched as a social media platform. In 2012, Google launched the Google Glasses. In 2013, the Chromecast was launched, and in 2014 Google acquired DeepMind and artificial intelligence research organization. The year 2015 sees Google create a new parent organization called Alphabet, with Google

© Jeremy Lloyd 2023
J. Lloyd, *Infrastructure Leader's Guide to Google Cloud*, https://doi.org/10.1007/978-1-4842-8820-7_2

becoming an entity of that. Giving a new structure of CEOs at the subsidiary level, this has helped Alphabet's diverse thinking and innovation pace. In 2016, Google launched the Google Assistant and the Pixel smartphone.

Another element that helps with Google's continued innovation is that Googlers get what is known as 20% time. This means 80% of their time is spent on duties their role demands of them and the final 20% is spent on ideas to move Google forward. These ideas could range from something fairly aligned to a Googler's current role to solve a challenge they face, or it might be a passion or dream they've wanted to pursue. Gmail was in fact created in this manner and now has 1.5 billion users.

That leads me onto talking about some other impressive statistics. The Google of 2022 has nine products that have over 1 billion users each. YouTube and Android have over 2 billion users as of data published in 2021/2022. Google's search engine accounts for over 85% of the global market share (Statista, 2022) and processes over 3.5 billion searches every day.

Note there are a host of other successful and failed products that Google has undertaken over the years. However, let's go back to 2008 and the launch of Google App Engine and look at the evolution of that product into Google Cloud as we know it today.

Google Cloud

As mentioned earlier, Google launched a product in 2008 called Google App Engine. This is renowned as the first product of Google Cloud. Since then, Google Cloud has seen continued growth in its portfolio of products and services. Notable product releases were as follows:

- Cloud Storage made generally available in 2010

- Cloud SQL announced in preview but wasn't generally available until 2014

- BigQuery made generally available in 2012

- Compute Engine made generally available in 2012

- Google Kubernetes Engine 2014

The pace of product launches and releases has increased year on year. There are now around 200 products and services on the platform. And over the course of 2021, Google Cloud made 1500+ product and feature releases, which equates to 4 releases per day.

As I've previously mentioned, Google has vast experience with consumers, and Google Cloud has vast experience with enterprises. This positions Google Cloud with the experience and insights to truly transform organizations.

Indeed the Google Cloud of today is positioned uniquely as the data cloud, the open cloud, the green cloud, the industry cloud, and the transformation cloud. I'll unpack each of these in greater detail in the "Why Use Google Cloud" section shortly; however, here is a summary.

Google Cloud as the data cloud offers "a unified, open approach to data-driven transformation that is unmatched for speed, scale, and security with AI built in" (Google Cloud).

Google Cloud as the open cloud, with a clearly defined strategy and commitment to open source, hybrid, and multicloud. Building products and services that serve developers and infrastructure/operations teams with consistent experiences no matter where their workloads are deployed.

Google Cloud as the trusted cloud, with Google's pioneering zero trust approach at the very core of their services and operations, a secure by default principle, and a commitment to helping improve their customers' security operations.

Google Cloud as the green cloud, the cleanest cloud in the industry; Google has been carbon neutral since 2007 and has a goal to run all their data centers 24/7 on carbon-free energy by 2030.

Other noteworthy points, Google and Google Cloud have a strong commitment to being the most diverse, inclusive, and accessible companies in the industry. Google is investing in a skills boost program that aims to get 40 million people trained on Google Cloud.

Google Cloud's mission is to "accelerate organizations' ability to digitally transform their business with the best infrastructure, platform, industry solutions and expertise." Google's philosophy on data is that you own it, not Google, and as I'll discuss throughout this book the controls and logs that help you to trust in that statement.

Google Cloud Core Components

Let's start with understanding more about the physical side of Google Cloud with regions, zones, points of presence, and the network.

Regions and Zones

In Google Cloud terms, a region defines a geographical location where your Google Cloud products and services run. Each region is made up of three zones (with the exception to this being Iowa which has four). A zone is where you deploy your products and services; it's the physical data center.

The data centers are custom-designed and built by Google and use the defense in-depth principles and a "redundancy of everything" approach. Each zone is to be considered as a single failure domain with its own power, cooling, and networking. Therefore, if you need high availability of your workload, you would deploy it across two or more zones within a region.

If a zone was to be affected by a hardware, software, or network failure, then those platform services and control planes automatically switch to another zone without interruption to Google Cloud customers.

Zones are connected through Google's network backbone, which provides most users with a direct private connection between the zone and your Internet service provider (ISP), more on the network later.

With 35 regions across 23 countries from South America to Japan, Google Cloud should have regions close to where you need them as shown in Figure 2-1.

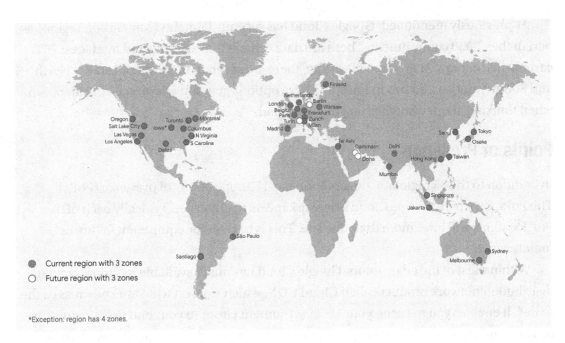

Figure 2-1. *Google Cloud's current and future regions*
Copyright Google Cloud

At the time of writing, there are nine new regions planned, which will all launch with three zones, meaning you won't need to sacrifice high availability if you deploy into a new region. Notable new regions are Google Cloud's first in the Middle East with Doha, Qatar, and the first in Africa with the announcement of the South African region.

Regions are named to denote first the continent; then a hyphen, followed by north, south, east, and west bearing based on the region's location within the continent; and then a number. The US regions break this rule by starting with a US prefix.

So for example, us-west1 would be in the United States and on the West coast, and europe-west1 would be Belgium.

Then finally, there is a zone suffix of a, b, or c. So europe-west1 becomes europe-west1-b to denote zone 2 within the Belgium region.

This is important because if you need high availability, you will need to ensure you deploy your workload into different zones within the region.

As previously mentioned, Google Cloud has recently launched low carbon regions as part of their 2030 commitment. These are data centers that are powered by at least 75% carbon-free energy. At the time of writing, there are seven of them spread across North and South America and two in Europe. These options give you additional consideration when thinking about where to run your workload.

Points of Presence

In addition to the 35 regions, Google Cloud has 173 edge points of presence (PoPs). The PoPs are where Google Cloud's network meets the Internet. Typically each of the PoP locations will have more than one site. This is to cater for equipment failure or maintenance.

Within most of the edge points, Google Cloud has made available its global content distribution network product called Cloud CDN, which runs on what are known as cache nodes. It enables you to cache your HTTP(s) content closer to your end users requesting it. These are the same CDN edge points used to serve Google.com to billions of users. However, it should be noted that Google.com also has a notion of Edge Nodes or Google Global Cache (GGC) of which there are roughly 7500.

The edge points of presence are connected to interconnection points. These are colocation facilities operated by 3rd parties across 113 locations as shown in Figure 2-2. Google Cloud partners with these facilities to enable Google Cloud customers to create a dedicated connection called a Dedicated Interconnect between the customer's on-premises locations and a colocation facility. This offers low latency access into a Google Cloud region.

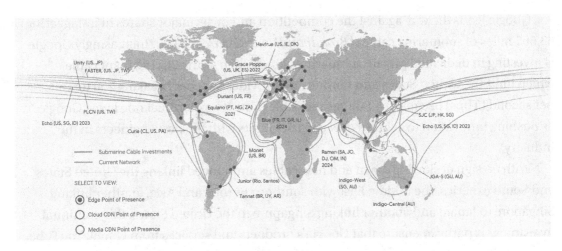

Figure 2-2. *Google Cloud's points of presence and current and future submarine- and land-based network links*

Copyright Google Cloud

Network

When it comes to building networks, Google knows a thing or two about that. Having been the world's Internet search engine of choice since the early 2000s, Google famously couldn't find the type of hardware available from existing network switch manufacturers that would give them the ability to scale and the bandwidth throughput required.

So they began developing their own with a vision that the hardware should be treated as a commodity and, instead, software should be used to control the hardware. So in 2005, they launched their top-of-rack networking switches and have been investing and innovating their network backbone ever since. In 2020, Google's network carries just under %20 of the world's Internet traffic (*The Global Internet Phenomena Report*, 2020). Google continues to show their commitment in this space "At Google, we've spent $30 billion improving our infrastructure over three years, and we're not done yet .... Google is committed to connecting the world and serving our Cloud customers"—Ben Treynor Sloss Google (Vice President, Engineering) 2018.

Google's network investments and innovation haven't stopped at land either. Having carried such a vast amount of global Internet traffic for over 20 years, Google needs to ensure content is available to users worldwide and fast. This has meant considerable investment in laying undersea cables, with USD 2 billion on networking alone in Asia Pacific since 2010 (*Economic Impact of Google's APAC Network Infrastructure*, 2020).

Google leads the way against the competition and owns major shares in a staggering 63,605 miles of submarine cables (*BroadbandNow Research*, 2021). Increasingly Google is investing in dedicated private submarine cables, such as the 2021 Dunant cable, which links the United States and Europe and provides a record breaking 250 terabits per second (Tbps) of capacity. Submarine cable industry experts acknowledge Google as pushing innovation to achieve new capacity limits with the best engineers in the industry.

With no sign of slowing down and new cables announced linking the United States and South America, the Middle East with southern Europe and Asia, another linking Singapore to Japan, and another linking Singapore to the United States, this continual investment is partly to ensure that Google's products and services from Gmail, YouTube, Maps, and more can continue to grow while also serving their existing customers' growing demands and partly enable Google Cloud customers who deploy products and services on the platform to reach their customers using Google's fast and secure network backbone.

So what does this mean to Google Cloud and your organization when you use it?

Well, it translates into better security with fewer hops between you and a Google Cloud data center as your data travels off the public Internet, higher availability as Google's network backbone has routing options as Google defines, and more available bandwidth which your workloads can consume which means lower latency.

In fact, "GCP has nearly 3x the throughput of AWS & Azure" (*Cockroach Labs, Cloud Report*, 2021). In 2021 over the Black Friday to Cyber Monday trading period, the ecommerce merchant Shopify which runs on Google Cloud was averaging 30TB per minute, which equated to 43PB a day and all with *"near-perfect uptime"* (Google Cloud, 2021).

So whether it's Google Meet which runs over the same network backbone and offers video calls with no lag between the United Kingdom and Seattle in the United States or even Melbourne in Australia or achieving near-perfect uptime while dealing with massive volumes of data, it has to be experienced to be believed.

Why Use Google Cloud

With a choice of cloud providers for you to choose from, how do you decide which platform to lead with?

That decision is multifaceted, but ultimately I believe that organizations will consume what they understand to be the strengths of a particular cloud provider. I have found that to not be the case when cloud provider selection has been an emotive decision. Such as making a selection based on having existing in-house skillset, or an existing relationship so the provider is trusted. Or it could simply be a like or dislike of a provider, which can be based simply on the experiences they've previously had with people who work at that provider.

If you look at the diversity of the existing customers that Google Cloud lists on their website and the case studies they have with those customers, you quickly learn that these organizations have understood how a relationship with Google Cloud is a collaborative partnership to take their use of technology and data to new levels. These organizations range from digital natives such as PayPal, Spotify, and Etsy to global organizations that have been in operation for decades, such as Deutsche Bank and P&G. They've chosen Google Cloud as their strategic partner in areas where Google Cloud has its strengths.

So what are Google Cloud's strengths, and what does Google want you to know about them?

Global Infrastructure

I've covered Google's global infrastructure in the Google Cloud Core Components section. Please see that section for more details.

Trust and Security

Security by Design

Google Cloud is designed and built around a defense-in-depth approach. That means there are progressive layers starting with the physical security of the hardware infrastructure, as in the actual data centers, through to operational security, such as how Google Cloud products and services (like Cloud Storage or BigQuery) are developed and deployed for us to consume.

Google custom-designs; their servers (removing components that usually introduce vulnerabilities, such as video cards, chipsets, and peripheral connectors); the underlying operating system (hardened version of Linux that has had all some tools and libraries removed and other controls moved into an unprivileged process that runs outside of the kerne); data center facilities and other safeguards like access cards, alarms, fencing and more.

Component vendors Google worked with are carefully vetted and regularly audited by Google to ensure the security and integrity of those components. This provides you with secure ways to communicate with Google Cloud, which means when you build and deploy workloads into Google Cloud, the way your end users consume the workload will also benefit from these security measures: be that from DDoS protection with Cloud Load Balancer through to default data encryption in transit, at rest, and many more.

Figure 2-3 gives a view of those infrastructure security layers. Start at the bottom with the physical infrastructure.

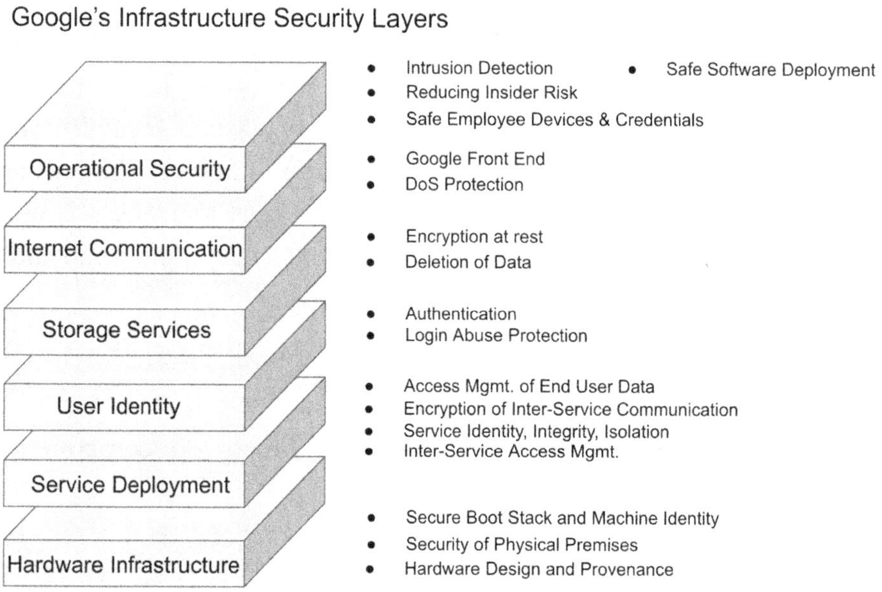

Google's Infrastructure Security Layers

- Intrusion Detection   • Safe Software Deployment
- Reducing Insider Risk
- Safe Employee Devices & Credentials

Operational Security
- Google Front End
- DoS Protection

Internet Communication
- Encryption at rest
- Deletion of Data

Storage Services
- Authentication
- Login Abuse Protection

User Identity
- Access Mgmt. of End User Data
- Encryption of Inter-Service Communication
- Service Identity, Integrity, Isolation
- Inter-Service Access Mgmt.

Service Deployment
- Secure Boot Stack and Machine Identity
- Security of Physical Premises
- Hardware Design and Provenance

Hardware Infrastructure

Figure 2-3. *The layers of Google's defense-in-depth approach*

Google operates a world-renowned dedicated security team. The team comprises hundreds of engineers who form part of the software engineering and operations division. Their activities are to do the following:

- Maintain the defense systems.

- Develop security review processes.

- Build and implement security infrastructure in alignment with Google's security policies.

- Monitor and detect security threats with tooling, penetration testing, and quality assurance measure, and perform security reviews and audits.

- Address information security threats.

- Oversee plans for the networks, systems, and services.

- Provide consulting services to Google's product and engineering teams.

Google's security team also consists of a dedicated team of security researchers, known as Project Zero. This team has been researching zero-day vulnerabilities in hardware and software since 2014. However, they received worldwide recognition for their efforts in discovering the Meltdown and Spectre vulnerabilities in 2017–2018.

And in case Google's security teams miss a vulnerability, Google has come up with a way to incentivize anyone in the world to identify vulnerabilities, called the Google Vulnerability Rewards Program, which sees a community of highly skilled people work hard to identify vulnerabilities and receive financial rewards that increase in value with the severity of the vulnerability. They've paid over $2 million to the community through this program. Of course, there is a leaderboard to gamify these so-called bug hunters into a friendly competition, which ultimately helps Google and you to benefit from a secure platform.

Encryption in Transit and at Rest

Google is a leader when it comes to encryption in transit and plans on staying there. Therefore, they continually invest in ongoing research and development in this space which only helps to keep Google Cloud customers and users of Google's consumer products safe.

All traffic into a Google Cloud data center routes through a custom reverse proxy known as the Google Front End (GFE). This detects and prevents malicious requests and Distributed Denial-of-Service (DDoS) attacks. The Google Front End is also used to secure connections between your device and the GFE and supports strong encryption protocols such as TLS. The workloads you want to build and run in Google Cloud can benefit from the features of GFE by using the Google Cloud Cloud Load Balancer, built on top of GFE.

For encryption at rest, the data stored in Google Cloud is split into chunks. A unique data encryption key is used to encrypt each chunk of data, with the key stored with each chunk. Key encryption keys (KEKs) then encrypt the data encryption keys. KEKs are stored exclusively inside Google's globally distributed and redundant central key management service (KMS).

Compliance Standards

When it comes to compliance, Google has a dedicated site called the compliance reports manager. This provides you with a single location to download third-party audits, certifications, and all other material related to Google Cloud's compliance with industry standards.

From an operational point of view, Google has a dedicated internal audit team that

- Reviews compliance and regulatory standards and laws from across the globe

- Assesses new standards to define control processes and systems required to meet them

- Facilitates third-party audits

Privacy

Google Cloud has publicly available privacy commitments:

1. ***You control your data.***

   Customer data is your data, not Google's. We only process your data according to your agreement(s).

2. ***We never use your data for ads targeting.***

   We do not process your customer data to create ads profiles or improve Google Ads products.

3. ***We are transparent about data collection and use.***

   We're committed to transparency, compliance with regulations like the GDPR, and privacy best practices.

4. ***We never sell customer data or service data.***

   We never sell customer data or service data to third parties.

5. ***Security and privacy are primary design criteria for all of our products.***

   Prioritizing the privacy of our customers means protecting the data you trust us with. We build the strongest security technologies into our products.

(*Privacy Resource Center, Google Cloud*)

Google logically isolates your data from other customers' data, even when the underlying infrastructure is shared. Google also provides you with controls over specific data sharing policies which you configure from within the Legal and Compliance settings within the Account setting in the console.

Data Deletion

Google provides a data deletion commitment that it can stand by due to their years of experience working with storage platforms, which process trillions and trillions of data elements. That deletion commitment doesn't come without its challenges though. When you store your data in Google Cloud, redundant copies are made using replication. That data replication could be local within a single zone, regional or global. This is critical for Google Cloud's products to offer you the high availability and scale your need.

When you click delete on a resource, project, or your account within Google Cloud, how do they process that request in a timely manner?

They've created a data deletion pipeline, which has different stages as shown in Figure 2-4.

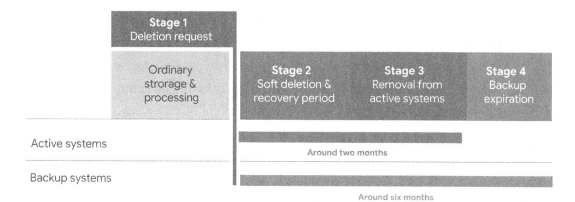

Figure 2-4. *Google Cloud's data deletion pipeline[1]*
Copyright Google Cloud (Data Deletion on Google Cloud Platform, 2018)

Stage 1 is the actual deletion request of a resource, project, or account that goes into the deletion pipeline.

Stage 2 is where the initial deletion request is typically actioned immediately. This means the pointers to your data get removed. However, Google does state there is a maximum of 24 hours where data can be in a marked for deletion state. Depending on the service, there is an internal recovery period of up to 30 days.

Stage 3 is where data deletion takes place in a couple of different ways depending on which Google Cloud product your data is being deleted from. Primarily data marked for deletion is marked as available storage and is simply overwritten over time, which is within 2 months of the deletion request.

The exception to this is Google Cloud Storage (GCS). Data marked for deletion in GCS gets deleted through an industry-standard technique called cryptographic erasure, which essentially deletes the encryption keys used to encrypt and decrypt the data. This process means that the fact that it takes 2 months to usually delete data from active systems through the process of cryptographic erasure makes GCS data unreadable and unusable the moment the key is deleted.

Stage 4 is where the removal from Google's backup systems is the same as stage 3. The process takes longer because the data is stored in aggregate snapshots. Backups expire regularly based on Google's predefined backup schedule, which is why this process can take around 6 months to complete.

---

[1]This image was created by Google Cloud, and is used according to the terms described in the Creative Common Attribution 4.0 License. Source: `https://cloud.google.com/docs/security/deletion`

However, Google does note that cryptographic erasure may occur before the backup containing the actual data has expired. In such situations, the data stored within the backup systems would be unrecoverable for the remainder of its duration in the backup systems.

Operational Privacy

From an operational point of view, Google has a dedicated privacy team separate from its security and product development teams. Their activities include the following:

- Review product design documentation.

- Perform code reviews to ensure privacy standards are met.

- Assist with releases for products that have strong privacy standards or that collect user data for administrative purposes.

- Oversee automated audit processes.

- Leads on continuous improvement initiatives around privacy best practices.

Transparency

Google strongly believes that trust is built through transparency. You'll find a large amount of publicly available documentation and whitepapers related to how Google handles activities like incidents, delegates privileged access, and handles information requests from governments and courts. Some of the controls Google provides are unique against their competitors, and Google continues to provide you with more controls against more Google Cloud products.

First let's look at Google Cloud's trust commitments:

1. **You own your data, not Google.**

2. **Google does not sell customer data to third parties.**

3. **Google Cloud does not use customer data for advertising.**

4. **All customer data is encrypted by default.**

5. **We guard against insider access to your data.**

6. **We never give any government entity "backdoor" access.**

7. **Our privacy practices are audited against international standards.**

(*Transparency & Data Protection, Google Cloud*)

Commitment 5 is interesting as Google is subject to a lot of policies imposed by governments and corporations. They believe we have a right to know how those policies affect privacy, security, and access to information. So they created a website which can be found at `https://transparencyreport.google.com/`. They were the first cloud provider to do this. In the site, you'll find reports that summarize the volume and nature of the various requests.

Incident response - Google handles incidents with a well-defined set of processes and procedures based around the Incident Command System (ICS) framework, originally developed by firefighters to tackle wildfires in California. The key concepts of ICS were adapted to be applicable to technology incidents. Google's framework is as follows:

- Identification, detection, and reporting through automation and manual processes

- Coordination, triage to assess nature and severity, and assigning an incident command who then assesses and aligns an incident response team, who then evaluates the effort

- Resolution, investigation, gathering of key facts, and addition of additional resources as needed. Containment and recovery, limiting damage while fixing the issue, and restoring affected systems. Developing a communication plan and communicating where appropriate.

- Closure a retrospective to capture lessons learnt, assign owners to any improvements that will take time to implement

- Continuous improvement, taking lessons learned, and improving processes to prevent the incident from occurring again

The full process is shown in Figure 2-5.

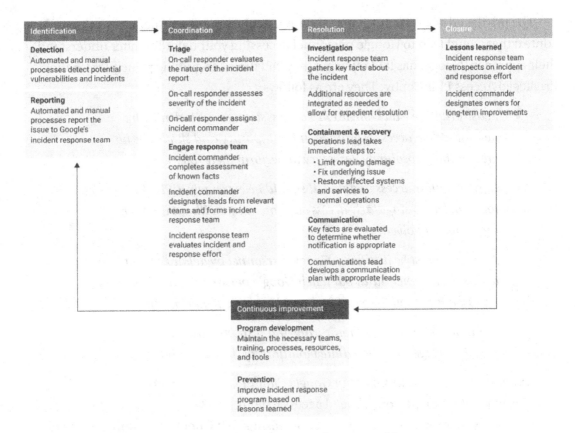

Figure 2-5. *Google Cloud's incident response framework[2]*
Copyright Google Cloud (Data Incident Response Process, 2018)

While all attempts and precautions are taken to ensure incidents do not happen when they do, Google has a good track record of resolving them in a timely manner. Google provides the history of outages and the root causes on this site `https://status.cloud.google.com/summary`.

Privileged access management - in the context of transparency, Google wants you to fully understand how they handle privileged access management. They've written a whitepaper devoted to this; see the summary for a link. It's important to state that by default Google personnel cannot access your data.

---

[2]This image was created by Google Cloud, and is used according to the terms described in the Creative Common Attribution 4.0 License. Source: `https://cloud.google.com/docs/security/incident-response`

The privileged access management whitepaper lays out the principles, limits, and context that would lead to Google personnel accessing your data. To better understand their approach, Google has laid out what they call their key guiding principles for their Privileged Access Philosophy. They are as follows:

- *Least-privilege – all Google employee system access is denied by default. When access is granted, it is temporary and should be no greater than absolutely necessary to perform their role.*

- *Limit singular access to data – it should be extremely difficult for Googlers to singularly access customer data without another individual involved.*

- *All access must be justified – Google personnel by default do not have access to customer data; but when Google personnel have privileged access, it is related to one of four valid business justifications.*

- *Monitor and alerting – monitoring and response processes exist to identify, triage, and remediate violations of these principles.*

(*Privileged Access Management in Google Cloud Platform, 2020*)

Why would Google personnel need access to your data?

Essentially there are a limited number of reasons that Google personnel will need to access your data; these are known as justification reason codes. There are four of these codes:

Customer initiated support - if you raise a support request with Google to assist you with resolving an issue, such as a Compute Engine instance not receiving traffic, then this request could result in Google support personnel who are working on the ticket with you being able to access your data. Note in cases like this, the Google support personnel would only be able to access low-sensitive data such as the Compute Engine name.

Outage or tool failure - in the rare instance of an outage or a tool failure, then Google personnel can access your data to perform a backup or recovery. This access is through tooling and is logged with the justification provided by the engineers and is audited and logged by Google's security response team. "Google will still generate Access Transparency logs that are visible to the customer during an outage if access to specific customers' data occurs. Engineers are not able to bypass the ACL for the resource in question under any circumstance, however, they will be able to access the data without customer approval." (*Privileged Access Management in Google Cloud Platform, 2020*)

Third-party legal requests - Google may receive direct requests from governments and courts asking for information. This happens to all technology and communication organizations. Once a request has been legally validated and it satisfies all of Google's legal requirements and policies, they will meet their legal obligations while taking measures to protect your privacy. One of Google's policies is to notify you if a request has been made directly to Google for information unless they are specifically prohibited by law. If a request is broad, they will seek to narrow that request to be more specific. The majority of requests are for Google Accounts and Gmail. A very small proportion relates to Google Cloud customers. These requests are what led Google to create the previously mentioned transparency report site.

Google-initiated review - these are also rare, but they are a review by Google personnel to keep your data safe and secure. A Google-initiated review is when checks need to be made in relation to security, fraud, abuse, or compliance breaches.

Google also provides you with the ability to monitor and control their access to data. This is done through two features. The first, called Access Transparency (AXT), gives you near real-time logs to easily audit the actions taken by the Google support personnel, answering who did what, where, and when. These logs can be collected and processed by any security monitoring tool, such as a security information and event management (SIEM) tool. This isn't turned on by default and will need to be enabled in the Google Cloud console. An active Google Cloud support package is a prerequisite at the time of writing to enable AXT.

The second feature is called Access Approval. This is another layer of control over and above the AXT. With Access Approval, Google personnel cannot access your data without your explicit approval. Notification for access comes through as an email or a Pub/Sub message, and you approve through the Google Cloud console.

Note that AXT must be enabled before you can use Access Approval, and Google does mention they may be unable to meet SLAs for chosen products due to support response times potentially increasing. Access Approval isn't available for all Google Cloud products. There is a list of products it does support available in the Access Approval documentation.

There are also some exclusions to Access Approval requests:

- System access to user content – these are programmatic processes that are authorized to perform activities like compression jobs or part of the content deletion process. These processes are subjected to Google's binary authorization checks to ensure job integrity.

- Manual access would be for cases when Google needs to comply with legal access requests and for outage access to resolve an outage or tooling failure. Both of these are described earlier in this chapter.

Key access justifications - if your organization needs the strongest levels of data access control, then you'll want to use Key Access Justifications in conjunction with Cloud External Key Manager (Cloud EKM). Cloud EKM is an externally hosted key management system that lets you store your encryption keys with a third party external to Google. Cloud EKM keys are hosted with providers such as Equinix, Fortanix, Ionic, Thales, and Unbound.

Using Cloud EKM means you have control over who accesses your external keys to decrypt data. With Key Access Justification enabled, it also offers an additional layer, which will allow you to approve or deny requests to use your external encryption keys. You also get visibility into every request to use your external encryption keys to change the state of the data.

What does this actually mean?

Ultimately, it means Google has no way to decrypt your data-at-rest without your approval. Requests will come with detailed justification, but you can deny any and all such requests.

Note, at the time of writing to enable this feature, you need to complete a form which is found on the Key Access Justification overview page. Also, please note that Cloud EKM isn't supported on all Google Cloud products. For a list of supported Google Cloud products, see the Cloud EKM overview page.

Third-party subprocessors - Google works with third parties such as customer support vendors. They maintain a public list of all their third-party subprocessors, the country they operate in, and the products and functions they perform. Third-party subprocessors must abide by the same compliance controls that Google does.

Data Cloud

When I consult with organizations who were early adopters of Google Cloud, the number 1 reason for their selection relates to data use cases. It might be down to Google Cloud's data analytics, databases, or artificial intelligence/machine learning capabilities. The fact is they trust Google when it comes to their data strategy. And that's because these forward-thinking, data-aware organizations knew that it was Google who led the charge to solve complex data challenges at scale, which is no surprise when you think back to their mission statement I mentioned earlier. When you combine their mission, experience, and Google's tendency to open source products and tools, it's a smart partner to pick. It enabled those early adopters to access products such as BigTable and BigQuery, which helped them solve complex data challenges faster than their competition. I will discuss the relationship that Google Cloud has with open source in the next section.

BigQuery, made available in 2012, was Google externalizing a product they called Dremel. Dremel essentially enabled Google to store records across different volumes in columnar storage. This allows Google to perform massively parallel queries across vast amounts of data in seconds. BigQuery gave that power to any organization on the planet.

Fast forward to today, Google and Google Cloud haven't stopped pushing boundaries of solving complex data challenges at scale through innovation and thought leadership. In turn, this leads to the creation of new products and services that become Google Cloud managed services for your use.

Of course, there are non-Google created industry standards and tools. In those instances, Google Cloud's openness continues, with Google Cloud publicly stating its open philosophy of "open source software and databases, open APIs, open data formats, and an inclusive partner ecosystem" (*Google Cloud Leads in Cloud Data Analytics and Databases*, 2020).

Google Cloud lives this out by ensuring interoperability with third-party services used for data ingestion, storage, processing, and analytics, such as Apache Spark, Presto, and others, and creating Google Cloud managed services that support industry standards such as Google Cloud's Cloud SQL, a fully managed service that supports PostgreSQL, MySQL, and SQL Server.

Not only is Google Cloud providing you with the most advanced data products and services, but they provide industry-leading reliability of those products, such as Cloud Spanner, a fully managed relational database that has an SLA of 99.999% that equates to just 5 minutes and 15 seconds of downtime a year.

Analytics/Intelligence

True to their word on democratizing access to data, Google Cloud develops data products to solve your biggest data challenges. They've enabled you to invoke machine learning capabilities using SQL query language with BigQuery ML. They've built products to simplify the user experience, time, and expertise required to build models with products such as AutoML. They've used AutoML to simplify further specific use cases, such as by providing pretrained APIs for images with Vision AI.

Then you have a machine learning platform called Vertex AI. It's a unified solution that provides users with an end-to-end workflow to build, deploy, scale, and manage machine learning models. You can easily access pretrained APIs and integrate with other products and services under the data category, such as BigQuery and Dataproc. And of course, there is integration with open source frameworks such as TensorFlow, PyTorch, and others.

What about data management?

Google Cloud is aware that as organizations adopt and grow their use of the platform, their structured and unstructured data is siloed within data lakes, marts, or warehouses. Enter Dataplex, a product that harvests the metadata stored across Cloud Storage and BigQuery. It provides a unified data mesh that enables you to apply consistent lifecycle management, classification, and quality tasks. This means you can centrally manage, monitor, and govern the data without any data movement as shown in Figure 2-6. Google refers to this as their intelligent data fabric.

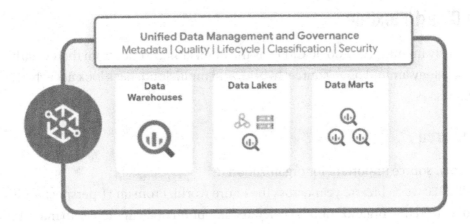

Figure 2-6. *How Dataplex unified data management fits with the wider Google Cloud data products[3]*
Copyright Google Cloud

What about business intelligence?

Traditional business intelligence (BI) platforms required a data team to perform complex tasks to derive insights. And you had to access a specific portal to see the visualizations. That doesn't fit in a world where data-driven decisions are critical to establishing and maintaining a competitive advantage.

Google Cloud's Looker platform, which they acquired in 2020, is a modern BI platform. I mean, it's been designed and built to enable users to more easily integrate their data intelligence within applications, websites, and other locations where they want to consume the data. It also has a SQL-based modeling language known as LookML. LookML aims to lower the skills required to use the platform.

Looker is also multicloud capable, enabling you to run the platform hosted in Azure, AWS, and Google Cloud, of course. It means you don't need to move your data which can help with data sovereignty challenges.

---

[3]This image was created by Google Cloud, and is used according to the terms described in the Creative Common Attribution 4.0 License. Source: https://cloud.google.com/dataplex/docs/introduction

Open Cloud/Flexible

As previously mentioned, Google Cloud as the open cloud comes from their clearly defined strategy around open source, hybrid, and multicloud. Let's look at each of those topics.

Open Source

Why is open source important for organizations?

Well, 2020 was a bizarre year across the entire world. From an IT perspective, it's well-publicized that organizations accelerated adoption of technologies to make remote working possible. Initially, organizations may well have reduced budgets in some areas to balance investments in software to enable remote working. A survey by Tidelift of over 600 technologists found that "44% of respondents reported that their organisations would increase their use of open source for application development" (*The Managed Open Source Survey, Tidelift*, 2020). This increase in the use of open source can be a way of saving costs and accelerating development by using open source libraries in your application.

While all the cloud providers now show their support for open source, Google has grown up with their ways of working going hand in hand with open source and the community. Their transparency discussed earlier is a testament to that.

In fact, Google publicly states that "open source is at the core of our infrastructure, processes and culture" (*Open Source by Numbers at Google*, 2020). Google is a large consumer of open source software, and we all benefit from their use of it, both in the consumer products and Google Cloud products. Google also strongly believes in giving back to the community, which we will look into shortly.

With a long history in open source, Google has created a dedicated team, the Open Source Programs Office (OSPO). OSPO's mission statement is "Bringing all the value of open source to Google and all the resources of Google to open source" (*Google Open Source*), which is proudly shown on their dedicated site opensource.google. I expect this relationship to continue to grow as the number of Googlers making commits to open source projects on Github has grown year on year, with Googlers being active in over 70,000 repositories in 2019 (*Open Source by Numbers at Google*, 2020), an increase of over 30,000 since 2015.

Google has quite an impressive history of developing products and turning them over to the open source community. Let's call out a few of their more well-known ones to give you some understanding of the sheer unrivalled scale of this: Android, Chromium (open source version of the Google Chrome browser), AngularJS (the web framework for single-page web applications), and a host of others. It doesn't start or end there though.

Let's look into products that Google has developed, turned over to the open source community, and then made available inside Google Cloud as products for us to consume and build upon.

Google's lessons learned from Borg (which is Google's cluster management service, which we discussed earlier) fed into the creation of Kubernetes (K8S), the container orchestration product. Google then turned Kubernetes over to the Cloud Native Computing Foundation (CNCF) to run as an open source project. Google still heavily commits to the ongoing development and the hosting costs of that development. In fact, with Google's support, Kubernetes has become "the highest velocity open source project in history" (Sharma, Cloud Native Computing Foundation). Google is also the number 1 contributor to CNCF, which is home to over 100 open source projects.

Google created their own managed variant of this that runs on Google Cloud called Google Kubernetes Engine (GKE), which greatly simplifies the deployment and management of Kubernetes, and AWS and Azure also now have their own managed services variants of Kubernetes.

Google's Brain Team also developed Tensorflow, the machine learning platform, and alongside the community they continue to develop and improve this platform. This is now available to use within Google Cloud as TensorFlow Enterprise or as part of Google Cloud Vertex AI, which is a platform aiming to provide all the machine learning tools you need in a single place.

Google's openness to publishing its research into solving complex problems has spawned entire generations of third-party products. In the early 2000s, it wasn't just the network scaling challenge mentioned previously that Google needed to solve. Google also needed to solve data processing on an unprecedented scale. To process data on the scale they needed, Google needed to look at how the data is stored. In 2003 they released the paper called "The Google File System," also known as GFS. This paper details a file system architecture that would enable Google to create applications to process data on a massive scale. The GFS paper also paved the way for the Hadoop Distributed File System (HDFS) and the entire Hadoop suite of products.

Another research paper related to solving massive-scale data processing led to Google publishing a paper with what they called the dataflow model. This research led the way to solve large-scale data processing for both batch and streaming methods. This led to the creation of Google Cloud Dataflow, which is available as a service to consume within Google Cloud. It also led to the creation of Apache Beam as the open source implementation of the dataflow model.

Google runs several initiatives to help contribute to open source that extends beyond the open source projects that Google uses, from Summer of Code, aimed at getting university students with some extra time on their summer holidays to work on contributing to open source projects, to Season of Docs, which sees open source organizations get help from the technical writing community to improve their documentation. Season of Docs sees technical writers contact the open source organizations that are part of the initiative and apply to be their technical writers. If the organization approves, they can apply for a grant through the Season of Docs initiative.

Other open source community outreaches are tools for open source developers to assess their code against common security vulnerabilities or open source dependencies.

Google is also affiliated with many open source organizations that help to keep the open source community alive, such as Apache Foundation, Linux Foundation, and others like the previously mentioned Cloud Native Computing Foundation which Google is a founding member.

Hybrid and Multicloud

A survey of cloud users undertaken by Gartner finds "81% of respondents using two or more providers," and in the same article, Gartner then goes on to predict that "By 2021, over 75% of midsize and large organizations will have adopted a multicloud and/or hybrid IT strategy" *(Cloud Strategy | Gartner IT IOCS Conference*, 2020).

So with organizations already using more than one cloud or having a multicloud strategy, what is Google Cloud's approach, and how can they fit your organization's multicloud strategy?

Google fully recognizes the multicloud reality and has several products designed to meet the common needs and challenges of not just an existing multicloud organization but also the organizations that still adopt cloud and need to modernize to survive.

Application modernization - one such challenge is the pace of software innovation within enterprise IT and the ability to migrate and modernize legacy workloads while ensuring operations are consistent and simple. Google Cloud's vision of the future of enterprise IT is laid out in a video by Urs Hölzle, SVP technical infrastructure, entitled "Hidden Forces: What's Next in Enterprise IT." In this video, Urs lays out how to bring the speed of development experienced in the consumer market to enterprise IT. To achieve this, Urs talks about what the enterprise would need: a software platform that is always up-to-date; is open source; accommodates legacy systems; and runs on-prem and in any cloud.

What is Google Cloud's answer to this?

Perhaps unsurprisingly, it's a software platform that is precisely those four elements mentioned above; it's called Anthos. Anthos provides a platform that enables you to build new workloads and modernize legacy workloads. And you can do that with or without moving them to the cloud as Anthos can run on-prem, AWS, Google Cloud, and Azure (in public preview at the time of writing). We will touch more on Anthos in a later chapter.

Multicloud data analytics and business intelligence - in a world with an exponential increase in the amounts of data we all generate, Google Cloud believes you should be able to perform analytics on your data where it currently resides.

BigQuery is the flagship product in Google Cloud's portfolio of data analytics tools, as mentioned in an earlier section. Google Cloud needed to bring that capability to other clouds. Enter BigQuery Omni, which enables you to use the same user interface, standard SQL query language, and APIs of BigQuery but against your datasets stored in AWS and Azure. This saves time and cost as those datasets no longer need to be transferred to Google Cloud storage before you can perform your analytics.

How has Google achieved this?

The Google Cloud product team responsible for BigQuery Omni developed it to run on Anthos, of course. So Google is certainly putting into practice what they are telling us. Google Cloud fully manages the Anthos clusters used to power BigQuery Omni. You just have to consume the product and query your data.

Organizations have data analytics needs that stem beyond SQL queries and into the business intelligence (BI) layer. Organizations are looking for a BI platform to fulfill multiple needs and use cases, from analyzing and reporting on data to embedded analytics within a workload built internally, all while keeping their analytics close to where their data resides and with native integrations into cloud data warehouses and databases.

For those needs, Google Cloud has Looker. Looker is a modern BI platform that aims to democratize data analytics by providing your users with self-service reporting and analytics capabilities. Looker has a query language called LookML, which you use to construct your SQL queries. With Looker, you can choose to host your Looker in AWS, Azure, Google Cloud, and even on-prem, should you need. Looker has integrations with cloud-native data warehouses and databases.

Why does this matter?

It means you can connect data sources within the same cloud provider, reducing latency and simplifying your cloud billing.

Cybersecurity analytics - Alphabet has a research and development subsidiary called X Development. X aims to solve the world's hardest problems (moonshots). X decided to take on cybersecurity analytics. Chronicle was born and moved to become part of Google Cloud in 2019. Chronicle can take in security logs from a huge array of products and vendors that create security products that generate logs. AWS and Azure logs are within that list. The reason they support so many sources is that they aim to do security analytics on a petabyte scale. When you start pulling in log data from firewalls, EDRs, load balancers, wireless networks, intrusion detection and prevention systems, operating systems, identity and access management, and more, then you are in large-scale analytics. You don't pay for the amount of data analyzed. Instead, the cost is based on the number of employees. This pricing model encourages you to ingest more data.

Flexible

What is flexible in a cloud computing context?

If we take the definition of flexible to be "able to be easily modified to respond to altered circumstances" (*Oxford Languages*), then in cloud computing, that would equate to easily being able to modify deployed resources to fit your changing needs. I'd also add that flexibility in this context would extend to it being easy to deploy new resources.

APIs - in Google Cloud, that translates to being able to use various means of interacting with Google Cloud to create new or modify existing resources. Google Cloud offers you that functionality through the Google Cloud console, Cloud SDK, or REST APIs. Within the Google Cloud console, it is the ability to open the Cloud Shell which essentially loads a private container with the Cloud SDK by default, meaning you can use what Google calls the GCloud CLI to interact programmatically to create new or modify existing Google Cloud resources.

Live migration - Google has to keep 100s of thousands of physical hosts updated and fully operational. This is a never-ending process, and Google needed a flexible approach to maintain the physical hosts in a timely manner but without impacting customers.

Virtual machines are mainly stateful, so terminating them to perform host maintenance wouldn't be good. So Google Cloud developed a solution that solves this for customers using Google Compute Engine (GCE) virtual machines. Transparent to you, Google provides the ability to live migrate from one physical host to another. In fact, this happens on a huge scale per month without issue, partly due to the fact that the average "blackout" period is just 50ms.

This live migration of your virtual machines requires no action on your part. This is a huge benefit to you, as it means Google won't notify you that you need to restart your GCE virtual machines. This does happen with other cloud providers, as the act of restarting your virtual machines on other clouds is used to trigger a move to another host, so that they can perform maintenance on the host running your virtual machine. With Google Cloud, your GCE virtual machines need a restart only when your operating system requires it after you've updated it.

How can Google Cloud perform live migration at such a scale?

This is thanks to Borg, which is Google's cluster management system, which is a huge differentiator for Google. Borg is complex, as the nature of what it does is incredibly complex, but in simple terms, Borg is essentially controlling thousands of physical hosts to ensure workloads and services that need to run have the capacity to do just that.

Most of the workloads managed by Borg, from Gmail to App Engine and even GCE virtual machines, are run as containers in what are known as Borg tasks. Google has designed tasks running under the control of Borg to allow for restarts at any time, as they are fault-tolerant and primarily stateless, which makes evicting or terminating lower-priority workloads and services to free up capacity for higher-priority workloads and services easier. As mentioned earlier, GCE virtual machines are likely to be stateful, so they won't work with this approach.

So to solve this required additional infrastructure, Google built what they call an instance manager. Instance manager understands the state of the running VMs, as well as their configuration. Instance manager runs like other Borg workloads (fault-tolerant, stateless). Borg was extended to allow jobs to be marked as migratable, which is what those jobs they want to restart or terminate a GCE virtual machine get marked as.

Side note, Google created Kubernetes based on the learning of Borg.

What this capability also means for you is that Google can be very flexible with the rate of change in your physical hardware. So improvements in hardware performance such as the latest CPUs from Intel and AMD, upgrading memory, and new network fabrics can be made available to you quickly.

That is a high-level overview of two complex areas of Google Cloud, Borg, and live migration. Testament to Google's transparency philosophy, they've written whitepapers giving you insights into how they do it. They are worth reading if you'd like to understand how Borg runs Google Cloud. The first is "Large-Scale Cluster Management at Google with Borg" and another that goes deeply into how live migration is possible: "VM Live Migration at Scale."

Sustainability

When it comes to sustainability, Google has been paving the way for years. Not only against their competitors in the cloud market, but they've also been leading the way against organizations of similar size globally. Google became the first major global organization to be carbon neutral in 2007, before most organizations were even thinking about it, let alone achieving it.

Google has now made a public commitment to be carbon-free by 2030. This is the most ambitious sustainability target in the organization's history. Google's sustainability strategy driving them toward that goal currently focuses around three pillars:

- Accelerate carbon-free and circular.

- Empower with technology.

- Benefit people and places.

To achieve the 2030 goal requires some serious rethinking of the traditional data center operations model. Google's challenge here is they need to use the clean energy that is already available for use in a particular data center, which isn't easy, and then you start to think about factors such as the clean energy produced through wind and solar has peaks and troughs. Google solved this as part of their initiative called carbon-intelligent computing. "Google can now shift moveable compute tasks between different data centers, based on regional hourly carbon-free energy availability" (*Using Location to Reduce Our Carbon Computing Footprint*, 2021). And they predict the available carbon-free energy using machine learning, taking into account weather forecasts and historical turbine data. This enables them to predict the power generated 36 hours ahead of time.

Google has also signed a first-of-its-kind agreement with a clean-energy startup called Fervo Energy. Using Google's capabilities in AI and machine learning and Fervo's leading expertise in advanced drilling techniques, the collaboration aims to supply a consistent 24x7 geothermal energy supply to the grid, starting with Nevada. Cocreating innovation in this space with industry leaders yet again shows Google's colors and commitment shining through.

The UK government is urging businesses to migrate to the cloud as a way of helping them to cut emissions. This is a trend that will likely play out in other countries across the world. IDC even predicts that "Cloud Computing Could Eliminate a Billion Metric Tons of CO_2 Emission Over the Next Four Years" (*IDC*, 2021). That's the equivalent of removing over 217 million petrol and diesel-powered cars off the road for a year.

Google's forward-thinking in sustainability has led to Google Cloud being renowned as the cleanest cloud in the industry. Google Cloud regions are now marked as low CO_2, which means the region is powered by carbon-free energy (CFE) for more than 75% of the time. At the time of writing, there are ten data center sites marked as low CO_2. Several of them are operating at 90% and above CFE. And to make it easier to select a low carbon region, the Google Cloud console has a green leaf icon next to those low carbon regions.

Once you have workloads running within Google Cloud, you can use their carbon footprint calculator to give you a measure of your Google Cloud estates' carbon footprint. This measure is useful when you need to report to governing bodies. It can also drive behaviors to show the impact of an unattended Google Cloud project or leaving a VM running idle or incorrectly sized.

With 90% of global IT leaders saying that improving the sustainability of their IT infrastructure is a priority (IDG), you can expect to see Google and Google Cloud continue to provide innovation and products that will help organizations meet their sustainability goals.

Google Cloud's commitment to sustainability and combating climate change doesn't stop with just their data center infrastructure. They focus on how they design and build their offices and their impact, with 17 million square feet being LEED-certified; preventing food waste from their cafes; and providing shuttles and promoting the use of electric vehicles and bicycles to access the offices. The last point alone has saved 40,000 metric tons of CO_2, the equivalent of taking 8,760 cars off the road.

Google has issued $5.75 billion in sustainability bonds, the proceeds of which will go on to fund environmentally or socially responsible projects. And as of 2020, Google has compensated for their legacy carbon footprint, making Google the first major company to be carbon neutral for its entire operating history.

Google uses the vast amounts of data they've captured through various means such as satellite imagery and geospatial datasets to detect and map trends on the Earth's surface. This has led to partnerships with Global Forest Watch to create a map of forest loss and Global Fishing Watch to track global fishing activity across the oceans. They released a Global Surface Water Explorer with the European Commission's Joint Research Centre (JRC) that measures and monitors where water is changing. They've mapped air quality and analyzed the surface area of 107 million rooftops to identify solar energy potential among other datasets made available to you to help inform your environmental, social, and governance (ESG) decisions.

Google regularly uses their insights gleaned from their data and their partnerships to publish whitepapers on specific topics or aimed at helping guide certain industries, such as their paper on "Closing the Plastics Circularity Gap" or specific guidance for the financial services industry. Google also publishes their environmental reports to show you the real data behind its numbers.

Of course, the perfect partnership to accelerate your sustainability decision-making is to take Google Cloud's datasets, combined with your data, and use Google Cloud's data analytics products and services to empower people from across your organization to identify meaningful insights.

Productivity and Collaboration

Since the launch of Gmail in 2004 and then Google Apps in 2006, Google hasn't stopped innovating in the productivity and collaboration space.

Google Workspace, previously known as G Suite, was designed and built for online collaboration.

As I've mentioned before, Google's products and services are designed to run as containers, giving Google Cloud the ability to scale those products and services easily. This was most evident when COVID-19 struck and forced countries to declare a state of lockdown. This left organization owners no option but to empower those that can work remotely to do that. With Google Workspace, you only need access to a browser and an Internet connection to be operational. As the number of users increases, Google Cloud increases the capacity of the product to ensure an optimal performant experience.

Third-Party Analysts

Where does Google Cloud lead according to third-party analysts?

You are most likely familiar with the quadrants used by market researchers such as Gartner, ISG, and Forrester, where leaders in the respective categories sit in the top-right corner of the grid. Well, according to their analysis, in the past couple of years, Google Cloud has been a leader in the following categories:

- Cloud infrastructure and platform services

- Cloud storage

- Data management for analytics

- Ad tech

- Full life cycle API management

- Content collaboration platforms

- Infrastructure-as-a-Service platform native security

- Public cloud development platforms

- Big data NoSQL

- Cloud data warehouse

- Enterprise file sync and share

- API management solutions

- Database-as-a-Service

- Cloud AI developer services

- Cloud database management systems (DBMS)

- Mainframe modernization

- Low-code platforms for business developers

- Streaming analytics

- Unstructured data security platforms

- Notebook-based predictive analytics and machine learning

- Computer vision platforms

- Continuous integration

- Data security portfolio vendors

This shows a huge diversity in where Google Cloud has its strengths. And by the time this book is published, there will undoubtedly be some additions to this list. Do keep an eye out for those announcements Google Cloud makes on their blogs website, and you'll be able to download the reports too. The Gartner reports can provide useful data points that can be added to your business case, especially if your use cases align with one of the quadrants where Google Cloud is leading.

Summary

Google offers organizations a genuinely unique partnership opportunity, from strengths in providing unrivalled insights into your current and future customers with the advertising side of Google to providing a mobile platform where you can engage with your customers and where organizations can empower staff with a wide range of Android supported hardware to solve all types of use cases.

Google Cloud's strengths are wide and varied, with deep expertise in specific industries. Going back to the opening of this chapter, I said Google's case study customers select Google Cloud for its strengths. Testament to that is you'll find a wide range of case studies that cover each of the capabilities I've just discussed.

Google Cloud offers a globally resilient, fast, and secure infrastructure. Google Cloud believes its products and services should be designed to ensure that you own your data and have the flexibility to move it as needed while also reducing manual tasks and configuration through automation. Google Cloud also wants you to be able to analyze your data quickly and efficiently using tools that don't require highly specialized skills or the need for you to move the data from cloud to cloud. Google leads in sustainability, with a 2030 pledge to be carbon-free. A number of their Google Cloud data centers are already powered using over 90% carbon-free energy. Google Cloud productivity and collaboration tools empower your workforce to work from anywhere in a secure way while also enabling your users to collaborate in real time, all underpinned by artificial intelligence and machine learning.

Finally, thinking differently and solving complex problems are what keep Google's and Alphabets' momentum alive. With world-leading innovation that's spanning over two decades, and available to Google customers to take advantage of through Google's products and services, it's hard to see why you wouldn't want to work with them.

It all adds up to products and services and a collaborative culture that offers organizations completeness of vision to modernize and innovate faster than they've been able to before.

Collateral - most of Google Cloud's security-related documentation and whitepapers offer CIO-level summaries. If you do not have time to read all the available documentation but need to seek further assurances, then at a minimum, look for the CIO-level summaries of the following articles and whitepapers:

- Google Infrastructure Security Design Overview
  `https://cloud.google.com/security/infrastructure/design`

- Encryption at Rest
  `https://cloud.google.com/security/encryption/default-encryption`

- Privileged Access Management in Google Cloud Platform
  `https://services.google.com/fh/files/misc/privileged-access-management-gcp-wp.pdf`

- Data Deletion on Google Cloud Platform
  `https://cloud.google.com/security/deletion`

CHAPTER 3

The Future of IT

"Prediction is very difficult especially if it's about the future."

—Niels Bohr, Nobel Laureate in Physics

First, let's get one point straight; you can't predict the future, and longer-term predictions around technology can be famously inaccurate, such as this prediction by American Economist Paul Krugman: "By 2005 or so, it will become clear that the Internet's impact on the economy has been no greater than the fax machine's." So rather than making bold claims about the future of IT, instead I'll look at trends that are here and growing momentum.

It must be acknowledged that before COVID-19 there had already been a growing trend toward the automation of product lines, remote working, and other industry innovations powered by technology advancements. However, when COVID-19 arrived in late 2019 to early 2020, it forced a global shutdown of industries the likes of which have never been witnessed before. We have seen an acceleration in many organizations' digital strategies out of necessity to survive. Now, more organizations than ever are using the Internet and digital channels to meet their customers where they are while safeguarding their employees during the pandemic. What the "new normal" looks like, we still don't know.

So, what does the future of IT look like?

To make some informed assumptions about the future of IT, let's look at some trends that affect the IT function.

Firstly, today's customers expect more than yesterday's, so it's fair to assume that tomorrow's customers will continue that trend.

IT's role within an organization has changed because IT's internal customers' expectations have changed. Not only do more people within your organization have requirements that IT needs to fulfill, but those requests are more varied than ever before. When IT can't fulfill, or it's a slow and complex process to fulfill a request, then

49

© Jeremy Lloyd 2023
J. Lloyd, *Infrastructure Leader's Guide to Google Cloud*, https://doi.org/10.1007/978-1-4842-8820-7_3

it's coupled with an increase in the number of non-IT personnel making decisions that affect the IT landscape, known as Shadow IT, as we discussed earlier.

In many organizations, IT is also being changed from a cost center to a profit center. This trend is often coupled with the organization's adoption of the cloud. However, IT also has to deal with many years of technical debt that can hold innovation back and hamper their decision-making.

There is increased public interest in data breaches, which means greater media attention and a bigger potential loss of reputation and revenue for organizations that get hacked and have data stolen. This is coupled with increased modern data privacy regulations such as the General Data Protection Regulation (GDPR). Gartner estimates that by 2023 65% of the world's population will have their personal data covered under such regulations (Gartner, 2020). This adds even more pressure and scrutiny to the IT function than never before. Organizations will need to consider where their data is stored and analyzed.

Back to the original question then, what does the future of IT look like?

With increased customer expectations putting pressure on IT to deliver more and faster, the future of IT will not be continuing to purchase physical tin to build and run your data centers. It will mean making use of the cloud for your workloads. It also means dramatically changing the ways of working to facilitate an efficient software delivery process. You should be able to deliver new features to production multiple times per day, and you should also be able to deploy into new regions globally with a few simple code changes, and doing all of that while knowing your software supply chain is secure.

Getting your IT function to that point will require changing from a Waterfall delivery approach to an Agile one. It'll also mean changing from a project-based approach to innovation and improvements to a product-based approach, and I'll discuss that later. And it'll mean shifting-left on capabilities like security, so you can embed tooling and perform checks earlier in the development lifecycle.

It'll also require automation of any remaining manual processes. Moving beyond using Infrastructure-as-Code (IaC) and toward a more end-to-end automated build, deploy, test, and release process, often referred to as continuous integration/continuous deployment (CI/CD), I'll cover this later in the book.

These practices will, in turn, help to improve the reliability and security of your workload while providing you with the ability to release to production more often. Now is a great time to start this journey if you haven't done so. As there are more enterprise friendly products and services from Google Cloud or third-party vendors, that all aim to help you improve your software delivery performance. Although this can be seen as a blessing and a curse, too much choice presents decision-making problems.

As mentioned earlier in this chapter, Urs Hölzle's vision is that "IT need a software platform that is always up-to-date; open source; accommodate legacy systems; run on-prem and in any cloud." Such a software platform would also help organizations tackle data sovereignty challenges.

Since Urs gave that statement, it's become clear that cloud providers need to extend their capabilities to edge locations and even within your current on-prem data centers. Products like the Google Distributed Cloud provide fully managed hardware and software solutions that enable local data processing and edge computing. Products that deliver that while providing consistent operations and security are key to meeting current and future customer needs.

What about the technical debt, I hear you say? Those workloads that you can modernize, should be. For those workloads that can't, operating a stable state is key. You should still move these legacy workloads to Google Cloud, and you should create the infrastructure using IaC. If they still receive updates, then you should automate that process.

You will empower non-IT employees to solve their own needs, while simultaneously IT provides guardrails and governance. One such solution would be for IT to provide Low-Code Application Platforms (LCAP) such as Google's AppSheet Automation.

What about the future of the infrastructure leader?

It is unlikely that every organization on the planet will move everything into a cloud provider. Our first generation of infrastructure leaders will, however, become relics. Organizations not utilizing cloud infrastructure at all will get left behind. Therefore, we will likely see second and third generations for quite some time.

Where does this leave you? Do you want to make a career out of infrastructure and become a leader within the field?

Following the guidance within this book will set you on the path to successfully operate and thrive in the evermore demanding, fast-paced IT world. Through changing your organization's current ways of working, adopting Google Cloud, and migrating and modernizing your workloads, your organization will see the benefits through value creation.

Summary

Essentially we can summarize that trends show internal and external customers have greater and more varied expectations that fall on IT to deliver. And IT needs to do that quicker than before while adding value to increase revenue streams and simultaneously managing and modernizing legacy systems. And if that wasn't enough, an organization has a greater spotlight on it if IT fails to store data in the right location and secure it appropriately.

The future of IT makes use of the cloud and changing current ways of working to turn IT from a cost center into a profit center, empowering non-IT employees to access technology to enable them to innovate while ensuring governance and controls are in place.

PART II

Business and Cloud Strategies

In Part 2, I will cover key elements you need to consider before moving to Google Cloud. Although even if you are partway through a migration, it's not too late to go back and revisit some of these elements. I will cover the different approaches that organizations can take when adopting Google Cloud. I will cover how to navigate your business case to justify the move to Google Cloud. Then define your cloud strategy and cloud operating model. I will discuss different migration and modernization strategies. Finally, I will cover the assistance you can get from Google and the partner ecosystem.

CHAPTER 4

The Four Approaches to Google Cloud Adoption

This chapter covers the four common approaches to Google Cloud adoption and details what to look for to understand which approach fits your organization. I also cover the steps to ramp up your adoption to the next approach.

Over my years as a consultant, I'm fortunate enough to have worked with many great organizations undergoing cloud adoption via various approaches. They'd have varying degrees of success. Some are getting it right and on track, while others have stalled or failed. I asked questions to try and understand what was working well and what caused stalling or failed adoption/migrations.

Time and time again, I'd see patterns emerge across areas such as the following:

- Current cloud usage/maturity

- Stakeholder alignment

- Current in-house skills and learning paths

- Vision, strategies, and objectives for adoption, migration, and modernization

There are milestones that can be identified and then used to help identify where you currently are with your cloud adoption capability. After consulting with a customer, I can usually bucket them into four categories:

- Shadow IT

- Tactical adoption

- Strategic adoption

- Organization transformation

© Jeremy Lloyd 2023
J. Lloyd, *Infrastructure Leader's Guide to Google Cloud*, https://doi.org/10.1007/978-1-4842-8820-7_4

Start your journey with me and this book by assessing and labeling where your organization is. Doing so allows you to more objectively challenge the current strategy or lack of, as is often the case. Let's delve deeper into these four Google Cloud adoption approaches. And as an infrastructure leader reading this, let me help guide you through what you need to do to get your organization toward strategic adoption and on a path to organizational transformation.

Shadow IT

Before anyone in IT has formalized an approach to the cloud, end users within your organization have likely signed up to a cloud service provider or some Software-as-a-Service products without IT's knowledge. Their intentions aren't malicious. They simply want to satisfy a business need they are responsible for. If IT can't provide services in a quick and easy process, then they are left with no choice but to solve the problem themselves.

Of course, Shadow IT isn't limited to organizations with no formalized approach to the cloud. Suppose your organization has a defined cloud strategy, but it's too restrictive or limited to a single cloud provider. In that case, the end users who need to fulfill a need will avoid IT and find an easier way to achieve the desired outcome.

And with Google Cloud specifically, I've seen another typical pattern that drives Shadow IT Google Cloud adoption. In this pattern, the organizations I engage with typically have a cloud first strategy (strategic adoption). Or are you undertaking an organization transformation with a particular cloud that isn't Google Cloud. They've progressed in their level of maturity with that cloud provider. They have security controls and governance processes in place. Infrastructure is deployed as code. Some even have robust continuous integration (CI) and continuous deployment (CD) processes.

Where this particular pattern differs is when I engage with the organization, it's directly with a business unit or workload-specific subject matter experts that aren't IT. Instead, these are data analytics or data science functions or a business unit outside of IT that has data skills. These teams are interested in or are already using Google Cloud because of its capability within the data analytics space. However, this is essentially classified as Shadow IT.

Any type of Shadow IT adoption can cause significant damage to your organization. Without IT's involvement, there is likely little or no governance or security considerations, which could easily lead to workloads not meeting compliance and regulatory standards. It could also lead to data loss and reputational damage.

How do you identify Shadow IT cloud adoption? The following are reactive steps you can take:

- Understand what new products and services have recently been released by the organization. Then align with IT to understand what parts of it they manage. Doing so should expose if IT isn't involved.

- Similarly, identify business units/teams producing new insights/ data for your organization. Again understand where analytics are performed, who is maintaining it, and what information security controls are in place.

- Engage a sales representative from the cloud vendors. Request information relating to the usage of pay-as-you-go billing accounts. There will likely be a process you'll have to go through to gain this information, but it will be possible.

- Engage with your finance and procurements team to identify any invoice-based cloud spend. Educate them on what you are looking for.

However, when it comes to stopping Shadow IT, it's far more effective to be proactive and understand what business units and users need from IT. Steps to help with that are as follows:

- Engage with the heads of business units and key decision-makers and ask them about their cloud usage. Delivered in a nonconfrontational way but you must understand their use case(s). Asking why five times can help you get to the root cause. The "five whys" is a known technique, and it does help.

- Understand each business unit's specific problems, needs, and goals by proactively engaging them. After extracting this information, align it with what IT can currently offer vs. what Google Cloud offers.

- Undertake a discovery and assessment of your current servers and applications (discussed in a later chapter). Doing so helps align that all new products and services are indeed known to you.

Tactical Adoption

Tactical adoption is defined as the adoption of a cloud provider by a business unit to meet a specific use case. In essence, in the tactical adoption approach, Google Cloud is used to solve a particular use case or multiple use cases. It might even be for data analytics, and I will explain why tactical adoption is different to shadow adoption shortly. These use cases might come about in the form of proof of concepts (PoC), proof of value (PoV), pilots, or minimum viable products (MVP). With this approach, depending on the size and decentralized nature of your organization, it's possible that two or more business units may be using Google Cloud in isolation from each other.

The main element that makes it tactical adoption, not just Shadow IT, is that IT is formally engaged by the business unit that needs Google Cloud. Due to that formal engagement, IT might control access and have some lightweight governance or a feedback loop to provide them an awareness of activities and a roadmap.

I've also found in these scenarios that the IT teams of some organizations have left the business unit to control and govern the Google Cloud environment. This is an error in my opinion, as one use case turns into two, three, or more and pilots/MVPs turn into production workloads. It's organic growth, and no organization is immune to that. It goes hand in hand with growing cloud maturity.

The more isolated the use case(s) are, the less IT wants to get involved. For example, performing data analytics on publicly available datasets that don't touch your on-prem and legacy workloads, then IT is happy not to be involved. However, if you need public DNS entries, single sign-on, or network connectivity into an existing data center or other cloud providers to ingest data, then IT will likely want more of a say in how Google Cloud is operating, and rightly so.

In tactical adoption, finance has likely been engaged to pay the bill by invoice and not a credit card. However, if IT is not controlling access to tactical Google Cloud adoption, then the same risks associated with Shadow IT are present here.

What's worse is IT has willingly ignored the request to let them control Google Cloud. I've found that this is because IT is already looking after one or more clouds and that those clouds contain production workloads, synchronized identities, and network connectivity.

Unchecked organic growth of Google Cloud in an ungoverned manner will leave IT with a larger problem in the future. At a minimum, once IT engages and defines governance, it'll require some rework to align those existing Google Cloud projects.

How do you identify this stage? Perform the preceding same steps listed for Shadow IT, but in addition, find the answers for the following:

- Which cloud providers does IT manage?

- Who is the person or team responsible for managing work identities (such as Active Directory) within your organization? Suppose a business unit needs to use their work emails for authentication. In that case, the team responsible for identity will know about any cloud-based identity synchronization.

- Ask the network team if any links are established with a cloud provider. And ask them to identify traffic inbound originating from one of the cloud provider's public IP ranges. All cloud providers publish these ranges, so this task is easier than it appears.

What about those more proactive steps?

If your organization is using Google Cloud in this manner and you want to progress to strategic adoption of Google Cloud, then

- Engage those business units, speak to the stakeholders, and understand their use case(s). If you are to take your organization forward to strategic adoption of Google Cloud, then you'll need to gather the information you need to support a business case.

- Familiarize yourself now with your company's business case template. It's highly likely that it's generic and will need molding to fit the narrative you'll want to show for the cloud.

- Start to populate a business case to justify a shift to embracing strategic adoption of Google Cloud. See the business case section for more details.

- Follow the guidance in this book to form your version of a cloud strategy, cloud operating model, migration, and modernization documents.

- Understand how you can use partners to accelerate adoption and start a partner selection process.

Strategic Adoption

When Google Cloud is selected as the primary cloud, or there is a balanced multicloud strategy with each cloud being made available for business units to consume, then the challenges are different. With this approach, IT is heavily involved, but it's the business driving the change, with IT being the facilitator.

To strategically adopt Google Cloud, you must define a cloud strategy and your target operating model. A CCoE is established, and several of the first team members will come from IT. Migration and modernization strategies will need to be created, and some workloads will have been migrated already.

How do you identify this stage?

- Your cloud strategy, cloud operating model, migration, and modernization documents have been defined and are known and have stakeholder support.

- There is an active program of works to adopt and migrate to Google Cloud underway.

- Partner(s) have been engaged to accelerate and/ or manage workloads in Google Cloud.

What can you do to move forward?

Just because an organization has stated that Google Cloud is the strategic cloud of choice doesn't mean it'll all go as planned. There will likely be a lot already in motion covering the technology aspect of adoption. To progress successfully or to move into the organization transformation approach, you'll need to do the following:

- Ensure current Google Cloud adoption, migration, and modernization workstreams have strong feedback loops, with clear accountability on who is making what improvements.

- Focus on the more cultural elements, the people side, the need for change, and a culture of improvement and innovation.

- Expose the root causes to the challenges facing the business and your industry. Understand what you require across people, process, and technology to solve them.

- Engage leadership to understand their perspectives on the organization's current market and competition and their vision, direction, and goals and, most importantly, their awareness of the need to change and their appetite for it.

- Coach and guide leadership on your discoveries of the challenges faced within the organization and how to approach solving them.

- Ask your leadership team to consult with a Google Cloud partner who can advise and assist with delivering digital transformation workstreams. If they prefer not to, then the minimum is they get mentorship from a leader who has taken organizations through a transformation. Your leaders are just like the rest of us, and they have to learn. Make it as easy as possible and attractive for them to do that.

Organization Transformation

An organization in this stage is less common, not least because an organization or digital transformation doesn't have a single agreed definition. I define it as an organization that has or is redefining its culture to stimulate innovation, collaboration, and agility under leaders with clear vision and direction. The key is the culture change and the people that drive process and technology transformation. Without them, transformation doesn't happen.

How do you identify this stage?

- A clear vision and goal(s) will have been defined by leadership. They will set a direction and help everyone within the organization be inspired and make decisions that move the organization forward.

- Leadership sets the drumbeat and models the cultural values.

- Clear guiding principles exist and resonate with the organization. They anchor people while simultaneously driving them on.

- A multidimensional program of works will be underway covering not just technology but also people and process aspects.

- There will be a renewed focus on technology and data more specifically, with more people within the organization using data to drive improvements across products and services.

- Innovation is driven by all business units, not just one small team that is part of the IT function. A culture of experimentation will exist to fuel the innovation.

- The organization's culture accepts failures happen and ensures that learning from those mistakes is a top priority.

What can you do to move forward?

- Continue to look for opportunities to make improvements across people, processes, and technology.

- Is every business unit and team working in an Agile way? Think about the Scaled Agile Framework (SAFe).

- Assess and understand what is working. You got to this point; invest time in ensuring that progress can continue.

- Stay closely engaged with stakeholders and leadership. Understand the goals and how they view progress toward them and their expectations on direction and performance to reach them.

Summary to Align Your Adoption Approach

Table 4-1 will help you quickly see what your current approach looks like within your organization.

Table 4-1. *A summary table of the cloud adoption approaches*

Shadow IT	Tactical adoption	Strategic adoption	Organization transformation
No formal adoption strategy	Use case-specific adoption strategy not led by IT	Formalized organization-wide adoption strategy with business outcomes	Formalized adoption strategy is part of other transformation workstreams aligned to business outcomes
New products and service being launched without IT involvement	IT is aware of new product and service launches and may have some involvement in cloud foundations	IT is fully engaged; a cloud adoption team structure exists including a Cloud Centre of Excellence	IT is fully engaged; a cloud adoption team structure exists; IT is set up to facilitate organization-wide innovation
No cloud operating model exists	Siloed cloud operating model exists but no strategy	Formalized cloud operating model exists. Day 2 operations are progressed with continuous improvement/ optimization	An evolved cloud operating model exists with function being shifted-left while maintaining governance. Day 2 operations are progressed with continuous improvement/ optimization
Credit card billing; procurement: just pay the bill and ask no questions	Centralized billing, procurement are aware, cloud is understood	Centralized billing with show-back model and financial operations capability	Centralized billing with show-back and charge-back model, mature financial operations capability
No engagement with IT to provide cloud services and operations	IT is a cost center	IT is a profit center	IT is a profit center
No cloud skills plan, any skills are in silos	Cloud skills increasing; champions exist but no formal learning plan	Formalized cloud skills plan, certifications gaining momentum	Culture of learning and improvement is engrained at all levels across the organization

(continued)

Table 4-1. (*continued*)

Shadow IT	Tactical adoption	Strategic adoption	Organization transformation
No active migrations to cloud	Use case-driven migrations are focused on lift and shift to VMs	Formalized migration workstream, with application rationalization and modernization. Lift and shift and move and improve approaches used	As per strategic adoption. There is also investment to refactor/rebuild legacy and do cloud-native development. And SaaS apps are widely used for commodity workloads

Cloud Adoption Meets the Four Generations

How do the four stages of cloud adoption align with the four generations of infrastructure leaders that I've previously described?

The four generations are based on your current state. It's where you are now and your current organizational and leadership capabilities with the cloud. The four cloud adoption approaches are how your organization is going to or is adopting Google Cloud. They get you to your desired target state. The four cloud adoption approaches are the vehicle to take you from your current location and drive down the road to your destination.

For example, if we were to take a first generation organization, there are four different ways they could adopt Google Cloud, although Shadow IT isn't an adoption strategy.

A first generation organization could adopt Google Cloud through tactical, strategic, or organizational transformation approaches. Each unlocks value back to the organization in different ways and times.

With tactical adoption, a first gen organization will only unlock value for the tactical use case.

Strategic adoption will see multiple technology-driven workstreams enabling value creation by hitting objectives and goals defined as part of the strategy.

Organizational transformation approaches can unlock the overall value of Google Cloud across the organization, with a culture of experimentation and innovation. Value creation could come from anywhere and at any time.

For a first generation organization to execute the cloud adoption approaches, they may hire leaders who've been through this before and can accelerate the adoption and migration workstreams. These would typically be second and third generation leaders with previous experience with cloud adoption.

Summary

Define which adoption approach your organization requires. Also, be aware of the generation of IT leaders within the organization. It helps you know what actions are required to progress with your cloud adoption.

CHAPTER 5

Business Case

In this chapter, I will discuss how you uncover the business benefits of Google Cloud. I will also cover two different business case approaches.

"We don't need a business case" or "a business case here is a waste of time, it's just a box-ticking exercise" are comments I often hear from customers. However, when their adoption stalls or progress is slower than needed, if senior leaders are not fully engaged or aligned, they won't offer the help required. By going through the proper channels and producing a well-thought-out case for Google Cloud, you'll find it easier to have active and engaged senior leaders become stakeholders, which is critical to successful adoption.

Regardless of your organization's industry, a business case exists as a single document, written to demonstrate the expected commercial benefits of an undertaking against its risks. The business case for Google Cloud can and should highlight how the key benefits of Google Cloud can relate to the value created for your organization.

When putting together the business case for Google Cloud or another cloud provider. It's easy to default to comparing the number of servers you on-prem with what they'll cost in the cloud. While that is an essential element, it's not the only way to demonstrate the value cloud can bring. Indeed, a business case for Google Cloud can be written to demonstrate commercial benefits through several different approaches.

Innovation

It can be used to justify the speed and agility benefits you can gain by moving specific workloads to Google Cloud. In his book *Be Less Zombie*, Elvin Turner describes these benefits as "units of progress." Elvin explains that the methodology is based on using products to do jobs for you. And those jobs represent progress, as in doing something "faster, better and cheaper."

© Jeremy Lloyd 2023
J. Lloyd, *Infrastructure Leader's Guide to Google Cloud*, https://doi.org/10.1007/978-1-4842-8820-7_5

Think about that for a moment. What jobs will you use Google Cloud for, and how does that relate to value for your organization?

The speed and agility "units of progress" have meant that commercial gain is through increasing release frequency. This means new features to get to production quicker, reducing the time to value and increasing customer satisfaction.

Google Cloud provides many other "units of progress" in addition to speed and agility. When consulting with organizations around their business case for Google Cloud, the common ones I use are scale, resilience, freedom, integration, simplicity, trust, reducing risks, security, efficiency, reducing effort, cost, stability, transparency, and confidence.

Consider adding to your business case a narrative around making use of Google Cloud products and services within Google Cloud to generate new revenue streams, such as performing data analytics on datasets within your application(s) and uncovering insights into your customers that can be used in numerous revenue-generating ways, from new ways to monetize your product or service to more accurate targeting of future customers by better understanding your current ones.

Delivering value fast can be a useful stepping stone to securing more budget, which you can use to drive further adoption and migration activities. It might add an extra step to your adoption journey, but I have this seen work in several organizations. Successful data analytics delivery on Google Cloud as the first use case will build trust and confidence with your stakeholders.

Operational Efficiency

A common commercial gain used in forming a business case for Google Cloud is based on becoming more operationally efficient by moving your entire data center into Google Cloud. This is based on the fact that purchasing tin and renting or owning the physical space to run your on-prem data center are more expensive than a cloud provider's pay-as-you-use model. While every business case will want to understand the estimated monthly cost for hosting your workloads in Google Cloud, I'd advise that your entire case for cloud isn't based solely on it. In Part 4, I'll cover more on accelerating the run cost estimation process with tools.

Being operationally efficient is also about automating deployments, streamlining the delivery of services, and having the right metrics to monitor for optimal performance. Combining these provides you with the ability to quickly and easily scale to meet peaks in demand. If your organization has workloads that have this type of traffic pattern, then again, the commercial gain should be estimated and provided within the business case.

Within the operational efficiency context, it's important to remember the narrative that being more operationally efficient is about reducing the time and therefore cost associated with those activities. If you are aware of processes that could be improved through the use of Google Cloud products and services, then find a way to measure that cost and add it to the business case.

Security

If your organization has suffered from a cyber threat, then you'll likely understand that there is a link between the cyber threat and a cost to the organization. That could range from loss of reputation and therefore loss of customers and sales to the cost of specialist security consultants to help you trace and resolve any breach. Use available and up-to-date survey data to add weight and credibility to the business case, such as the statistic that the average cost of a data breach is $4.24 million (*Cost of a Data Breach Report 2021*).

Reliability

If your on-prem data center has had incidents that have affected workloads, caused downtime, and therefore had a commercial impact, then being able to define what the impact was in monetary terms is a useful metric. The average cost of a serious or severe infrastructure outage is $100,000, (*2021 Data Center Industry Survey Results*). If you lack data points on the cost of downtime, then use industry survey data.

If your workload's reliability issues aren't infrastructure and are, in fact, more related to software, then while simply moving to Google Cloud won't necessarily improve that. It'll certainly provide the products and services your development teams can use to improve their software delivery performance and reliability.

Again, estimating improvements in that area to commercial gain will strengthen your business case. The DevOps Research and Assessment (DORA) team at Google Cloud uses the calculation shown in Figure 5-1 to show the cost of downtime.

Figure 5-1. *The calculation for the cost of downtime*

The common theme across the approaches is to demonstrate that costs avoided should be considered as returns. For example, let's suppose by moving to Google Cloud you can avoid 3 hours of infrastructure outages a year at $100,000 an hour. You've avoided $300,000 in costs that would have been incurred. Instead of simply saving that money, it should be reinvested as it would have been budgeted for.

Sustainability

Finally, do not overlook that running your workloads inside Google Cloud will dramatically reduce your IT infrastructure's carbon footprint. Power Usage Effectiveness (PUE) is the standard measure for a data center's efficiency. A PUE of 2.0 would mean for every 1 watt required to power infrastructure, another watt is needed to run those ancillary services such as cooling. The goal is a PUE as close to 1 as possible. Google Cloud's most efficient region has a measure of 1.06, and overall across all regions the measure is 1.10. This is dramatically better than the industry average of 1.57 according to Uptime Institute (*Uptime Institute 2021 Data Centre Industry Survey*).

Business Critical Events

The last one is typically in the wake of a response to a business critical event, such as changes in regulations like the US government executive order in May 2021 that requires enhancement to support chain security, which came after the SolarWinds attack. Other business critical events could be mergers, acquisitions, or divestitures; the end of support for mission-critical technologies (hardware and/or software); and, finally – one I've found quite common of late – data center facility closure and serving you a notice of termination of the contract, leaving you no option and usually not as much time as you'd like to exit the data center.

Rapid Business Case

In situations where the organization wants to assess the cost of a move to Google Cloud but is keen to make quick decisions and accept a little more risk, then the rapid business case is what you need. The aim is to determine the cost of running your current workloads on Google Cloud. And if you are planning to accelerate migration with a Google Cloud partner, then it would include estimated partner costs to migrate the workloads.

However, given cloud providers have been in existence since 2006, it is unlikely that you'll wake up one morning and suddenly decide you need to build a rapid business case to justify a move to Google Cloud if nothing on your end has changed.

A rapid business case, meaning a shorter time to decision, will have come about due to several internal or external factors. If you are not the person issuing the request for the business case but tasked with putting it together, then ask whoever issued the request what has changed since yesterday, last month, or last year?

Often this rapid method can be a precursor to a detailed business case, used as material to catch the eyes of C-level executives. So knowing what internal or external factors have changed will enable you to add more dimensions than purely focusing on cost reduction.

A rapid business case often accepts the default benchmarked on-prem costs from data center discovery tools, while this will greatly speed up the creation of the commercials. It must come with a warning that your on-prem costs could be significantly higher than the benchmarks.

The rapid business case should also use publicly referenceable data on cost avoidance as per my examples of security incidents and infrastructure outages.

A rapid business case for Google Cloud in its simplest form would cover the following:

- Total cost of ownership analysis of your on-prem infrastructure costs vs. Google Cloud running costs (use only automated discovery and assessment tooling)

- The high-level benefits that would be realized vs. the risks of doing nothing

- Migration costs, such as dual-running infrastructure costs, Google Cloud migration specialist partners, team overtime

- Estimated cost reductions or cost avoidance

For my rapid business case template, please see the website infrastructureleader.com/resources.

What level of detail does your business case need?

Depending on the size of your organization, the rapid business case might get you past the first door, but you have another that you'll need to get through. This usually happens in larger organizations where the cultural changes required to adopt and operate a cloud environment affect many people. It means the decision-makers need assurance that the benefits of the cloud are worth the challenges of the journey. In these cases, you'll often need to create a detailed business case.

However, be sure to understand who the decision-makers are. As there is nothing worse than putting hours into the business case, then presenting it to the decision-makers only to have them tell you that someone else also needs to be involved. And equally important is understanding the impact a move to the cloud will have on their role, business unit, and teams. You'll need to try and cater for them within your business case. Failure to tackle this now during the business case stage will likely cause a slowdown and stagnation of your Google Cloud adoption.

Detailed Business Case

The detailed business case requires additional time and effort. This is because the detailed business case brings additional data points, such as the current state of IT and data around the workload landscape, including what can be retired, replaced, migrated, etc. It will also include data on the actual costs for personnel, hardware, power and cooling, network, storage, and maintenance charges over a multiyear period. Maintenance costs from vendors will increase the older the hardware gets. So ensuring you have the true costs for maintenance is key to understanding the potential cost savings you can unlock by no longer owning the hardware.

A detailed business case will also benefit from data points to back an opinionated viewpoint you are trying to give. For example, if you are trying to align the value of a product such as Anthos, then using data from a third-party analyst report on the return on investment of Anthos can give credibility to your case. Google has consolidated all current third-party analyst reports on this page `https://cloud.google.com/analyst-reports`.

Your detailed business case should also have accurate data points for the cost of security incidents or infrastructure outages. Look for data points such as the durations involved and the number of teams working dedicatedly to resolve the issues. Then work out the IT labor costs from that, and add to that loss of revenue throughout the duration (finance teams should be able to help) and, finally, any longer revenue loss as a direct result of issues, such as a customer terminating a contract due to incidents or outages.

As I've previously mentioned, Google Cloud data centers are exceptionally energy-efficient, and a growing number of those data centers are powered by carbon-free energy. To get a metric to benchmark against Google Cloud, you'll want to find out what your server's kilowatt-hours (kWh) are and the CO_2e/year of the manufacturing process. CO_2e/year information is available from the server manufacturers' websites like Dell. Google also has some industry benchmarked CO_2e data that can be used against your specific estate, but it will still require a few inputs like your kWh. Speak to a Google Cloud sales representative or Google Cloud partner to find out more.

At a high level, your detailed business case for Google Cloud should cover the following:

- Current state assessment, including details on challenges and aspirational targets/goals

- The quantifiable benefits that would be realized by migrating to Google Cloud vs. the short- and long-term risks and costs of doing nothing

- The detailed multiyear total cost of ownership analysis of your on-prem infrastructure costs vs. Google Cloud running costs, with a clear return on investment shown (combination of automated discovery tooling and data gathered manually from various sources)

- Migration costs, such as dual-running infrastructure costs, Google Cloud migration specialist partners, team overtime

- The high-level outcomes from a detailed analysis of the workload landscape and the expected future state. For example, how many workloads will be retired vs. rehosted vs. replatformed

- Estimated migration timeline with some metrics upon which progress can be measured

- Learnings and observations from a pilot, proof of concept, or Shadow IT usage that may have taken place

- Innovation initiatives that can leverage Google Cloud and most importantly the "units of progress" this enables and value it creates

An antipattern that I've seen more than a few times is writing a business case on a per workload basis. It's usually in global organizations where decision-making is decentralized. Avoid it, as it'll slow the overall progress of migrating to Google Cloud. Instead, work to identify the root cause of why it can't be approved for all workloads and understand who is involved in making that decision. Engage with them and work to understand and resolve how the process could be simplified and accelerated.

Integrating with an Existing Business Case Template

Your organization will likely have a business case template you must use. A larger and decentralized organization will likely have several variations or templates for specific business units. Firstly ensure you are using the correct template. Next, you'll need to understand how to align the information captured in the rapid or detailed business cases and get that to fit into the template. More often than not, this will entail adding additional fields that you can populate the information.

Once you are happy you've added all the information you captured, read the business case end-to-end. For that first pass, I often pretend that I am about to stand in front of a packed meeting room or video call and talk it out loud. And if you feel brave enough, join a virtual meeting with just you in it and record yourself delivering it. Or deliver it in front of some peers and ask for their feedback.

I try to make written notes of the areas I stumble on or am unsure about or if my content doesn't flow or a sentence doesn't make sense. I find that writing notes helps to maintain focus, and attention isn't diverted to yet another application on the screen.

With the second pass, I aim to resolve most if not all of those identified areas and instead will focus on typos. Then finally, ask a peer to review it end-to-end. Once you've taken their feedback, you are ready to submit it.

Be Aware of Competing Priorities

Your organization only has so many people who only have so much time upon which to do their work. Your organization may also have set budgets for programs/projects, which may be carved out by business unit, country, or another way.

Time and time again, I've worked with organizations that have put together a good case for the cloud, only to find they have too many competing priorities that take away the people or the budget required for cloud adoption and migration. So don't fall into that trap. Identify all current and planned workstreams from across the entire organization and understand how that affects the people and budget you need.

Summary

You will likely need to write a business case to justify the move to Google Cloud. Start with a rapid business case and then a detailed business case. Identify the "units of progress" that move your organization forward. Understand what costs can be avoided and how that can create funds to invest in a Google CloudGCP migration. Use industry survey data to add credibility to points where you lack potential financial impacts. Identify competing priorities that will affect the available budget and bandwidth of the people you need.

CHAPTER 6

The Cloud Strategy

> "Without strategy, execution is aimless. Without execution, strategy is useless."
>
> —Morris Chang, CEO of TSMC

In this chapter, I will cover why you need a cloud strategy defined and what should be included within it.

Your organization will likely have several different strategies defined by your executives. Strategies of interest to us will be the business strategy and the technology or IT strategy. Each will have elements you'll want to be aware of before writing the cloud strategy. First, let's address the fact that not all strategies are of the same quality. To what degree you'd happily say your organization has well-defined strategies is another question! In fact, "74.6% of organizations have an IT strategy process they feel is ineffective" (*Build a Business-Aligned IT Strategy*).

Let's quickly look at a typical business strategy to set some relevant context with a cloud strategy. A business strategy document will be time-bound, often for 3 years with well-established and larger organizations. Within the business strategy, you'd expect to have items such as the following covered:

- The organization's purpose, vision, and direction
- Key performance indicators and goals
- Customers and target markets
- Marketing strategy
- Finance strategy
- Operations strategy

© Jeremy Lloyd 2023
J. Lloyd, *Infrastructure Leader's Guide to Google Cloud*, https://doi.org/10.1007/978-1-4842-8820-7_6

Your organization will also likely have a technology or IT strategy. A McKinsey & Company survey found that executives' posture toward a technology strategy has changed since 2017. It's a shift that has accelerated due to COVID-19, from 48% of executives using technology to reduce costs in 2017 to just 10% in 2020. The majority (38%) of respondents now choose to invest more in technology to make it a competitive advantage (McKinsey & Company, 2020). Within the technology strategy, you'd expect to see the following:

- IT key performance indicators, objectives and goals, and how they align with the business strategy

- Budgets and investments

- Technology roadmap, which might include cloud

- Asset and workload life cycle

- Partners and alliances

- Operational efficiencies, cost optimization, automation of processes

- Risks and issues

What is a cloud strategy then?

Simply put, a cloud strategy lays out the function cloud has within your organization. It has directions and guiding principles and details the alignment with the business's outcomes.

So, where does a cloud strategy fit, and why do you need one?

First, let me start by saying a cloud strategy is not meant to be a long drawn out document. It should be concise and simple to understand. I've seen customers with it as a dedicated document, or within a technology strategy, or as part of a digital transformation strategy. What matters more is how this cloud strategy aligns with the business strategy and helps the business achieve its desired outcomes and goals.

It's also important to ensure your cloud strategy is accessible to all. It should not be hidden away and never used. Trust all employees with knowing the cloud strategy. I'd advocate that you proactively get the cloud strategy sent out through as many channels as possible (email, internal social platforms, posters on office walls, etc.).

Simply making the cloud strategy available in this manner will greatly help to reduce Shadow IT. And instead, orient the organization toward the cloud strategy. Some of the best cloud (or even technology strategies) I've seen don't use documents and thousands of words at all. They use modern web tools that help bring the strategies to life in a more storytelling narrative, such as Adobe's Spark that is now part of the Adobe Creative Cloud Express platform. Spark is an online web tool, which also handily means anything you create can be accessed via a URL.

I'd also advise that you share your cloud strategy with partners such as your Google Cloud account team and any Google Cloud partners and MSPs. Doing so allows them to understand the vision and direction and how they can align services to help accelerate you on that journey. If your cloud strategy is aligned to the business and value creation, why wouldn't you want to get there faster?

Without a cloud strategy, anyone within the organization can decide to consume a product or service from a cloud provider. There is no real guidance on the official position on cloud usage from IT. It's the role of the cloud strategy to join existing domains such as governance, security, operations, and compliance and what these mean in the context of the cloud.

For a template to get you started, visit infrastructureleader.com/resources.

So, what exactly is in a cloud strategy?

The cloud strategy should cover the following elements:

- Version

- Executive summary

- Current state

- Financial models

- Alignment to business strategy

- Guiding principles

- Security

- Compliance

- Risk management

- Governance

- Ways of working

- Objectives and key results

- Implementation plan

You can alter sections of the cloud strategy to fit your organization's current alignment of roles and responsibilities. Typically the more regulated the industry, the more dedicated teams are focused on security, compliance, risk management, and governance. Bear this in mind when writing the cloud strategy.

The cloud strategy should be consumed as an input document when defining your cloud operating model, which we will discuss later.

Who should create the cloud strategy?

I've worked with organizations where the creation of a cloud strategy is an individual responsibility. I've also worked with organizations where several different teams coauthored it, and I have engaged in consulting during its creation. One thing is always true: for a cloud strategy to be effectively implemented, it requires buy-in from key people within your organization, be they key peers or senior leaders.

So, how can you get people to buy into your cloud strategy?

You have to understand how implementing the cloud strategy could affect them. To do that, you have to put yourself in their shoes. If you cannot do that, consult with those key people. Let them read the document and then ask them how they feel the cloud strategy affects them and their team? Listen for their answer. Give them the space and time to answer. Then follow up with another question: what challenges do you see with the implementation? You could ask them what challenges their team members would see. Again listen and make some notes about what was said.

To implement your cloud strategy, you'll need to allay these fears and challenges and win the support of those key people. So let me unpack each of the areas within the cloud strategy and guide you on the contents.

Version

Like any important document within an organization, having a simple version number can greatly help track the evolution. Those changes will undoubtedly occur as priorities change within the business. It may mean there are some changes required to the cloud strategy. Likewise, as your organization's cloud adoption progresses, you'll find changes or extensions of the strategy to ensure it provides relevant guidance and direction are required. For the actual version control, I usually propose a simple table with columns: version number, data release, and the authors who made the changes.

Executive Summary

The executive summary should capture the what and why of the cloud for your organization. Keep this section concise; think of it as an elevator pitch.

Current State

This section should detail how IT currently operates. Is it a centralized or decentralized function? Detail the challenges, risks, and issues currently faced and how they align with the organization's technical debt.

Financial Models

Establish a financial model that outlines how your organization will pay for its cloud usage, with cloud providers offering pay-as-you-go models through to direction and indirection agreements. This section should detail the impact of the shift from CAPEX to OPEX and, at a high level, the controls and mitigations that must be in place. Any associated risks with the CAPEX to OPEX shift should be exposed here and documented under risk management.

Various financial commitments can be made against an individual Google Cloud product or service (discussed in Part 6). This section should detail the considerations that should be taken into account by the consumers of cloud products and services. Advise them before making such purchases. And aid them in making those decisions, which will be financially beneficial over the longer term.

Finally, you should define if you will be using a show-back model. Consumers of those Google Cloud products and services are presented with the costs for informational purposes, or a charge-back model, where cross-charging mechanisms exist to pay for their consumption.

Alignment to Business Strategy

For this section, a lot of what has been written in the business case can be reused here. It's the alignment of the benefits that the cloud can bring the organization, coupled with the desired business outcomes. If your organization has never created a business case for the cloud, use the approach I've used earlier in this book to align cloud benefits with your business outcomes. Again think about Elvin Turner's "units of progress" and how that progress aligns with those desired business outcomes.

Define the process and responsibility for assessing and measuring the alignment cloud to business outcomes.

Guiding Principles

This section should contain statements that help consumers of the cloud make decisions that they know align with the organization's cloud strategy. It's these principles that can help prevent Shadow IT decisions from occurring.

I am not here to define your principles for you. Instead, let me show you the areas your guiding principles should cover:

- The priority of each service model. Software-as-a-Service (SaaS), Platform-as-a-Service (PaaS), and Infrastructure-as-a-Service (IaaS).

- The priority of each deployment model from the public cloud, private clouds, hybrid to on-prem infrastructure, as in are you cloud-first.

- The definition of the terms to be used to define your existing workloads future state, as per the six R's approach (discussed later).

- State what your position is on automation: is there an automation-first approach?

- Define how teams approach security, as in security by design/default (a shift-left approach).

- Guidance around a team's size; think about when a team becomes too big.

- If your organization is multicloud, define how a cloud is selected and if there is guidance on the use case.

- How to control costs or guide users on their responsibility and the impact of costs.

- How products and tools are to be selected. Think about the right tool for the job approach vs. being more prescriptive and blanket standardization of a limited number of tools. Think about if tools for certain functions must support multicloud.

- How do the consumers of cloud approach innovation. When do they need approval to experiment?

Security

Your organization might have a set of security principles, guidance, processes, or all three. They provide the guardrails needed to ensure your organization's users, workloads, and ultimately data remain safe. It's quite likely that the responsibility of creating and maintaining those standards sits with an individual or team. I'd advise you to engage with them while working on this section of the cloud strategy. And if your organization doesn't have a set of defined security principles, now is a good time to write some.

I would also advise using a cybersecurity risk framework (sometimes known as a cloud compliance framework). Use an established and reputable body, such as the NIST Cybersecurity Framework or the Cloud Security Alliance's Cloud Controls Matrix (CCM). It's a common mistake made by security teams that feel the need to create their security standards. This leads to a never-ending cycle of questions as you educate the wider organizations on your standards. And it can lead to security becoming perceived as gatekeepers and blockers.

The NIST Cybersecurity Framework (NIST CSF) gets your organization to describe the key outcomes of cybersecurity risk across five functions, which the NIST CSF describes as follows:

Identify - "Develop an organizational understanding to manage cybersecurity risk to systems, people, assets, data, and capabilities."

Protect - "Develop and implement appropriate safeguards to ensure delivery of critical services."

Detect - "Develop and implement appropriate activities to identify the occurrence of a cybersecurity event."

Respond - "Develop and implement appropriate activities to take action regarding a detected cybersecurity incident."

Recover - "Develop and implement appropriate activities to maintain plans for resilience and to restore any capabilities or services that were impaired due to a cybersecurity incident."

Another mistake is to reuse current on-prem standards. Be aware of those current standards, and describe where they integrate with the Google Cloud shared responsibility model. But do not simply use your current standards. For example, you'd align current VM security standards to Google Cloud's IaaS. But those same standards wouldn't apply to PaaS or SaaS, where you do not manage the underlying virtual machines.

The cloud provides you with the ability to improve current security standards. Detail the current security challenges, risks, or areas of improvement. Align them to controls you'll put in place to raise those standards and solve the current challenges.

This section should also tie into a broader organization security strategy if you have one. Securing your workloads on Google Cloud is critical. So is securing your users and the devices they use as it'll be those devices that are used to log in to Google Cloud.

Data Classification

Within the security section, you should specify the sensitivity of the data that will reside in Google Cloud. Most organizations have data classification standards. Ensure you align with them. You should also describe at a high level the measures that will be put in place to control and protect the data. I explain more about this in Part 6.

Compliance

This section of the cloud strategy should list all regulatory and compliance standards your organization must comply with and detail how you'll aim to satisfy them. Certain workloads or even specific services within a workload (e.g., a payment processing service) must comply with standards such as PCI-DSS. Think about data sovereignty even if you aren't in a highly regulated industry. Now country- or continent-wide, rules about the processing and transferring of data exist, such as the European Union's General Data Protection Regulation (GDPR).

When detailing how you'll satisfy the standards, aim to give guidance in the form of statements, such as describing how your cloud consumers should select a Google Cloud region. For example, select the Google Cloud region closest to your operating country and do not select based purely on the lowest latency.

You might specify that before using a new Google Cloud product or service. The public documentation is read to confirm data does not get sent outside of the country or continent from where your resources reside. For some standards, it might be that you point them toward the Google Cloud compliance reports manager, which provides the certifications and documentation related to how Google Cloud satisfies the standard, leaving you to ensure any customer responsibility will be met by your additional guidance.

View compliance as part of a cyclical process, and review tooling such as Cloud Security Posture Management tools. They can simplify your ability to secure workloads and data and maintain compliance. If a tool is going to be used, then detail that within this section.

Risk Management

Organizations of any size should have a risk management life cycle process when using the cloud, either as a dedicated function or part of a security team's function for small-mid-sized organizations. Simple misconfiguration could lead to a breach of security. So managing risks associated with the cloud and putting the mitigations in place are fundamental.

This section of the cloud strategy should detail if you will use existing risk management frameworks or implement a new framework to cover cloud risk management. Your risk profile changes when using the cloud. In the security section of Part 6, I will go deeper into how.

If you are unsure how to get started with cloud risk management, start by performing a cloud risk assessment against the following:

- Assess against your organization's current capability across the topics and functions in this book, for example, the risk of not having a cloud operating model defined or the risk of not having migration and modernization strategies.

- Cybersecurity. Start by assessing information security risks of workloads or individual servers against the confidentiality, integrity, and availability (CIA) of the data they contain. I'll cover CIA in more detail in the security section.

- Compliance. Assess against the risk of not meeting the standards you must comply with like GDPR.

- Migrations. Assess them against downtime incurred and estimated revenue impact.

Risks can be identified in several domains. The above points, combined with implementing a framework such as the NIST Risk Management Framework, will help to highlight, manage, and put mitigations in place to reduce your cloud adoption risk profile.

Google now offers a Risk Protection Program. This is essentially a specific product that combines an insurance package, cocreated by Google and the insurance underwriters (Munich RE and Allianz currently), with tooling from Google that will generate reports related to your security posture. If your organization needs this or has purchased it, then detail that within this section of the cloud strategy.

Governance

This is the "how" section. Everything within the cloud strategy is closely linked. How will you know security principles are being met? How will you monitor that compliance standards are adhered to? How will you monitor risks and any changes to the risk profile? How is the cloud strategy itself going to be adhered to? Who is responsible for that? You can't be a one-person gatekeeper and have all things cloud-related channeled via you. If you weren't there, how will adoption continue in alignment with the strategy?

Your organization likely has a governance framework such as COBIT or ITIL. If so, take the time to understand your organization's implementation of it and how it can be amended to fit the cloud environment. In Part 6, I will detail more guidance around adjusting your IT governance for Google Cloud.

When I am talking about cloud governance with my customers, I often find that this drives some of the guiding principles. For example, if one of the governance processes is to ensure infrastructure is secure, consistent, and repeatable, then having a guiding principle related to the automation of Google Cloud products and service is key to driving the behavioral changes you need.

Ways of Working

Taking full advantage of what the cloud can offer means that the current ways of working need to change. The cloud strategy should address how your organization will tackle behavioral change in a cultural change program. It should set out to allay fears around job security. Failure to ensure your team's physiological safety is a way to guarantee your adoption will be slow or stagnate and leave you unable to fulfill the desired outcomes.

This section needs to cover direction setting around any changes from the current IT operating model. This section doesn't define what or how the cloud operating model looks. That's covered by the dedicated document of the name (covered later on). So by direction setting, I mean against areas such as the following:

- Will you establish a Cloud Centre of Excellence?

- Are certain IT functions that are currently decentralized going to become centralized?

- How will the teams responsible for adoption, migration, modernization, and day 2 operations be resourced? Internal team members currently fulfilling other duties, new hires? Think about the cloud skills required at the start of your journey.

- And will they be run as a project team? Going from one to another or like a product team whereby they are responsible and accountable for its complete life cycle?

- The delivery style, will you use Agile, Wagile, or a mix of other styles?

Within this section, you should also lay out skills paths for roles affected by the cloud. Table 6-1 includes column headings of the current role name, a short description, and skills required, followed by the future state of the role using the column's future role name, short description, and future skills required.

Table 6-1. *Current roles and skills mapped to the future roles and skills*

Current role name	Short description	Current skills required	Future role name	Short description	Future skills required
Infrastructure engineer	Responsible for the build, maintenance, and decom of physical and virtual servers	Server imaging, backup/restore, configuration scripts VMware	Platform engineer	Responsible for provisioning Google Cloud resources	Infrastructure-as-Code concepts, Terraform, Cloud Build, source control, continuous integration, continuous deployment

This section of the cloud strategy isn't meant to be a learning and enablement plan. Instead, it should be the input needed and help set direction for those responsible for creating learning and enablement plans. See the skills chapter for more details.

Objectives and Key Results (OKRs)

It's pretty likely that one or more objectives are behind your organization's adoption of the cloud. Understanding the problems the cloud is solving and the benefits the cloud can bring is essential before you set OKRs.

This section of the cloud strategy should detail those objectives in a clear and easy-to-understand form. The objectives shouldn't include numbers. Once the objectives are defined, you need to detail the key results that help you to know whether the objective is on track or has been achieved. These should be specific and time-bound.

Objectives related to cloud adoption and migration can span a vast range. Here are some common ones I've seen in use with some key results underneath. Please replace the specific numbers with what is achievable and relevant to your organization:

- To be known as a technology organization that does (insert relevant industry-specific wording)

- To have 50% of candidates apply directly through our website or LinkedIn by mm/yyyy

- To have our competitively differentiating workloads running in Google Cloud by mm/yyyy

- To modernize our competitively differentiating to use Google Cloud managed services by mm/yyyy

- To turn our infrastructure team into platform engineers with 60% of the team certified on Google Cloud by mm/yyyy

- To make 100% of Google Cloud infrastructure changes on competitively differentiating workloads through continuous integration/continuous deployment methods

- Be invited to talk about our products and services at an industry event by mm/yyyy

- To decommission our on-prem data centers

  - Number of workloads moved by mm/yyyy

  - Reducing amount of data stored on on-prem storage appliances to x by mm/yyyy

  - Number of physical racks (or servers) decommissioned by mm/yyyy

  - Number of data centers decommissioned by mm/yyyy

  - Percentage of IT budget spent on on-prem associated cost vs. Google Cloud by mm/yyyy

- Improving agility, speed, and scalability through the use of Google Cloud

  - Number of workload modernizations in-progress by mm/yyyy

  - Number of modernized workloads in production by mm/yyyy

  - Number of cloud-native products in production (or it could be used to measure products in development) by mm/yyyy

- To increase software releases for (name of product or service) to x per week

- Number of daily active users on Google Cloud

When creating your OKRs for Google Cloud adoption, migration, and modernization, think back to the "units of progress" that I mentioned previously. It's possible to position a unit of progress as the objective and then define the key results around it that demonstrate your progress toward achieving it.

Implementation Plan

During my work, I've reviewed many cloud strategies for small and mid-sized organizations through to global household names. I find that people overlook the plan to implement the cloud strategy. The plan should define who needs to do what next to deliver it.

I also find it's best not to try and write every action required for an adoption journey as it'll inevitably change. Instead, across each element, define the next one to three actions required to move it forward and, most importantly, who is responsible for them. Then hold a short agile standup style meeting every week or two to keep tabs on progress.

Summary

You can avoid a stalled or failed Google Cloud adoption by creating a cloud strategy for your organization. Form opinions and write definitions for each of the elements I've laid out. It's okay if they change as your cloud journey progresses.

Form a team to work together on different elements, as Cloud adoption isn't a solo endeavor. Ensure your stakeholders are aligned, specifically around the alignment to the business strategy. Ensure you have the actions and accountability defined that will lead to progress.

Cloud Operating Model Strategy

In this chapter, I will cover what a cloud operating model is, why you need one, the different types, and how to align your future state toward one.

Once your cloud strategy is written, you need to define how that will be made a reality. That's where your cloud operating model comes in, also referred to as a target operating model. The cloud operating model is the arrangement of your organization's teams to functions and responsibilities that deliver value and outcomes.

What is an operating model?

You might not be surprised that if you asked ten leaders, you'd likely get ten different answers. Even if you asked ten leaders within your organization about your current operating model, you'd likely get various answers. In business terms, "an operating model is the blueprint for how value will be created and delivered to target customers" (*Gartner*).

So what is an IT operating model?

An IT operating model "represents how an organization orchestrates its I&T capabilities to achieve its strategic objectives" (*Gartner*). What that means is how day-to-day activities performed within IT add value and move IT toward defined objectives, a simple explanation of a profoundly complex area that has seen the creation of many different frameworks.

Okay, so finally, what is a cloud operating model?

So based on those two earlier definitions, a cloud operating model is the blueprint that aligns the domains required to operate and innovate in the cloud to team responsibilities that support business outcomes.

Why do you need a cloud operating model?

© Jeremy Lloyd 2023
J. Lloyd, *Infrastructure Leader's Guide to Google Cloud*, https://doi.org/10.1007/978-1-4842-8820-7_7

Your current organization will have an established IT operating model. It's likely evolved over the years and is probably not often discussed as it is accepted as the standard way of working. When workloads run on physical infrastructure that you own and manage, it means the focus of the IT operating model is on stability, not change. This often led to lengthy change management processes, with all teams having to review and approve changes even if the change in question had no impact on one of those teams.

On the more extreme side, I've seen change management processes for a financial services organization that had 15 levels of approvals and took around 3 months to go through the end-to-end process. However, for most organizations, it's common that this type of change process would take about 2 weeks or be built to fit into when the change advisory board (CAB) would meet.

In the cloud, that operating model will hold back the true agility you'll want to harness. As Google Cloud can be available on-demand and from anywhere means a traditional IT operating model doesn't fit anymore. You can no longer wait 2 weeks for CAB to approve your change to a product or service in Google Cloud.

If you want to reduce the time to value of your products and services, then you need tooling and processes that enable automated security policies and testing, releases to production to be frequent with monitoring in place, and autoscaling to meet demand in one region or many, all with appropriate feedback loops in place to ensure lessons are learned and improvements to the processes are made.

Before you define your cloud operating model, you must truly understand the workloads you'll be moving to Google Cloud. If your estate primarily consists of commercial-off-the-shelf (COTS) software that you run as virtual machines, then you are not in control of how often the vendor makes new releases. Instead, you control when and how you update the software on those virtual machines.

Moving large numbers of virtual machines to Google Cloud that are running COTS software will mean that your needs and your cloud operating model will look different, compared to an organization with in-house development teams that build and deploy software used by internal and external end users.

In the latter scenario, the teams have complete control over their release cycles and are ideally situated to modernize their workloads to take advantage of Google Cloud managed services and PaaS products which will help them to realize many benefits, such as resilience, scalability, availability, and the ability to release to production quicker.

It's pretty likely you'll have a mix of both, so it's worth understanding what percentage of your workloads are COTS vs. internally developed.

CHAPTER 7   CLOUD OPERATING MODEL STRATEGY

So how can you define your cloud operating model?

There is no perfect cloud operating model. Not only does every organization have different needs or maturity levels, but the world of cloud computing is constantly evolving. It simply doesn't stand still. And so there are always improvements to be made. All of this will alter what your cloud operating model looks like.

What your cloud operating model looks like is driven by several different factors:

- The type of workloads within your current estate (COTS vs. internally developed) and what percentage of each you have.

- The migration pattern you use (the R framework): are you lifting and shifting on-prem COTS and internally developed workloads? Or will you lift and shift the COTS but modernize your internally developed workloads to cloud-native?

- The strategy around prioritizing the cloud services models (SaaS vs. PaaS vs. IaaS).

- The way your IT function currently operates (centralized vs. decentralized) and the strategic vision of future operations.

- The OKRs you've defined within the cloud strategy. If you don't have OKRs defined (I'd suggest you do that first) or alternatively, write down what are the outcomes your organization is looking to achieve by adopting Google Cloud.

Three Common Cloud Operating Models

While working with many organizations on their cloud adoption, I've identified three common patterns to a cloud operating model, each with its advantages and disadvantages. There are of course other variants, but these are the common patterns that most variants stem from. They are as follows:

- Decentralized operations

- Centralized operations

- Hybrid operations

Decentralized Operations

In the decentralized pattern, your organization is likely global with a current decentralized IT operating model. In this pattern, each isolated team will have to seek guidance by referencing the cloud strategy. Google Cloud is centrally procured to maximize your buying power. And your organization node and cloud identity are set up and configured by IT.

The aim is to ensure all who need access can get it and self-serve their needs. Each isolated team will then be able to set up the Google Cloud folders and projects they require and the network connectivity needed to migrate and manage their workloads.

Advantages of This Pattern

Proactive and engaged workload owners/teams will rise to the top and become Google Cloud champions. You can identify them through their Google Cloud consumption.

The teams closest to the workload are in control of migrating (or building cloud-native versions) and managing it. If something goes wrong with the infrastructure or a new release, a single team can solve it, which typically leads to reliability improvements from the automation of common tasks to the use of other Google Cloud products and services that modernize and help to improve the workload. In a decentralized pattern, this happens faster than in the other two patterns due to the self-sufficient nature of the teams.

The Disadvantages of This Pattern

There is no CCoE to own the cloud foundations. In this pattern, a Google Cloud organization node and Google's identity provider (Cloud Identity) are usually the only elements a central function has set up.

No CCoE means there are no best practice landing zones for the workloads. And it means that cloud skills will need to be learned by the teams through trial and error. However, I've found that even in a decentralized approach, as everyone knows they have a common platform, there is organic growth in sharing what is or isn't working. How quickly that process takes partly depends on your organization's culture.

Eventually, a definition of what good looks like becomes apparent. However, some teams will have rework to conform to newly defined standards. Depending on your size and scale, that could be significant and require you to form a cross-skilled specialized team to assist those decentralized teams in getting to the new standards. This brings us to the second pattern.

Centralized Operations

Are where all the functions required to operate a workload in the cloud centralized, from cloud foundations to operating system maintenance and software vendor updates? This operating model pattern is a good fit for organizations that do not have hundreds of landing zones to maintain, and the workloads are primarily all COTS.

Therefore, the primary objective is to provide a stable platform for the workloads. You achieve this through consistent standards, policies, tools, and training. In this model, the central teams manage the cloud foundations, landing zones, and workloads, typically starting with a single CCoE team.

The Advantages of This Pattern

It avoids the pitfalls of the decentralized pattern by ensuring a centralized team (CCoE) defining standards and keeping the Google Cloud projects and workloads in compliance. The CCoE will design and deploy the cloud foundations and create the modules required to create landing zones. The CCoE should develop automated procedures for new releases and updates to workloads. The CCoE can create development and test environments to be identical to production environments.

The Disadvantages of the Centralized Pattern

It will almost always start with a single centralized team. And as workloads migrate and other new workloads are built and deployed to be cloud-native, the team can find itself a bottleneck and struggling to balance priorities, which leads to growing the size of the team. This growth is acceptable if carefully managed.

Keeping to the principles of small teams means you can more easily split the team and grant them more specific responsibilities. For example, one team might be responsible for all consumer-facing workloads, while another all backend data analytics workloads. Or you might split out security, networking, and financial operations or a similar combination.

Another disadvantage of this approach is that developers and operations are still not working as a cohesive team. The centralized team's focus is on stability and automation and not innovation.

This continual growth of the centralized teams moves you toward the third pattern.

Hybrid Operations

In this pattern, cloud foundations are centrally managed, but each landing zone is owned and managed by the team responsible for the workload(s). This pattern enables those responsible for workloads that need stability to prioritize that. And those teams responsible for workloads that create a competitive advantage for your organization can prioritize using Google Cloud managed services and PaaS products and services. This pattern enables teams to organize themselves and their ways of working (Agile/Waterfall, etc.), all while the centralized teams ensure standards are adhered to.

A typical nuance of this pattern that I've seen brought in is a centralized operations function. This is a different team from the CCoE. Instead, this team is performing day 2 operations for business units that lack the skills and/or budget to get the necessary skills to manage the workload themselves.

The Advantages of This Pattern

In hybrid operations, workload teams can migrate and modernize in the manner and timescale they need. Workload teams can benefit from the best practices, landing zone modules, and architectural patterns created by the CCoE. Workload teams also have the freedom to make improvements to their workloads by using CI/CD release processes and using Google Cloud managed services and PaaS products.

The CCoE provides the cloud foundations and guardrails to ensure workload teams have freedom but stay in compliance with the organization's standards.

This approach also allows you to adjust centralized functions as demand is identified, such as the centralized operations team.

The Disadvantages of This Pattern

The centralized team can often feel like they are guardians, telling people the tasks and activities they should perform and informing them when they don't meet the standards. Often the centralized team would prefer just to do the work themselves.

The key is that if you've had to grow into this pattern, your organization will likely be of considerable size. The centralized team needs to ensure that the organization's desired outcome is what is motivating them and ensure there is an acceptance that, to adopt and migrate to Google Cloud at scale, they cannot simply do it alone.

I've also seen that the centralized teams in this pattern directly assist with migration and modernization activities. Suppose the workload team is inexperienced and not proactively engaged in Google Cloud training and enablement plans. In that case, it can leave the central teams in a position whereby they are now an operations team for the workload.

That is when you either introduce the centralized operations team. If you do that, then ensure you define strict criteria required for a workload to become managed by that team. Otherwise, it becomes the path of least resistance, and you'll find workload teams become less agile and able to modernize at pace.

The centralized teams will naturally expand to become teams designed to serve specific functions, similar to the centralized model.

Evolving Your Operating Model

Just as migrating to the Google Cloud is a journey that can take organizations months to years, so is evolving your current IT operating model to fit the future needs of your organization. The cloud operating model that you define at the start of your Google Cloud migration journey is unlikely to be the same once you are partway through your migrations. And it'll likely change again once you've moved all workloads to Google Cloud.

As I've previously mentioned in this book, people are the most challenging part to change. There is also plenty of research that is publicly available that confirms this is the case.

So to successfully transition to your defined cloud operating model, you will need to have a plan. When advising organizations I work with, I often refer to this plan simply as the transitional operating model and have this as a dedicated section within any material produced to define the cloud operating model.

By putting a transitional operating model in place, you are accepting that there is a transitional state. This means the team members who have responsibilities expect things to change. They are more open to the fact it's not perfect. A transitional operating model helps to activate the team's learning mode. And when combined with any feedback they provide means your cloud operating model becomes a better fit for your organization's needs.

The transitional operating model should address what and how your preferred cloud operating model will be implemented.

Have a section of the cloud operating model dedicated to the transitional stage. It should detail who is responsible for each function that makes up your current IT operating model. Then use the direction set within the cloud strategy to define the team's structure and align the responsibilities.

For example, if your cloud operating model defines establishing a Cloud Center of Excellence (CCoE), then your transitional operating model should align what functions the CCoE performs as soon as the team is established. The CCoE will evolve as the needs of the organization change. See Part 3 on cloud adoption teams for more details.

To create some data points to measure your transition to your cloud operating model, you can put in place an OKR. Such as the following examples:

- Number of teams using the cloud operating model

- Number of teams enabled for cloud operating model

- Number of requests received by the CCoE/central teams

- Number of post-migration incidents logged

- Number of cloud operating model improvements in the backlog

The purpose of this OKR is to expose bottlenecks and see the adoption of the cloud operating model and improvements in service delivery.

Summary

Review and understand the factors that influence your cloud operating mode. Align the strategic vision to a cloud operating model pattern such as decentralized operations, centralized operations, or hybrid operations. Establish your transitional operating model plan, describing how to get from the current state operating model to the desired cloud operating model. Ensure you have strong feedback loops to help evolve your operating model. Define OKRs to help you measure your progress.

CHAPTER 8

Migration Strategies

In this chapter, I will discuss the different migration strategies, how they align to Google Cloud's migration terminology, how you identify and manage risk in the migration stage, and how to work with your IT outsourcer during the migration (if you have one). Finally, I will cover Google's Rapid Assessment and Migration Program to guide you on the journey.

Talk of strategies, and people instantly feel insecure, unsure what a good strategy looks like or how what's in their head can be translated into pretty visuals and clever buzzwords. Fortunately, things are slightly better defined when it comes to having a migration strategy.

However, when I speak to customers, they still try to find their solution to this problem. Stuck in the analysis paralysis stage, some have too much data on their workloads, some have too many stakeholders with competing priorities, and others have little to no data and no idea where to begin.

In 2010 Gartner introduced the concept of 5 Rs, with the aim to guide decision-makers tasked with solving the directive of "Move some application to the cloud" (Watson, 2010). The 5 Rs in 2010 were Rehost, Refactor, Revise, Rebuild, and Replace. Google Cloud's R framework consists of 6 Rs:

- Rehost

- Replatform

- Refactor

- Replace

- Retire

- Retain

© Jeremy Lloyd 2023
J. Lloyd, *Infrastructure Leader's Guide to Google Cloud*, https://doi.org/10.1007/978-1-4842-8820-7_8

Google Cloud will sometimes refer to the Rs by different terminology. I will detail those alternatives and the definition of each approach. When Google defines its R's framework, they discuss each approach in the workload context. Remember that a workload can be a single server or many. It's important to recognize that you might use more than one approach to get a workload migrated.

Of course, these 6 Rs alone won't provide any value unless you use the 6 Rs to discuss each workload currently in use and decide that workloads fate. In Part 4, I'll show you how to achieve this with a couple of methods I use with my customers.

Rehost or lift and shift – this approach is taking an existing server from your source environment and moving it to the target environment. There should be little to no modifications required.

Use this approach when you have time-bound events to migrate, such as the termination of a lease on a data center and the urgent need to improve infrastructure stability or reduce infrastructure CAPEX. It requires the least operational changes as you are still running servers.

Replatform – move and improve or improve and move. This approach sees modifications made to improve the server. Typically this is by adding cloud-native functionality, but in the case of improve and move, it's upgrading an OS or libraries and binaries to a newer version ahead of moving.

Use this approach for workloads that need improving to be able to run in the cloud, as is the case with improve and move. Or the migration to the cloud is seen as a chance to make improvements that enable you to deliver value faster or improve reliability to meet business objectives, such as containerizing the workload with Migrate to Containers.

Refactor – rip and replace, rebuild, or transform. This approach starts with business requirements and designs cloud-native workloads that meet those requirements. Design cloud-native workloads with cloud architecture best practices in mind. This approach doesn't always mean you design the workload from the ground up. It might start with one or two services of hundreds that make up the workload.

It is used for workloads that competitively differentiate your organization but are now legacy in how they are written, updated, and maintained. This approach offers an excellent chance to revisit the tech stack used, helping to remove vendor lock-in for services such as databases.

Replace – use replace on workloads that fulfill commodity functions for your business. Replace with a SaaS version or a competitor's product, commonly used to reduce the number of vendors that need managing or to consolidate and standardize on a strategic vendor of choice, perhaps after a merger or acquisition. Also, it might be that the workload has reached its end of life. And newer, more up-to-date products exist that are market leaders and/or simply align better to business needs and objectives.

Retire – do not migrate to the cloud and decommission the servers and infrastructure relating to this workload.

It is used in conjunction with a Replace approach, as in a workload has reached its end of life, and the function it fulfilled you replaced with something newer. Sometimes it's used in isolation, as in there is simply no requirement for the functionality the workload fulfilled.

Retain – this sees the workload not being migrated to the cloud and usually means it stays in its current physical location but not always. It might mean moving to a colocation facility or a private cloud.

It is used when strict data sovereignty or other regulatory compliance standards must be met. More often these days, a retain approach makes use of products like Google Distributed Cloud. This enables you to use Google Cloud products and services managed by Google but physically located on-prem, in a colocation data center or Google edge network.

Considerations

Figure 8-1 helps you position the different approaches and on a basic level where they might be applicable. It also shows you that approaches can be dynamic. As in, you may lift and optimize a VM, then subsequently improve it to run as cloud-native in a container.

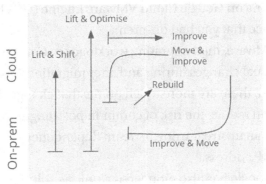

Figure 8-1. *Migration approaches use case alignment*

Different components of a workload can also have different migration journeys. For example, you might lift and shift a web front-end server but move and improve the SQL server to Google's Cloud SQL (a managed version of SQL). Take these dynamic journeys into account when planning a workload migration journey.

You need to write the definition of which Rs you will use and what they mean to your organization. Try not to reinvent the wheel; using definitions that are publicly referenceable makes it easier for everyone to understand the terminology. Put your definition in a location that others within the organization can easily find. I usually suggest to customers a single slide and to have it stored in the same location as the cloud strategy document.

Migration Risk Management

Within the cloud strategies risk management section, I have called out how to approach cloud risk management. However, what about risks associated with a migration to the cloud? How can you mitigate them?

First of all let's explore the risk that by moving to the cloud, your workload won't function as it did before. There are several ways to mitigate and control this risk. If the workload has a non-production environment, this could be replicated to Google Cloud using Migrate to Virtual Machines, previously known as Migrate for Compute (M4C). Testing can then be performed against your non-production environment. Secondly, Migrate to Virtual Machines can create test clones, meaning you don't have to migrate your non-production to test that it will function in Google Cloud. Use the same approach when replicating your production environment to Google Cloud.

You can mitigate the risk for VMware workloads by using a lift and shift approach with the workload landing on Google Cloud VMware Engine (GCVE). This offers you the same VMware experience that you had on-prem.

If you don't have VMware, then migrating workloads to Compute Engine is another product requiring minimal changes during and after migration. You can use the lift and shift approach. However, there are more touch points that change. Through the testing I describe above, you can reduce the risk of common post-migration issues such as a blocked firewall port or an upstream/downstream dependency not communicating with the new Google Cloud IP address.

And on that note, Google has also pioneered a unique solution to help de-risk your server migrations to Google Cloud. It enables a conceptually similar network extension from the on-prem network to your Google Cloud network, just like a Layer 2 extension between two on-prem data centers. This reduces migration risks enabling you to migrate VMs from on-prem to Google Cloud without changing the IP addresses during migration. This resolves common issues with tight dependencies on VM IP addresses, typically caused by hard-coded IP addresses in application interface configurations and firewall rules.

It's called Hybrid Subnets, and it uses Proxy ARP to enable you to create overlapping subnets between your on-prem and your VPCs in Google Cloud. For example, if you have a range on-prem of 10.10.0.0, you can create an identical range in Google Cloud. You continue to migrate the servers using M4C, but now those common issues previously mentioned aren't an issue.

Working with Your IT Outsourcer in a Cloud Migration

Many organizations have, over the years, outsourced more and more of their IT functions. Often this was done as a way to reduce operational costs and overheads and reduce risks by being able to hold others accountable. Let's understand the outsourcer's perspective to understand the challenges this model can present and find some solutions. The outsourcing leader will want your organization to have a stable operation with all your systems being available per the SLAs agreed within the contract. If no SLAs are breached, the outsourcer is doing its job well, and the customer should be happy with the service they are receiving.

What happens when a change needs to be made?

As we've previously discussed, change in any context brings fear of the unknown. So cue rigorous (and usually slow) change process with change advisory boards (CAB) that meet every 2 weeks. When you own the physical infrastructure and operate the data centers, focusing on the availability and security of the physical kit is critical. Tracking changes made in order to mitigate risk is also vital. However, tracking those changes can be like finding a needle in a haystack.

When you no longer own the physical kit or the data center and are using the cloud, availability and security are still critical, but the risks' focus has moved up the stack to the products and services running the workload.

So how does an outsourcer work with you to unlock the potential of Google Cloud while ensuring they still meet their SLAs and find ways to reduce risk?

There are a few different options that depend on the relationship you have with your outsourcer.

Some organizations have not had a great time with their current outsourcer. They want to replace them or insource the work.

There's the 'work with' approach, where you engage the outsourcer to perform the move to Google Cloud. This approach will require additional costs from the outsourcer.

There's the collaborative approach where you work with your current outsourcer but bring in a Google Cloud specialist partner. That partner brings the skills and knowledge of migration and modernizations to Google Cloud and can leave the knowledge with your outsourcer when they disengage.

Finally, there is a hybrid approach, where you insource workloads that competitively differentiate your organization and leave all your commodity workloads with your outsourcer or Google Cloud specialist partner to move to Google Cloud and manage.

When working with an outsourcer, I have seen migrations stall due to communication. So whichever option you take, ensure the leaders from each side sit down together, discuss the goals you want to achieve, and give clarity into roles and responsibilities.

Google Cloud Rapid Assessment and Migration Program (RAMP)

To help guide customers through migrations to Google Cloud, Google has created the Rapid Assessment and Migration Program (RAMP). RAMP has six key pillars that simplify the cloud onboarding process and accelerate your ability to perform workload migrations.

The pillars of RAMP as defined by Google Cloud are as follows:

Guidance - Google is providing documentation in the form of whitepapers, reference architecture patterns, and best practices.

Training - Google's Qwiklabs online learning platform has a host of courses.

Tools - Google has Migrate for Compute Engine to move servers and Migrate to Containers, to move servers to containers.

Partners - Google Cloud has thousands of partners to assist you with migrations.

Google Cloud Professionals - get access to experts from Google Cloud and Google's own professional service organization.

Offers - Google can provide incentives in the form of credits to reduce your Google Cloud costs or funding for a Google Cloud partner to work with you.

(*RAMP up Your Cloud Adoption With New Assessment and Migration Program*, 2020)

Entering into the program is a great way to accelerate your Google Cloud adoption. Your team will upskill faster than if they were to undertake the journey by themselves. You can lean on experts from Google and the approved Google Cloud RAMP partners to guide you around common mistakes and blockers. That said, you can use Google Cloud migration journey or any other migration framework, without having to enter into Google Cloud's specific migration program. However, RAMP will start you off with a free discovery of your data center, which I highly advise. Treat RAMP as your starting point in the journey.

Summary

Define your organization's definition of the Rs framework. Document migration risks that you foresee. Only by doing so can mitigations be put in place. Communicate joint goals and outcomes if working with an existing IT outsourcer. Engage with your Google Cloud field sales rep and inquire about RAMP, starting with the free data center discovery.

CHAPTER 9

Modernization Strategies

In this chapter, I will cover what a modernization strategy is, why you need one, and what goes into it.

Gartner defines workload or application modernization as "the migration of legacy to new applications or platforms, including the integration of new functionality to provide the latest functions to the business." In the context of Google Cloud, this means migrating on-prem workloads to Google Cloud and utilizing new Google Cloud products and services to improve the workload's ability to serve the businesses' needs.

What are the benefits of modernizing your workloads? Organizations look to modernize their existing workloads to solve their current challenges. These challenges directly impact your customer's ability to do business with you, such as a performance bottleneck on a website or an inability to integrate two systems or challenges such as a service that goes down regularly or is taken down to deploy a new release.

I've previously mentioned the Gartner Rs as a framework in the context of a migration from on-prem to cloud. The Replatform and Refactor Rs, or, as Google refers to them, move and improve, improve and move, rebuild, and transform, are the approaches most aligned with modernizing workloads. Having worked with numerous customers on migrations that contained workload modernization, I found you can undertake varying degrees of modernization during a migration.

There are relatively trivial Replatform modernizations such as an operating system (OS) upgrade. This can be performed by a migration tool if the OS can perform in-place upgrades. Or of course, this can be done as a pre-or post-migration task. Then there are deeply complex modernizations such as refactoring a monolithic application running on a mainframe and written in COBOL.

I've found that formalizing your organization's modernization approach helps to unblock decision-making about modernizing your workloads. I usually advise the creation of a modernization strategy document.

© Jeremy Lloyd 2023
J. Lloyd, *Infrastructure Leader's Guide to Google Cloud*, https://doi.org/10.1007/978-1-4842-8820-7_9

The following is a sample table of contents. I will expand each section a little to give you context of what each should contain. Your modernization strategy should include the following:

- Guardrails

  - Modernization approaches

  - Boundaries

- Modernization roadmap

  - Premigration modernization

  - In-flight migration modernization

  - Post-migration modernization

- Workloads to modernize

  - Baseline metrics for improvement

- Skills and team structure

- Products and partners

Guardrails

Modernization approaches – as previously mentioned, there are several different approaches from Gartner's Rs to Google own take. This section should detail which approaches you will use during your migrations and the definition of what they mean within your organization, described in Table 9-1 to give clarity and order. You should provide practical patterns that align with the migration approach. For example:

Table 9-1. *Modernization approach definitions*

Migration approach	Description	Patterns
Replatform	An OS upgrade or a change of DB to a managed service	In-place OS upgrade Database migration Database replication
Refactor	Changing code and deploying services to run on cloud-native products	Functional decoupling Strangler Fig

Continue to update the table when you identify new patterns.

I advise setting some boundaries for the Replatform and Refactor approaches during an on-prem to Google Cloud migration. Failure to do so can leave you with teams working on deeply complex modernizations for months or longer. A simple catch-all boundary is to set a time limit upon which to complete the modernization. Otherwise, it defaults to a lift and shift, and once that is completed, the team can look at modernization efforts again.

Modernization Roadmap

The modernization roadmap aims to build upon the definitions in the migration approaches section, providing the reader with guidance upon which they can make decisions that set their direction.

Premigration modernization is also known as improve and move. Here you detail what premigration modernization should or could take place and any criteria that will help your organization quickly and efficiently decide if the workload needs premigration modernization activities. For example:

Table 9-2. *Premigration modernization criteria and high-level tasks*

Criteria	Premigration modernization
OS is SUSE Linux Enterprise Server (SLES) 10/10 SP4	Network boot OS upgrade to 11 SP4 through SUSE Service Location Protocol (SLP) server

In-flight migration modernization is the act of modernizing while you move workloads. Typically this approach will involve specific tools created for such a purpose. Detail the criteria that guide the reader toward the modernization pattern and the required tool. For example:

Table 9-3. *In-flight modernization criteria and high-level tasks*

Criteria	In-flight migration modernization
Non-production SQL Server 2008/2012/2014 databases	Database migration to Google Cloud Cloud SQL using Database Migration Service or tools like Striim
Production SQL Server 2008/2012/2014 databases	Database replication to Google Cloud Cloud SQL using listed above
	Becomes database migration once non-production migration has been completed
SUSE 12, 12 SP3, and 15 web servers where Migrate to Containers fit assessment is excellent fit or good fit	Run on Google Kubernetes Engine (GKE); migrate using Migrate to Containers

Post-migration modernization, also known as move and improve, is typically where the majority of modernization patterns sit. Post-migration modernization stretches from automating regular tasks using Google Cloud products and services or configuring your workload using Infrastructure-as-Code (IaC), through to modernizations like decoupling a monolith into microservices that run in containers or running your data warehouse in a managed service. Again clearly detail your post-migration modernization patterns within a table such as Table 9-4.

Table 9-4. *Post-migration modernization criteria and high-level tasks*

Criteria	Post-migration modernization
OS is Server 2008 R2 or 2012 R2	In-place OS upgrade, using Compute Engine automated gcloud process
Web servers that have peaks and troughs in demand and/or require availability in more than one zone	Stateless Managed Instance Group (MIG)
Stateful workloads that require resilience and frequent updates and/or require availability in more than one zone	Stateful Managed Instance Groups (MIG)

Workloads to Modernize

How do you define your in-scope workloads? Your organization is likely using more workloads than you know (Shadow IT). That is why a discovery process using tooling and questionnaires is key to understanding your organization's current workloads. I'll discuss the discovery phase in Part 4.

Once you have your list of workloads. The next key consideration is how do you know which to lift and shift vs. a move and improve, improve and move, or transform?

I guide my customers through a process known as workload categorization. This process sees you put workloads into four categories: low value, high value, noncritical, and critical. I discuss this process in detail in Part 4.

With workloads categorized, you define what's in scope for modernization and define a priority order. You'll naturally want to first modernize workloads with the greatest urgency and highest business impact. However, this route often leads you to undertake complex workload modernizations and learn many lessons. Depending on the severity and impact of those lessons, it can change the organization's appetite for further modernization.

A better approach is to learn those lessons on low-risk workloads. Identify workloads that fit the criteria for modernization but have a smaller user base or low impact on your customers, revenue, and brand reputation. As the team's capability to modernize workloads grows, they can take on more complex modernizations.

To decide on the risk vs. urgency of modernizing a workload, you'll need to bring specific data points for each workload. Data such as the following:

- Business and technical owners

- Number of users (internal/external)

- Workload lifecycle

- Criticality (low, medium, high)

- Complexity (simple, medium, complex)

- Value to the business (low to high)

- Security posture (very bad to very good)

- Time taken from code written to being in production

- Deployment frequency

- Failure/rollback frequency

- Time to recover (TTR) from failures

These data points help you to identify that workload's limitations more clearly.

Once you have the data points, give each workload a modernization risk (low, medium, and high) and an urgency. As previously mentioned, you should start with low-risk and move on to medium-risk and, finally, high-risk modernizations. However, do base your decision on the urgency factor as well. For example, you might have a workload that, in its current state, has limitations that cause financial impact (such as an inability to scale to meet demand). Use a quadrant, such as Figure 9-1 to apply your data points and to help prioritize which workloads to modernize.

Figure 9-1. *A quadrant to help you prioritize workloads to modernize*

Skills and Team Structure

Does your organization have the right skills in-house to perform the modernization activities? You need a blended team centered around three key aspects:

- Technical knowledge of the workloads/applications

- Technical knowledge of Google Cloud's managed services and PaaS products

- Experience with modernization approaches and tooling

This section of the modernization strategy should define the following:

- The skills required

- The number of teams

- Where the team members will be resourced from

- How the modernization team structure will look

Keep the knowledge of Google Cloud and modernization skills within a defined modernization team and the workload/application knowledge within the team currently responsible for it, as shown in Figure 9-2. This workload team then augments the modernization team for the duration of the modernization effort. Have the business and technical workload owners be part of the modernization effort. It will help to unblock decisions that could otherwise cause delays.

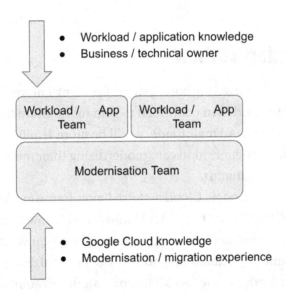

Figure 9-2.   *How a modernization team works with a workload/app team*

Tools and Partners

This section of the modernization strategy needs to set the direction on the tools and partners the modernization team will have available to them to complete their work. Business leaders have often asked me about how to speed up modernization activities.

One common element to improving modernization velocity is empowering the team with the right tools. Being aware of tooling that can accelerate activities is crucial. More importantly, let the modernization team have a way to procure and put those tools to use quickly. There are Google Cloud and some third-party tools that you should consider. Often, the team can assume what tools they need before they start, but it's not until they start modernizing workloads that they fully understand their tool requirements.

Furthermore, engage with a modernization partner from Google Cloud's partner program to accelerate modernization activities. Google Cloud modernization partners will bring previous experience in having delivered the different approaches, tools, and ways of working. Using a partner will help to bring your teams up to speed quickly and ultimately achieve your outcomes faster than doing it alone. You can use a partner to run your modernization team or simply augment a team you manage. Your modernization strategy should detail how you plan to use partners to accelerate your modernization initiatives.

Mainframe Modernization

Mainframes have been the powering core systems for many enterprise organizations since they arrived in 1943 and then continued to gain momentum through the 1950s and 1960s. If your organization has a mainframe, you'll be more familiar with the challenges and costs of running one. Organizations are modernizing their mainframe applications to keep pace with today's demands.

Recognizing this trend, Google Cloud acquired mainframe modernization company Cornerstone in 2020. Cornerstone built a tool known as G4, now known as the Google G4 platform. The G4 platform and Cornerstone acquisition represent 25+ years of experience in mainframe application migrations and modernizations. In 2021, this led to Google being named a leader in the ISG Mainframe Modernization software quadrant.

The G4 platform provides an automated approach to understanding the composition and interdependencies between all your mainframe applications. This gives you the data points you need to make informed decisions around your modernization strategies.

There are several different mainframe modernization strategies, each providing different outcomes that will be more or less suitable for meeting your current needs. Modernizing your Mainframe applications is often a multistep journey, with potentially multiple destinations depending on the mainframe data and applications you have. You might need to use two or more modernization strategies to achieve your desired outcome.

The different mainframe modernization strategies are as follows:

Retain – applications continue to run on the existing infrastructure but are encapsulated behind an API. Often this is the first step of the journey to decompose mainframe applications.

Rehost (emulation) covers two patterns. The first is rehost to a mainframe as a service offering, such as IBM Power on Google Cloud. This approach has minimal risk but also provides fewer benefits. The second is to recompile the code on x86 architecture and rehost on Google Cloud using emulation tools from organizations like TmaxSoft and Lzlabs.

Refactor (G4 platform) has two patterns: line-by-line conversion of code to Java or dot net. The second is building new applications from the metadata of the legacy code. The first pattern enables you to modernize while maintaining the business logic and process from potentially millions of lines of COBOL code. The second pattern allows you to move to a new architecture pattern, such as microservices. Google Cloud's G4 platform can be leveraged to automate the discovery, assessment, and code conversion of mainframe applications.

Reimagine is greenfield application development where you understand the business processes and requirements and write new code in a new application to meet them. This approach can take considerable time and proves an expensive route.

Replace is where you purchase commercial off-the-shelf (COTS) software to fulfill the needs of one or more of your Mainframe applications. This approach can cause considerable business change. Users of Mainframe applications will have to adjust their ways of working to the COTS software's capabilities.

The different strategies have a trade-off between the cost, effort, risk, and time vs. the value, as shown in Figure 9-3.

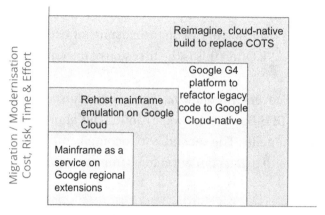

Figure 9-3. *The different mainframe modernization strategies against cost, effort, risk, and time against the value*

Migration and Modernization Decision Trees

Pulling your migration and modernization strategies into decision trees can allow team members to visualize a direction of travel with minimal reading. Of course, once they know their direction, they can review the specific documents to understand the approaches, patterns, tools, and other considerations.

Google Cloud has produced two decision trees that I typically start with when consulting with my customers. These usually evolve into something a little more bespoke to fit a customer's strategy as migration and modernization programs of work progress.

Figure 9-4 helps orient the viewer into understanding what to migrate to cloud vs. replaced vs. retained on-prem.

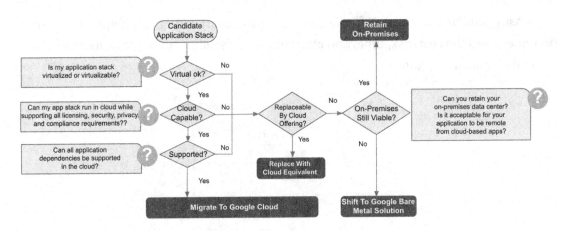

Figure 9-4. *Decision tree to help identify what you migrate vs. replace vs. retain*

Figure 9-5 focuses on how you modernize the workload. It helps you understand lift and shift vs. lift and optimize vs. move and improve paths.

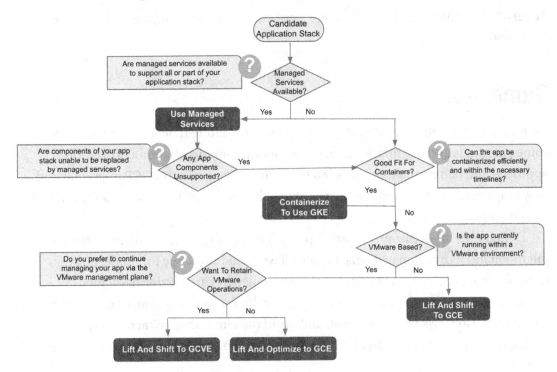

Figure 9-5. *Decision tree to help identify how you modernize your workloads*

Lastly, similarly to the mainframe modernization chart earlier, it is helpful for teams to understand the cost, risk, time, and effort of each migration strategy against the value gained as shown in Figure 9-6.

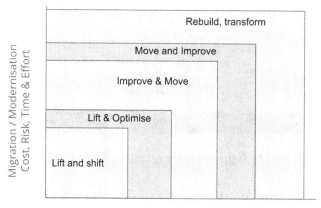

Figure 9-6. *Modernization strategies against cost, effort, risk, and time against the value*

Summary

Create a modernization strategy document using the outlined table of contents. Put some guardrails and boundaries in place by clearly defining what modernization approach and patterns to use during an on-prem to Google Cloud GCP migration and how long the team should spend on a workload before handing it back to a lift and shift migration team.

Define your modernization roadmap detailing premigration, in-flight, and post-migration modernization patterns. Define all workloads in scope for modernization using the workload categorization approach detailed in Part 4. Prioritize which workloads to modernize first by giving each workload a low, medium, or high risk. Start modernizing low-risk workloads first, and avoid the temptation to tackle the big complex workloads. They can come after your team has learned some valuable modernization lessons.

For Mainframe modernization, understand the data and applications used on the Mainframe and plan what each application's modernization journey should look like.

CHAPTER 10

Accelerate with Google and Partners

In this chapter, I cover engaging with Google Cloud and Google Cloud partners and why you should do that.

Googlers and Office of the CTO

Google Cloud is a large organization, and knowing how to get help can seem daunting, but, fortunately, it's not. Google Cloud has a sales function with teams of people they call field sales representatives (FSR). These FSRs are assigned organizations to look after. Some of those organizations will already use Google Cloud, and others might not. There are customer engineers as well. These talented people are more technical in their background and can provide guidance and advice on Google Cloud products and services.

If you want to discuss your journey to Google Cloud, then simply visit the Google Cloud contact page to connect through online chat or phone or submit a short form, and they will contact you. You can, of course, contact a Google Cloud partner. And in turn, they can assist you with establishing your Google Cloud relationship.

Google also has a function they call the Office of the CTO (OCTO). The OCTO team comprises ex-CTOs from various industries and senior engineers covering specialities such as artificial intelligence/machine learning, containers, security, high-performance computing, etc. OCTO also has a holistic view of the products and services other Alphabet (Google parent company) subsidiaries are building, such as Waymo, Google's self-driving car project, or DeepMind, Google's team of AI specialists.

Google Cloud also has a professional services team known as PSO (professional services organization), focused on helping large organizations get the most out of Google Cloud products and services on a large scale, typically on multidimensional programs of work.

119

© Jeremy Lloyd 2023
J. Lloyd, *Infrastructure Leader's Guide to Google Cloud*, https://doi.org/10.1007/978-1-4842-8820-7_10

Partner Ecosystem

Google Cloud has seen enormous growth in the number of partners wanting to join their partner program in the past few years. There are now thousands of Google Cloud partners globally, providing expertise across various industries. Google Cloud buckets partner into three models:

- Sell partners where the partner integrates Google Cloud offerings into their portfolio and sell these to their customer and provide indirect reselling.

- Service partners provide consulting and integration services and Google Cloud authorized training.

- Build partners create solutions that integrate with and/or run on Google Cloud to complement or enhance Google Cloud products and services; build partners offerings are available on the Google Cloud Marketplace.

Partners can be active in one or more of the engagement models. Partners can also attain technical designations from Google. These are known as expertise and specialization. These help you understand the partner's focus, experience, and quality of the service they deliver. Some partners will also cover Google Marketing Platform, such as the Google partner I currently work at, Publicis Sapient. These partners are known as being able to provide the 'One Google' story, which is essentially to bridge the marketing / advertising side with the cloud.

Expertise shows that the partner has demonstrable growth and customer success across solutions, specific industries, or technologies.

Specialization is the highest-level technical accolade that Google Cloud awards partners. It requires an established Google Cloud practice within the respective specialization area with proven, repeatable customer success and proven technical abilities, vetted by Google and assessed by a third party. To achieve a specialization requires a partner to obtain certifications + the expertise + customer success.

When it comes to partner selection, understand what you are looking for. Typically Google Cloud-only partners are renowned for delivering in an Agile-style approach, making progress and getting to value faster than a traditional partner might do.

Look at the partner's specializations. Do they align with your needs and strategy? Have they got experience solving the challenges you face and in your industry? Do you need a Google marketing / advertising partner as well as cloud? When I speak to customers, they want to consolidate suppliers and partners. There is a burden when managing tens to hundreds of these relationships. If that resonates, look for a partner with more of an end-to-end capability, one that can truly take you on a journey, even if you only need them for part of that journey now. Having the relationship in place with all supporting legal paperwork for when you need them again is useful.

Why should you use a partner?

The right cloud partner does not work reactively with you on a specific point-in-time challenge, and then you never hear from them again until you reach out to them. No, the right cloud partner has diverse capabilities and offerings and engages with you proactively to build a relationship. Using their depth of experience, they'll guide you through the pitfalls and trends, having worked with other organizations within your industry. They will be able to meet you where you are at and then accelerate your organization in that given capability.

Managed Service Providers (MSPs)

A Google Cloud approved MSP is a partner who has been consistent in their ability to obtain and maintain the specializations they hold over several years. And they pass the strict criteria to qualify as an MSP. A third party audits Google Cloud MSPs annually to ensure they meet Google's standards across multiple domains. As someone who previously worked for a Google Cloud MSP (Appsbroker) and was involved in the annual audit process, I can confidently say Google Cloud is setting the bar high for MSPs. In turn, this means you know you can engage an MSP with a high degree of confidence in their ability to deliver. MSPs must have a high proliferation of Google Cloud certified individuals within the organization.

A huge plus to partnering with an MSP is their connections to Google Cloud's engineering teams. It means the MSP can directly provide any product feedback or escalations you might need to the engineers responsible for the product.

When looking for an MSP, look at the specialization they hold and whether it aligns with your workloads and use cases of Google Cloud.

At the time of writing, there are less than 40 MSPs globally. All Google Cloud partners, including the MSPs, can be found on the Google Cloud website.

Summary

Assess your adoption, migration, and modernization timelines, and understand if a specialized Google Cloud partner is needed to accelerate your journey. Assess what you need to manage in-house against commodity workloads that a Google Cloud MSP can manage for you. Engage with Googlers to understand what assistance they can offer you. Engage with a partner who has proven experience in the areas you require.

PART III

Organizational Readiness and Change

In Part 3 of the book, I will cover the organizational readiness and changes required in advance of adopting and migrating to Google Cloud. This part will therefore focus more on people and processes.

CHAPTER 11

Cloud Adoption and Cultural Change

> It is not the strongest of the species that survives, nor the most intelligent; it is the one most adaptable to change.
>
> —*Charles Darwin, British Naturalist*

This chapter covers how to unite your people to get behind a cloud adoption program and what Google's Cloud Adoption Framework covers and how to use it.

No matter where you are currently on your journey to Google Cloud, I'm sure you've either directly or indirectly come across migration projects or cloud adoption initiatives that have stalled or failed. Often they stall after one or more workloads have been moved. Things might not have gone as planned, end users were unhappy and logged help desk tickets as their work was affected, and ultimately the people involved in the migration got blamed. It creates an uneasy atmosphere where taking calculated risks to move the workloads feels like sticking a target on your head.

Another reason for stalled or failed adoption is when an organization has started with a highly ambitious application development project. You know the sort of project I mean; it's the one with a multimillion dollar budget and detailed plans spread over multiple years. The only right decision made on these projects is they selected to build them on cloud infrastructure, not on-prem. These big-budget projects aim to be cloud-native but often never make it to production due to the project's delivery model.

I have witnessed both of these firsthand across several customers. It's not the fault of the technology, as that's proven to more than satisfy the demands of customers big and small the world over. No, it's down to us, the people, and our willingness and the speed at which we accept change. Change means there will be things you don't know. And because of that, change often brings feelings of nervousness and fear of the unknown.

© Jeremy Lloyd 2023
J. Lloyd, *Infrastructure Leader's Guide to Google Cloud*, https://doi.org/10.1007/978-1-4842-8820-7_11

That can lead people to resist the change. If this happens with your team or people within other key teams that you'll need to onboard into Google Cloud, try to uncover their rationale for these feelings and alleviate their concerns.

Look to resolve resistance to change quickly. It doesn't help the individuals involved nor the wider cloud adoption strategy to simply gloss over it and shy away from having a difficult conversation. Consider if other roles are more suitable for those individuals. It reduces the impact on cloud adoption strategy, and the individuals concerned feel more comfortable in their working environment.

Fear also triggers other negative emotions such as sadness and anger, especially when there is a lingering but likely unfounded notion that a move to the cloud means job losses. However, this has proven not to be the case. A survey conducted by Logicworks across 400 IT decision-makers in 2020 shows 86% believe a shortage of qualified talent will slow down cloud projects in 2020 (*Logicworks Report - Challenges of Cloud Transformation*, 2020). So even if a move to the cloud sadly resulted in job losses, those newly acquired skills learned during migration should serve anyone well in finding a new role.

Unite with a Purpose, Guide with a Mission, and Deliver Through Objectives

What type of culture is required to flourish in the cloud?

To overcome the complex challenge of cloud adoption, you must get your colleagues to learn new skills to challenge themselves to operate outside their comfort zone. It's easier said than done. If you can unite teams with a sense of purpose, it will help understand why change is needed. If the organization you work for has a strong sense of purpose and a reason for its existence, it can make this easier, such as Google's, which is "To organize the world's information and make it universally accessible and useful" (*Our Approach – How Google Search Works*), or Sony's "To be a company that inspires and fulfills your curiosity" (Sony).

You can join the organization's purpose with project-specific mission statements that inspire colleagues to work together on a journey to Google Cloud. You will also want to define objectives, again making them specific to the move to Google Cloud and targets that the teams aspire to achieve. I previously discussed setting objectives in the cloud strategy chapter, so I won't cover them again here.

While there is a relationship between purpose and change, it goes via missions, objectives, and workstreams, as shown in Figure 11-1.

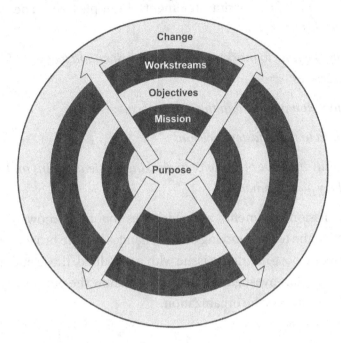

Figure 11-1. *How change starts with a purpose*

Purpose

If your organization's purpose is less well defined, then work with your colleagues to describe·a purpose for the move to Google Cloud and write some supporting mission statements.

Whenever I am in a meeting room or, more recently, addressing groups via online video conference calls, and I ask what your organization's purpose for adopting Google Cloud is, I get a lot of blank faces. A few prompts can get people to discuss their thoughts. So use my example purpose as a conversation starter to define your organization's Google Cloud adoption purpose.

Our purpose is to empower every colleague in our organisation with the right technology to move us forwards.

Mission Statements

After your purpose, you define mission statements. Examples would be as follows:
We will achieve this by:

- *Reducing the time to market with faster product and feature releases for our services*

- *Put innovation potential in the hands of colleagues*

- *Using data to make faster decisions*

- *Continually improve our service by making efficiency gains and technology advancements*

The purpose, mission statements, and objectives should be known and accessible to all, not just limited to the teams working on the changes but the broader organization. So if at any point there is a post-migration issue with a workload, those end users affected (should still log a ticket for investigation) will at least know the purpose and mission of the team and how that affects the organization.

Psychological Safety

Right now, I know you might think that a move to the cloud is only successful if you have the right culture. And you don't have that type of culture in your organization. It's not something that any organization I have worked with has had from day 1. Instead, it's about sowing the seeds and growing the momentum for change. This can start with a simple set of guiding principles. It's most likely that you or a fellow leader within your organization has already defined some guiding principles. Dig them out, dust them off, and see if they just need mild adjustments to be relevant.

"Do unto others as you would have them do unto you." You need to foster a blame-free culture and cultivate psychological safety. How? A good start is not blaming anyone else when an issue arises. Unfortunately, assigning blame is easy, and we often do it without realizing it. Having this principle at the forefront of people's minds will help to make that happen. Research by the DevOps Research and Assessment (DORA) shows that inclusive and psychologically safe teams lead to improved performance.

A blame-free culture goes hand-in-hand with the agile mindset. I'd advise hiring or contracting an agile coach to set the standards and train and enable teams on the agile ways of working. Focus on an agile approach to Google Cloud adoption and migration in the first instance, but there is no doubt the scope should extend far beyond IT. An organizational goal should be to operate in a more agile manner.

Give people clarity on what changes will happen to their role as the organization adopts Google Cloud. Advise them on their options; perhaps there is another role instead, and a move to Google Cloud can be the catalyst for positive change.

The COVID pandemic dramatically altered how we work in IT. As I write this, organizations are trying to find the balance between working from home and office-based days. If your teams are now 100% remote, ensure you focus on providing a safe environment.

Identify Key Decision Makers and Get Them on Side

As mentioned earlier, being an infrastructure leader means guiding others with opinions and action. However, before you jump in with your opinions on moving to Google Cloud, you must first identify the key people in your organization that you need to engage. Get answers to these questions:

- Who are the key people?

- What is their role?

- Is that role a decision-maker, influencer, or both?

- From what you know so far, are they for or against cloud providers?

- By getting them onboard with adopting Google Cloud, how does that help make the move to Google Cloud a reality?

If your organization maintains an up-to-date organization chart, it might be helpful to use that to jump-start identifying who you need to engage. I've asked my customers to whiteboard their organization chart during the early stages of establishing a case for Google Cloud. And we whiteboard the answers to those questions until we have a targeted list of people to engage.

After any whiteboard sessions, ensure that you store the information in a table like the one shown in Table 11-1. As your Google Cloud adoption grows momentum, new people will join the teams and the program of work. This table can be used for them to understand who is or isn't involved.

Table 11-1. *Key people and roles and how they can assist with Google Cloud adoption*

Name	Role	Decision-maker or influencer	For or against cloud?	Progress toward Google Cloud adoption
Gary Deacon	Network Manager	Decision-maker	Neutral	Would enable us to establish connectivity between on-prem and Google Cloud
Bill Jones	Senior Developer	Influencer	For cloud	Can influence the Development Manager that new projects should be cloud-native
Douglas Ingram	Vice President of Engineering	Decision-maker	Against	Can set a cloud-first strategy and assign budget to migrate existing workloads

The size of your organization, how decentralized it is, and the industry you are in will define how many people you need to engage. Generally speaking, you'll need to identify decision-makers and/or influencers who operate in the following capabilities:

- Senior leaders/stakeholders
- Information security
- Governance and compliance
- Networking
- Business and technical application owners
- Culture

The quickest route to gaining momentum to move to Google Cloud is to engage with more key decision-makers than influencers within your organization. However, if a particular decision-maker isn't within your sphere for some reason, that's when you'll want to engage with people who can influence that decision-maker.

The minimum engagement is a stakeholder and business and technical application owners. Failure to do so can result in your adoption and migration strategy being too infrastructure-focused.

With your table of names to hand, it's time to speak to those contacts. When you engage the key people, start with a big question: what are your greatest concerns if we move to Google Cloud?

Listen to those concerns, and write them down. Unpack any vague words such as costs, security, downtime, and skills. You need to unpack them down to action items, and you can't make an action out of nouns like downtime.

You need to understand why they have these concerns. Unpack each concern one at a time. Let's take a security concern as an example. Ask questions such as the following:

- What specifically are your security concerns?

- Can you give an example of that?

- Does that concern stem from a current or past issue?

- Is this concern based on a challenge you've faced or been made aware of by colleagues?

Tail off your conversation with a final question to make it real for them.

- If our infrastructure was running in Google Cloud, how would that affect everyone around you?

This question is trying to elicit a detailed response about specific people, teams, or functions that this person deals with. If you know some of those people's names, give a prompt, "what about Alice and her tasks?".

Your aim from these interactions with the key people is to get beneath the surface of any blockers they might have or put in the way. Those blockers can stall or prevent adoption and moving workloads to Google Cloud. You must define a list of action items that lead to progress. To do that, you need them to make that concern real, to bring it to life. Only then can you understand their perspective.

Listen to any tone changes they make to emphasize words. Make a note of those words. Do they require further unpacking? If so, then frame the word back to them as a question. For example, let's say you identified a tone change for the word risk.

What does risk mean to you? Can you give me an example of a risk?

Successfully navigating these conversations and bringing decision-makers on side are critical to enabling you to be the leader who unlocks Google Cloud adoption for the organization.

Finally, these key decision-makers must make hundreds to thousands of daily decisions. During cloud adoption, that number will increase. Make it as easy as possible for them to make those cloud adoption-related decisions.

Product Mindset over Project

It's common that when I first engage with an organization that is preparing to or already undertaking a migration to Google Cloud, that team from the customer is a project-based team. Either they are permanently on a project and go from one project to another, or they are part of a business as usual function and have a percentage of their time to work on the Google Cloud migration workstream. While it works and is likely deeply embedded in the organization's structure and ways of working, it's not necessarily the best way of operating.

A product-focused approach focuses on value generated for the users of the product. It requires truly understanding the product's users and their needs. You define measurements of success around outcomes.

You might think this is only applicable to organizations that write their software. Well, it's also very relevant to organizations who purchase commercial-off-the-shelf software. When a third party designs software, they cater to wider user requirements, potentially making the software not meet all your organization's needs. Instead, focusing on your users and their needs better enables you to align with commercial software that meets them. It also allows you to periodically assess the suitability of the commercial software against your user's needs.

It's a significant cultural change, and successfully navigating it will require that you get a stakeholder involved. The change goes hand-in-hand with a shift to a culture that embraces change, accepts failure as a learning opportunity, is nimble, and continuously seeks improvements. This type of change needs those senior leaders within the organization to buy in and drive.

Site Reliability Engineering

The move to the cloud means changing your current ways of working. Cloud enables you to bridge silos that have long existed between developers and operations. DevOps is a term you will no doubt be familiar with. I will focus on Google's Site Reliability Engineering (SRE). If you are familiar with DevOps, you can view SRE as a specific implementation of DevOps.

What is SRE?

SRE is what you get when you "treat operations as if it's a software problem" (Google Site Reliability Engineering). It's a concept that was pioneered inside Google in 2003 by Ben Treynor Sloss.

Applying SRE at the core of Google product engineering has ensured the stability and availability of their products while they grow at an unprecedented scale, from search to YouTube and Android to Google Workspace. Indeed the SRE books written by Google give good clarity and direction on what SRE is and how to apply it, which has led to widespread adoption within organizations like Spotify and Netflix.

"In general, an SRE team is responsible for the availability, latency, performance, efficiency, change management, monitoring, emergency response, and capacity planning of their service(s)." *(Google - Site Reliability Engineering)*

In Part 6, I cover optimization in day 2 operations. This is a continual process of ongoing service improvement. Google's SRE approach provides clear responsibilities for those day 2 optimizations.

You may find some workloads require an SRE in day 2 operations. While other workloads that are commercial off-the-shelf software don't, the SREs themselves must possess developer and operations skills. Getting the right skills in your SRE function is key to doing SRE properly. It's typical to meet SREs at my customers who just perform some automation and keep the workloads running. This is not SRE. A true SRE should be more than capable of working in your development team and also just as capable of being in your infrastructure/platform/operations team.

Google Cloud Adoption Framework

To help guide organizations adopting Google Cloud, Google created the Google Cloud Adoption Framework (GCAF). GCAF centers around two different dimensions. The first is a cloud maturity scale, which aims to show you where you currently are on a Google Cloud adoption journey and where you need to head next to get maximum benefits from Google Cloud. The second dimension exposes the workstreams that need your focus, ownership, and actions to move the organization and Google Cloud adoption forward.

First, let's look at the GCAF cloud maturity scale. The scale has four themes and three phases, as shown in Figure 11-2.

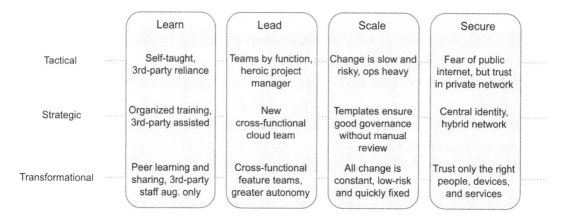

Figure 11-2. *The GCAF maturity scale*

In the GCAF, the four themes (Learn, Lead, Scale, and Secure) form the core foundations upon which Google defines cloud readiness. Learn is about upskilling your technical teams, identifying how engaged they are, how effective the results are, and working with experienced partners.

Lead is around having executive-level stakeholders backing a move to the cloud. It's having teams in place that are cross-functional, collaborative, and self-motivated in the context of the cloud.

Scale is essentially around improving the operational efficiency of the cloud services you run or will run. It's about ensuring your design thinks about scale and uses Google Cloud managed services that you automate provisioning and deployments of the infrastructure through continuous integration (CI) and continuous deployment (CD).

Security, last but not least, is about your ability to protect your workloads running in Google Cloud from unauthorized and inappropriate access. It's having a robust security posture that covers cuts across all the themes, essentially providing organization-wide continual improvement against measurable security objectives, working together cross-functionally to reduce risks.

Within each theme, you have different maturities.

Your current business practices in each theme determine which phase you are in, tactical, strategic, or transformational. I believe there is a phase before your organization gets to tactical adoption. It's Shadow IT, which I discussed in Part 2.

How can you quickly understand which phase of maturity your organization is in?

Google provides an online Cloud Maturity Assessment that you can populate and get the results instantly. It can yield useful data points about how others perceive your current state. Each question has five answers, and you can select only one of those five.

I'd advise you to get your identified key decision-makers and influencers to fill it in and ask them to send their results to you for collation. Ask them to send you the results URL, and you can compile the data.

Create a simple summary of each question by counting the number of people who selected each answer. I usually put this into a simple table that lists the question in the first column and then the total number of responses for each of the five options per question. For example, if 15 people responded, the data for the first 2 questions would look like Table 11-2.

Table 11-2. *GCAF results table*

Question	Answer 1	Answer 2	Answer 3	Answer 4	Answer 5
1	5	7	3	0	0
2	2	4	7	4	0

To analyze the results quickly, I would suggest you simply identify the most common answer for each question. Then cross-reference with the Google Cloud Adoption Framework whitepaper PDF `https://services.google.com/fh/files/misc/google_cloud_adoption_framework_whitepaper.pdf`.

The second half of the GCAF PDF details each theme and what you should do to be tactical, strategic, or transformational. You will need to take your average answer for each question and align it to what the GCAF says you should be doing. This process shouldn't take long and is to give you an indication of your current maturity level.

If you want to go to another level of detail in your analysis, look to identify patterns in the responses based on who was filling it in. You could group by roles, team, department, business unit, or country. This analysis can yield insights into a team of champions blazing a trail or some underperformer who might need additional support to upskill.

To group the questionnaire results, simply add a column specifying the metric you want to group by as shown in Table 11-3. Add additional columns if you want to group by role, team, department, business unit, or another logical unit relevant to your organization.

Table 11-3. *Expanded GCAF results table*

Question	Role	Team	Other metrics	Answer 1	Answer 2	Etc.
1	Product owner	Product management		3	2	
2	Solutions Architect	IT		2	1	

The process for identifying the most common answer and then aligning your organization to a GCAF's maturity is the same as described earlier.

What do you do with the analyzed questionnaire results?

Schedule a meeting with as many key decision-makers and influencers to deliver your summary of your organization's current maturity based on the questionnaire. Encourage debating over the result of each question. What does it mean? What should you do about it? Who can own the actions related to it? These are the types of questions you want to hear from your meeting attendees. If you don't, then start asking them yourself. Give a healthy silent pause after you've asked a question. You need to get people thinking and talking.

Ensure you allow enough time for questions and debates; do not rush your delivery of the summary. If you run out of time, schedule a second meeting to finish it. And remember, you don't need to be the one with all the answers. Give enough time for those who might have answers to speak. Before the end of the meeting, give a summary, and list any actions and the owners of those actions. Ensure you have a way to track who owns what actions and inform them how often you'll want to hear about their progress.

The second dimension is built around the people, process, and technology paradigm, as shown in Figure 11-3.

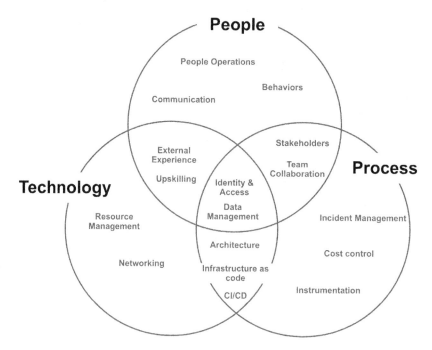

Figure 11-3. *The second dimension of the GCAF*

This dimension aims to break down the numerous moving parts of cloud adoption into digestible workstreams, which GCAF refers to as Epics. This Agile methodology term essentially means a large isolated body of work that gets broken down into multiple smaller user stories.

User stories define an end goal of a particular user. It's that user's story, the what and why, not the how it's done. Let's bring that to life and look at an example. Let's pick the Infrastructure-as-Code (IaC) epic. That epic alone offers me no context or goal upon which to start working on it.

What about IaC? Who needs IaC? Why do they need it? What are they using it for?

Instead, you need the next level of detail and you need a user story. I will show you the what and why in an example for the IaC epic:

- As a platform engineer, I want to automate the provisioning and configuration of Google Cloud resources (the "what") so that human error is eliminated and configuration is consistent (the "why").

Agile terminology lesson over, the key to using the GCAF in the Agile epic and user story methodology is to ensure you have defined who those users are. So ask yourself these questions in the context of Google Cloud adoption: who will be involved? What is the name of the role they will fulfill (future Google Cloud role, not current role as it might change)?

The aim of the GCAF is for each of the epics to have a stakeholder. Note the stakeholder might be responsible for more than one epic.

The last piece here is selecting which epics you need to start with. GCAF suggests you focus on the epics inside the four adoption themes for a minimum viable adoption approach.

A quick side note, from a practical perspective, you might foresee that managing all these epics, stakeholder mappings, and user stories becomes a resource burden. I suggest you use an Agile tool that lets you create a backlog and start to put it all into that tool like Trello or Jira. Ensure you invite others into the tool as this information should be widely known. Your organization likely has one or more of such tools in use already. Rather than purchasing another tool, use what the organization is already familiar with.

So, should you base your entire Google Cloud adoption strategy around the GCAF? It depends on where your organization is on the journey to Google Cloud. If your estate is still mainly on-prem based, then the GCAF maturity questionnaire might seem like a future step, not the next.

To be classified as tactical in your Google Cloud adoption, you need to have some current Google Cloud use cases within your organization, be they Proof-of-Concepts (PoC) or production pilots. That said, your organization will likely use the cloud for some use cases by now. It's probably just a case of Shadow IT.

If you suspect Shadow IT usage of the cloud, your next step is to engage the broader organization to uncover who is using what, why they are using it, and how much it costs (licensing, hosting fees, etc.). The data points you capture will be helpful to feed into a business case to formalize Google Cloud adoption and get you the GCAF maturity scale.

If you have some PoCs or production pilots within your organization, then the GCAF maturity questionnaire should be your next step.

Summary

Unite the team with a common purpose to drive change. Provide psychological safety; it's more important than ever in this hybrid working model that now exists. Understand if you have the right people to fulfill the SRE function. Read the Google Cloud Adoption Framework PDF. Discover the Shadow IT within your organization. If you have some known Google Cloud usage, get key decision-makers and influencers within the organization to take the GCAF maturity questionnaire.

CHAPTER 12

Cloud Operating Model Readiness

In Part 2, I discussed three common cloud operating model strategies. In this chapter, I'll focus on what you should consider in advance to prepare your organization for a new operating model.

Security Readiness

It's likely that you have a person such as a chief information security office (CISO) or a team for information security. They might be dedicated to that function or have to wear a few hats that are often closely coupled with security, such as risk and incident management, governance, and compliance.

Regardless, you will have a process to engage the security function across areas such as change management or how to consult them for review and approval of documentation during design phases.

When your workloads are running in Google Cloud, securing them is still a critical function. In the cloud strategy section within Part 2, I included security. Your cloud strategy should guide the frameworks you'll be using in the cloud. I've also covered the required skills and the learning paths available earlier within Part 3. Now let's drill into processes that may need adapting.

Accountability

Shared responsibility model – what you are responsible for changes when your workloads run in Google Cloud. I discuss this in more detail in the security section of Part 6. Prepare yourself by assessing what security is currently responsible for. Ensure the security team is aware of these changes under the shared responsibility model.

139

© Jeremy Lloyd 2023
J. Lloyd, *Infrastructure Leader's Guide to Google Cloud*, https://doi.org/10.1007/978-1-4842-8820-7_12

Compliance standards – review your current compliance standards for specific guidance related to cloud environments. Clearly define the security standards required to operate workloads in Google Cloud safely. These standards might start as a minimum viable set of security standards. You can always iterate and improve them. Being too strict will potentially cause blockers to Google Cloud adoption and migration.

Operational Security

Incident response – understand the current process for handling incidents, specifically how you triage security incidents. Whoever does the triage must understand how to identify a security incident in Google Cloud. When the workloads run in Google Cloud, will your security team have the right skills to assist with any required investigation?

Monitoring – how are you currently notified about incidents? Through customers and/or alerts? What tools are you using? Will they be used in Google Cloud (are they compatible), or will Google Cloud's cloud operations be used? Ensure service level indicators (SLIs) are recreated in Google Cloud to provide you with the same monitoring capability.

Audit – what tools currently analyse log files? Will they be used for Google Cloud logs? There are different types of logs generated within Google Cloud. They are as defined by Google's documentation:

- Admin activity logs API calls or other actions that modify config or metadata of resources.

- Data access logs API calls that read the config or metadata of resources and user-driven API calls that create, modify, or read user-provided resource data.

- System event logs for Google Cloud systems (not user actions) that modify config of resources.

- Policy denied logs a deny of access to a user or service account because of a security policy.

You will want to ensure relevant ones are enabled and that the log files are in a location that is accessible to any tools used for log analysis.

Threat detection – what processes and tools do you currently have in place? Are those tools suitable for monitoring Google Cloud? Or are Google Cloud's native products and services better suited? Compared with on-prem, the likely attack vectors change as all Google Cloud's products and services are available over public REST APIs.

Technology and Architectural Guidance

Google Cloud managed services – in the shared responsibility model, Platform-as-a-Service (PaaS) products and services put less responsibility on you than Infrastructure-as-a-Service (IaaS). The security team should provide guidance on how PaaS/Google Cloud managed services can reduce attack vectors.

Security design principles – assess any current principles, and put in place ones conducive to driving a shift-left mentality, that is to say, considering security in the design stage.

Often performing an assessment of your current security standards against key pillars I've defined above can provide you with a gap analysis. This will form the backlog of policy, process, and tool changes required to operate securely in Google Cloud.

Governance Readiness

How do you prepare your governance for Google Cloud adoption and migration?

As I previously mentioned, the governance function should sit within a cloud office. So establishing the cloud office and having the right people who can provide governance oversight of your Google Cloud adoption and migration is the first step.

It's also by ensuring alignment with the cloud strategy. Governance should focus on the cloud strategy's security, compliance, risk management, and OKR sections. Put in place the controls and measures to understand if your organization is adopting and migrating in the manner defined. I'll discuss governance, risk, and compliance in a day 2 operations context later in the book.

Lastly, the governance function should also be aware of the need to adjust controls as new workloads migrate, and the organization's Google Cloud maturity grows. This approach means that appropriate controls should be in place in alignment with the category of workloads you are migrating. For example, a static content website might be one of your first movers. Since all the data on this workload is publicly accessible by design, the controls you put in place should reflect that.

Migrations can stall or struggle to get started when the controls are too strict. As during adoption, the teams working on Google Cloud are yet to have the skills and experience to find ways to keep moving forward or challenge what's in place.

Operations Readiness

In Part 6, I've provided you with the required considerations. In addition, ensure that you clearly define how the transition between migration and modernization teams to operational teams will take place, what artifacts are required, what support will be provided, and by whom.

Summary

Understand the changes in security accountability and what this means to your current operational security. Understand how different Google Cloud products and services have different security responsibilities. Define where the cloud governance function will sit, and put appropriate measures in place that reflect the sensitivity of the data/ workloads that will run. Understand that controls will need to evolve as your adoption and maturity grows.

CHAPTER 13

Skills

In this chapter, I will cover how to build your organization's Google Cloud capability, how to cross-skill team members with AWS or Azure skills, the available Google Cloud's learning paths and certifications, and how to build certification momentum within your organization.

Prioritize your skills plan.

As mentioned earlier in the book, the cloud skills shortage is attributed directly to stalling cloud migration projects. Furthermore, even if a business was to identify a pocket of proactive, qualified IT talent, the pace of cloud innovation, new business pressures, and the need to evolve have made the ability to keep that talent relevant over time a real challenge. That's where formalizing your approach to provide learning paths that lead to Google Cloud certification is crucial to reducing the risk of stalling.

I was working on a cloud adoption strategy with an organization in the United Kingdom. They understood the importance of training and ensured their team members attended instructor-led training sessions annually. When I asked what the outcomes they expected of investing in training their team members were, it was to ensure they have the skills needed to do their role successfully.

However, they benchmarked against the current role, not a future role catering for Google Cloud skills. In these instances, you need to formalize some learning paths and give the team members a career path, which makes it easier to align more relevant learning paths and skills required. Also, consider if providing them with career options for future roles outside their current team or business unit would work within your organization.

When I questioned my customer about the investment in training over the years and how many team members were now certified, the answer was surprisingly few. I asked them what they do when a team member passes an exam, and the answer was not much.

© Jeremy Lloyd 2023
J. Lloyd, *Infrastructure Leader's Guide to Google Cloud*, https://doi.org/10.1007/978-1-4842-8820-7_13

Getting certification momentum requires some upfront planning. Having certified people within the organization helps to increase Google Cloud adoption. It can also attract others to work for your organization, as they want to work in a company with certified people. It shows them some insight into what the organization's culture is like.

There are two types of required skills.

So what skills do you need within your organization to adopt, migrate, modernize, and manage workloads on Google Cloud?

The answer to this question depends on what type of workloads are within your organization, whether commercial off-the-shelf (COTS) software makes up a high percentage of the overall estate or internally developed software does.

However, it is a question that I often get asked early when consulting with organizations. There are hard or technical skills and soft skills. Successful cloud adoption and migration require teams with the right mix of both.

I'll cover the soft skills first as I won't go into specific details about these in this book.

Adoption, migration, and modernization team's soft skills are as follows:

- Bias for action

- Ability to communicate

- Working well in a team environment

- Desire to learn and be able to learn from mistakes

- Ability to listen to others

How to Get the Skills You Need

When I was advising a global organization with decentralized IT function on their adoption strategy, their default answer to getting Google Cloud skills within the organization was to centralize the IT function and hire hire hire. I vetoed that and said to them you have local IT personnel who are more than capable if you provide them with the following:

- Psychological safety by informing of their purpose; their new function in a cloud environment

- Jointly created learning plans that are specific and aligned with the cloud strategy and future role

- The time upon which to learn the new skills

This different approach not only reduced the new hire count by several hundred; it also changed the cloud adoption rollout strategy and put skills enablement at the center. There are other benefits as well, as your existing personnel don't require onboarding like new hires. They also know your workloads and processes. So ensure you look at the people you have within the organization as they provide a way to accelerate your Google Cloud adoption.

Building the Capability

Earlier, I mentioned that successful adoption, migration, and modernization teams need a mix of technical (hard) and soft skills. I've covered the soft skills, but how do you build a Google Cloud capability with the right mix of technical skills? My approach uses four phases:

- **Early learning** starts with reading, watching, and attending any training material available. If they already have cloud skills, guide them to begin with Google Cloud for AWS or Azure professionals. But otherwise, this phase doesn't need to be focused or structured. Just get them to consume any information before there is an urgent need for the skills.

- **Job-specific learning** – understand their current capabilities, and then steer and guide the teams with Google Cloud defined learning paths that end with a certification.

- **Learn by doing** – use the free tier to experiment, and encourage your development teams to do the same; you might even set them to task on a specific activity such as the migration of a non-production low priority workload.

- **Learn by sharing** – identify the Google Cloud champions, those who show a genuine interest and drive to progress with Google Cloud. Support and encourage them to create a community to learn and share their experiences with other team members.

Across each of these four phases, track learning progress, understanding data points for each team member on areas like what articles or videos have they watched, what did they find most helpful from the material, and would they recommend the material to others.

Lightweight tracking of progress can be done during scheduled 1:1s or in a short meeting. The early learning phase will provide you with a useful understanding of who is self-motivated to learn Google Cloud and likely to be a future Google Cloud champion.

Cross-Skilling from AWS or Azure

When planning your Google Cloud adoption, there are three common reasons that you'll want to ensure you can cross-skill team members who have AWS or Azure skills:

- Your organization currently uses one or both of those clouds and therefore have skills in-house.

- You can't find enough skilled Google Cloud people to recruit.

- You don't have the budget required to grow a team of new hires.

Cross-skilling team members should still follow the four-phase plan I mentioned earlier to get their Google Cloud skills and certifications. Google has produced specific content to accelerate the learning with their Google Cloud Fundamentals for AWS Professionals, with the same being available for Azure.

Learning Paths

Google has created learning paths that cover all the key roles required to operate in Google Cloud, from data engineers and infrastructure engineers to SAP architects to data scientists, packed full of curated video and written content, quests (with hands-on labs), quizzes, and some paths aligned to certification at the end. At the time of writing this book, quests are available via Google's e-learning platform Qwiklabs or via a recently introduced initiative called Google Cloud Skills Boost, which has a dedicated website.

You have to enroll into a quest, and this requires credits. When you sign up, you'll get a certain number of free credits. Once used up, you can purchase additional credits. The Cloud Skills Boost initiative aims to get 40 million people trained on Google Cloud, and the website has over 700 learning resources available.

Back to the credits, I feel this can, if left unmanaged, create a bit of a perceived barrier of entry into having your team enroll in quests and undertake some learning. The new Cloud Skills Boost initiative at the time of writing, has introduce a monthly or annual subscription to access the content, including the Qwiklabs.

Check `cloudskillsboost.google` for the latest information. Start creating the right culture by ensuring your teams know that you can purchase subscriptions and credits when needed.

Table 13-1 looks at how current roles within your organization align with future cloud-enabled roles and the learning paths from Google Cloud to help your team members get there. For more information on these learning paths, please see `https://cloud.google.com/training#learning-paths`

Table 13-1. *Mapping of current roles to future roles and the possible learning paths*

Current roles	Future roles	Google learning paths
Infrastructure Manager, Head of IT, Head of Operations, Head of Applications, Head of Engineering, product owner	Cloud Infrastructure Lead, Head of Cloud Operations, Head of Cloud Applications, Head of Cloud Engineering, product owner	Cloud Digital Leader
Infrastructure or Data Center Engineer	Cloud Engineer, Cloud Architect	Cloud Engineer, Cloud Architect, Hybrid and Multi-cloud Cloud Architect
Networking	Network Engineer	Network Engineer
Security	Security Engineer	Security Engineer
Solutions Architect	Cloud Architect	Cloud Architect, Hybrid and Multi-cloud Cloud Architect
SAP Architect	SAP Architect, Cloud Architect	Cloud Architect, Hybrid and Multi-cloud Cloud Architect
Developer	Cloud Developer	Cloud Developer, Cloud DevOps Engineer
Tester, DevOps or Site Reliability Engineer	Cloud DevOps Engineer	Cloud DevOps Engineer
Application Support	Cloud DevOps Engineer, Collaboration Engineer	Cloud DevOps Engineer, Collaboration Engineer
Data Analyst	Data Analyst	Data Analyst

(continued)

147

Table 13-1. (*continued*)

Current roles	Future roles	Google learning paths
Database Administrator	Data Engineer, Database Engineer	Data Engineer, Database Engineer
Database Engineer	Database Engineer	Database Engineer
API Developer	API Developer, Cloud Developer	API Developer, Cloud Architect/Engineer on Apigee (hybrid), Cloud Architect/Engineer on Apigee (private cloud)
Data Scientist	Data Scientist/Machine Learning Engineer	Data Scientist/Machine Learning Engineer, Contact Center Engineer

Note that you may have other roles within your organization; it's key to understand what those roles are and the skills of the people currently fulfilling them. As you'll see, I suggest that some roles have multiple learning paths. I feel this gives the team members upskilling into those new roles a more rounded understanding.

The other point to note here is that you should train everyone using Google Cloud on the basic security measures your organization will put in place to protect your workloads and data.

Aside from Google Cloud's material, there are numerous other public third-party sources where training material is created and published faster than ever before. Some of this requires subscriptions, and other sources are freely available.

There are also Google Cloud accredited training partners. As part of your cloud adoption strategy, you might consider using a single partner to accelerate your technology adoption and migration and understand and create tailored training plans to fill your skills gaps.

I'd love to hear what learning resources you found useful. Please contact me via my website (infrastructureleader.com).

Certifications

Does your organization pay the entry fee for any exams you take? If they do, then great. If you are unsure, it's a sign that it's not known, which is a potential blocker to people taking them. If they don't pay for exams, why not? If there is a training budget, then there is no reason why an exam at $200 or less couldn't come from that budget. If there is no training budget, then speak to your human resources team about the benefit of having certified team members. Certifications are proven to have a meaningful business impact.

According to a survey by Google, 71% of Google Cloud certified individuals report becoming certified enabled or will enable their employer to get more business, increase work with existing customers, or help scale up their business (*Google Cloud Certification Impact Report*, 2020). Certification also provides numerous benefits to your career, from pay rises to additional responsibilities or even a new job.

Google Cloud certifications are split into three categories, Foundational, Associate, and Professional, as shown in Figure 13-1. Certifications exist to cover breadth with the Cloud Digital Leader and Cloud Engineer and then depth with the eight Professional certifications.

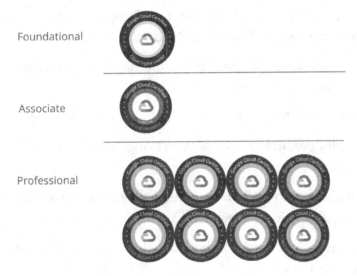

Figure 13-1. *The Google Cloud certifications*
Copyright Google Cloud

A Google Cloud Associate and Professional certifications expire every 2 years from the certified date. The Cloud Digital Leader expires after 3 years. Certificates expiring every 2 years are now standard among the cloud providers. It's an excellent way to ensure people are keeping their skills current. The certifications provide a superb end goal, but there is a need for structured learning through the learning paths I discussed earlier.

The first step to getting your team certified is understanding their current capabilities. Are you a decision-maker who defines your team's learning plans? Then you need to capture the current state of the team's capability. I'd advise you to create a questionnaire in Google Forms. I find treating this process similar to how you treat a performance review works best. Send a questionnaire to the team to populate their answers. Then discuss each response with each team member individually during a 1:1.

Using a Likert scale (which gives the responder a range of answers from one extreme to the other) gives you a method of measuring current knowledge level, which produces quantitative data points upon which you can more easily measure progress. These are some of the questions I ask. How you frame them is crucial, as it helps the reader digest and visualize what you are asking of them. Questions need to be tweaked to cater for the team you are assessing.

Please rate the statements per the following scale: 1, strongly disagree; 2, disagree; 3, neutral; 4, agree; and 5 strongly agree.

- I understand cloud computing, the shared responsibility model, and the business benefits of using the cloud.

- I understand how our organization's priorities and goals align with the use of the cloud.

- I can deploy products and services on Google Cloud through the GUI.

- I can deploy products and services on Google Cloud through automation.

- I can design solutions to enable faster deployments to production using Google Cloud managed services.

- I can design solutions to scale horizontally using Google Cloud managed services.

- I can design secure solutions that protect our data and brand reputation.

- I understand the principles of Site Reliability Engineering (SRE)/DevOps.

- I can apply SRE/DevOps principles to improve our current development and operational processes.

- I can design solutions that improve the observability of systems.

And so on, use the above examples to help you write your questions. And use the data captured through this approach as that team members' baseline. Work with them to suggest an appropriate role and learning paths.

Building Certification Momentum

The size of your IT function will determine how large the task is to get a high percentage of teams trained and certified. However, coaxing one or two team members to follow a learning path and take the exam to get certified isn't the end goal. You'll need a plan to build some training and certification momentum.

The early learning phase discussed earlier provides evidence highlighting who will likely be a Google Cloud champion. You'll need these Google Cloud champions to evangelize for others to join them on that journey; it's key to creating momentum as shown in Figure 13-2, but it's not that easy.

Figure 13-2. *Building certification momentum by starting with champions*

Consider getting team members certified the same way you'd approach a product or event launch. Have a stakeholder back you in this initiative. You should create a timeline and plan for regular, clear, concise communications. You'll want to create some buzz and excitement around it. Have someone responsible for getting people to participate. Consider asking those interested to sign up using a basic online form. Ask them to select all learning paths and certifications that interest them. Hold "ask me anything"-style sessions with those Google Cloud champions who are already certified. And publicly celebrate those who pass an exam and plan how you can reward them.

One approach I propose is to focus a certification initiative launch on a specific certification. Once a few people get certified and rewarded, it can become infectious. This approach is suitable for small and large organizations.

During the journey, plan inclusive events, be they in-person or online. These could be anything from short lunch and learns from a particular Google Cloud champion or a subject matter expert from a partner or Google Cloud. Or host entire daylong hackathons, where you encourage the teams to solve current challenges your organization might face or create new innovative ideas but all built on Google Cloud.

For those who may not be successful in passing an exam, prepare a retake plan that covers the additional support you'll be able to provide them. Do this before you launch your exam initiative. That way, when they inform you of their result, ensure to be encouraging and supportive in your language. Then provide them with the retake plan to help them a second or third time. I talked about the importance of psychological safety previously. Ensuring they know it's okay to fail the exam is key to getting people certified.

As part of that retake plan, consider in-person training from a Google Cloud accredited training partner or certification boot camps. Contact your Google or Google Cloud training partner sales rep and inquire about their scheduling and how many spaces could be made available for your team.

Of course, there is a good chance you'll need to run several certification initiatives to get the number of people you need to be certified. Learn lessons along the way, and take that feedback as a backlog of improvements to be made before you launch another initiative.

Cloud Digital Leader

Google Cloud has released its first nonengineering-focused exam, Cloud Digital Leader, aimed at anyone who needs to understand how technology can align to achieve business goals. It assesses general cloud knowledge, Google Cloud-specific knowledge, and then Google Cloud products and services. Google describes the exam as "The Cloud Digital Leader exam is job-role independent. The exam assesses the knowledge and skills of individuals who want or are required to understand the purpose and application of Google Cloud products" (*Google Cloud, Cloud Digital Leader*, 2021). This exam fits nicely into the model of being an infrastructure leader (either decision-maker or influencer). Whichever you would classify yourself as, this exam is worth having.

From a decision-maker's perspective, studying the material needed will give you a well-rounded understanding of cloud computing and Google Cloud-specific knowledge. This knowledge should prove useful in your day-to-day as you work to move your infrastructure to Google Cloud. From the influencer perspective, having this exam reinforces that you are blazing a trail.

Your colleagues will be curious to know how easy or difficult you found it and what material you used to study for it. Entertain all of these conversations; they help to reinforce you as an infrastructure leader with wisdom to share. These interactions also offer a chance for you to show humility. Telling them how easy you found it (even if you did) is your pride speaking and instantly puts the other person in a position whereby they feel inferior. Avoid doing this at all costs.

Instead, if they ask you directly how easy or difficult you found it, reframe your answer to focus on the material Google has produced that they can use as a study guide. I often respond to that type of question with, "It sounds like you might be worried about the difficulty of this exam. Google has created a learning path with supporting material to help guide you." It might appear like such a small, unimportant encounter. Still, I assure you that giving someone an inferiority complex doesn't help your organization's bigger picture move forward. This guidance applies to any certification. Try to instill this type of culture within your organization.

For exam preparation material, Google has released a series of dedicated Qwiklabs as part of their Cloud Digital Leader learning path (`https://cloud.google.com/training/business#cloud-digital-leader-path`).

The exam comprises of multiple-choice and multi-select questions. Some practice questions are available on the Cloud Digital Leader page (`https://cloud.google.com/certification/cloud-digital-leader`).

In-Person and Online Events

From community groups and webinars to summits and conferences, Google Cloud has plenty of year-round learning opportunities.

Like the other cloud providers, Google Cloud has an annual conference where they make new product announcements, showcase customer success stories, and get the product teams to speak about the products, use cases, and roadmaps. The content is always made available online to consume. Google's key conferences to watch out for are Google Cloud Next, which is around October each year, and Google I/O, a developer-focused conference.

To ensure you find all events at the time of writing, you have to visit a few different sources:

- The Google Cloud homepage has an events page, misleadingly listed under the Why Google dropdown.

- Google Cloud OnAir is a website where you can find up and coming webinars as well as past webinar and digital events.

- Developer-focused regional events and digital events can be found on the "Google Cloud Developer Center" website.

- Local community groups known as Google Developer Groups (GDG) can be found on developers.google.com/community, or the c2c community website c2cglobal.com.

Summary

Assess your team's current technical capabilities. Define the roles your organization needs in the future, and then create learning paths for those roles. Ensure that the organization pays for people to take exams. Engage with other leaders within your organization to tell them the benefits of getting their team members certified. Get those leaders to take the Cloud Digital Leader exam. Encourage team members to attend a mix of in-person and online events.

CHAPTER 14

Cloud Adoption Teams

> Great executives become organization architects, taking a systemic look
> at capabilities – processes, governance, culture, competencies, technolo-
> gies – and build them into the organizational machine expressly designed
> for a particular strategy.
>
> —*Ron Carucci*

In this chapter, I will cover the teams required to adopt and migrate to Google Cloud successfully. I'll discuss what functions they perform and how they evolve.

There is no one-size-fits-all approach to the teams and structures required for Google Cloud adoption and migration. However, some common teams and functions they perform do appear time and time again in successful adoption programs. These teams are shown in Figure 14-1.

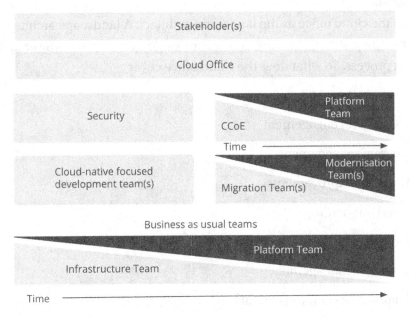

Figure 14-1. *Common teams required for Google Cloud adoption*

J. Lloyd, *Infrastructure Leader's Guide to Google Cloud*, https://doi.org/10.1007/978-1-4842-8820-7_14

This is not your organization chart. These are teams you require to adopt, migrate and modernize to Google Cloud, and then operate thereafter. Think about how these teams have touch points with current business as usual teams. Look to identify blockers to any transitions that will need to take place. Engage the leaders of those teams early and help them understand what it means for their team and what you require of them.

The platform team is an evolution of your current infrastructure team. As Google Cloud changes the nature of what the traditional infrastructure team has to deliver, as this book covers, the term platform team or platform engineering becomes more appropriate. For now, I will focus on the cloud office and cloud center of excellence teams.

Cloud Office

The cloud office is often referred to as the cloud business office, cloud adoption office, cloud management office, or cloud program office. Its purpose is to have a centralized holistic view of your organization's adoption, migration, and modernization workstreams. The name you decide to give this function doesn't matter. What matters more is that the team exists, is known throughout the organization, and is focusing on putting efforts into the right areas to achieve the outcome of accelerating your Google Cloud adoption.

I position the cloud office as the landscape architect. A landscape architect advises on the site planning, and the landscape design then oversees the creation and development process. So what does the cloud office cover:

- Cloud strategy and governance

- Comms and engagement

- Program management

- Adoption improvements

- Cloud onboarding

- People and skills management

- Cloud risk management

- Financial operations (FinOps)

Each of these responsibilities requires different skill sets, and therefore I would advise you assign the responsibilities to appropriate people. Decide if these people will go full-time on their assigned roles within the cloud office or if part-time is adequate.

In my experience, part-time assignments often mean the new cloud office responsibilities get neglected as business as usual and other competing priorities take precedence. Aim to have the team full-time. If part-time is the only option, then ensure you put some metrics in place. It will enable you to tip the balance to having full-time assignments. Let's look at each of these responsibilities in more detail.

Cloud Strategy and Governance

The cloud office should have a direct line of communication and regular reporting to a stakeholder sponsoring the cloud adoption program. The cloud office is responsible for creating the cloud strategy and governance overlay, which includes defining the governing standards and then ensuring compliance with them.

Comms and Engagement

Cloud adoption means change and potential disruption to services. Communicating with people across every part of the organization is critical. I advise the people responsible for comms and engagement to ensure they use the 4MAT learning system by Dr. Bernice McCarthy. This system aligns with how our brains are wired and covers the why, what, how, and so what in sequential order.

Putting the system to effect, you need clear messaging that helps people to understand the following:

- Why changes are going to be made, as in why the infrastructure needs to change.

- What is happening, keeping the concepts simple.

- How it affects them.

- So what if it goes wrong.

Program Management

Cloud adoption can be run as a single workstream or broken down into multiple; this largely depends on the size and complexity of your organization. Regardless, as this book explains, there are many moving parts. You'll likely have several teams on different aspects of cloud adoption. Ensuring consistency and alignment with the business case, cloud strategy, and cloud operating model is where the program management function comes in.

Program management is responsible for reporting to the stakeholders about progress made, covering adoption, migration, modernization, people enabled for Google Cloud, and skill increase. They also need to report blockers to adoption that the program team require escalating.

Adoption Improvements

As soon as you have adoption, migration, and modernization work underway, the teams will learn valuable lessons. Aim to capture those lessons and ensure you make the improvements.

Cloud Onboarding

The responsibilities within cloud onboarding center around the objective of empowering people across the organization to be able to consume Google Cloud products and services quickly, while also adhering to any guardrails, covering your current people and new hires.

People and Skills Management

The cloud office's people and skills management function is responsible for enacting what I have discussed within the skills chapter earlier.

Cloud Risk Management

While this is a function of the Cloud Office, see the cloud strategy risk management section in the book detailing what is required.

Financial Operations (FinOps)

Again, this is a function of the Cloud Office. However, later in the book, I cover it in greater detail within the FinOps section.

Cloud Center of Excellence

When I speak to any second or third generation infrastructure leader (the ones who are partway through or have been through an on-prem to Google Cloud move), I start by asking a few different open-ended questions. I aim to understand what didn't go well and the challenges they currently face while moving to Google Cloud. I also want to learn what went well for them. As I mentioned before, writing this book came about because I listened to what these leaders said and realized they needed a way to accelerate their learning based on the learnings of those who've gone before them.

In the case of what went well during Google Cloud adoption, usually establishing a Cloud Center of Excellence (CCoE) was up there, although do keep an eye on the CCoE team members having too high standards to start with, as this can lead to some stalling. Increase standards as more critical workloads move to Google Cloud and the team's proficiency increases.

So what is a CCoE?

A CCoE is an organic team focused on driving activities related to cloud adoption. What do I mean by organic? The CCoE's core functions change over time as the organization's cloud maturity changes. What you need from your CCoE at the start of a move to Google Cloud is not the same as what you need from your CCoE once your move is nearer to completion. Therefore, the people within the CCoE at the start might not be the same toward the end.

The CCoE team is your Google Cloud, champions, ambassadors, advocates, and rockstars. These are just some of the many terms I've heard leaders use to describe their CCoE team members. With the cloud office as the landscape architects, think of the CCoE as the landscape gardeners. The landscape gardener does everything from creating the structures like a pond, paving, paths, and fences to material selection and the actual planting.

Filling your team with champions/rockstars isn't easy. As I discussed earlier in the book, there is a cloud skills shortage that affects cloud migration projects.

An even greater challenge to filling your CCoE with champions/rockstars is data from a 2021 Global Knowledge survey of 9500 IT professionals. It states that there is only one Google Cloud certification in the top 10 list of certifications that IT professionals plan to pursue that year, despite the survey finding that Google Cloud certified architects and data engineers are number 1 and 2 highest paid respondents in North America (*Global Knowledge 2021 IT Skills and Salary Report*). I mentioned Google's plan to combat this earlier with their cloud skills boost initiative.

With that data in mind, cross-skilling AWS and Azure experienced individuals is an option worth looking at. See the earlier section in the book for more details on that. And as I also mentioned earlier, train your existing team members.

Why does it matter?

Establishing a CCoE is high on the list because this skilled team is the enablers of Google Cloud adoption. A top-down directive to move to Google Cloud will only get you so far. You need a self-motivated team of Google Cloud champions/rockstars making it happen. They are the ones who build the momentum you need as an infrastructure leader. You just need to steer them in the right direction. Some senior leaders/stakeholders within your organization may not see the value in creating a CCoE. Go to them armed with how they will keep driving your Google Cloud adoption and migration.

What does the CCoE do?

As mentioned, your organization's cloud maturity defines what you need your CCoE to do and who needs to be in it. Going back to the four defined phases of cloud adoption

- Shadow IT, sporadic use, organic growth

- Tactical adoption, proof of concepts, proof of value, specific use cases

- Strategic adoption

- Organization transformation

For details on what each phase is, please see Part 2. I will briefly summarize each to set the context and then expand on what the CCoE does during that phase.

Shadow IT

Google Cloud is being used without IT's knowledge, adopted by a non-IT business unit/team for a specific use case. It is doubtful that you'll have a CCoE. You'll probably not even know who is using Google Cloud, let alone what they use it for. All you can do if you hear or suspect that Google Cloud is in use is engage with those using it and follow my guidance from Part 2.

Tactical Adoption

In tactical adoption of Google Cloud, you have a Google Cloud organization hierarchy defined. IT is aware of the use of Google Cloud for particular use cases. IT might be controlling access, or they may be more hands-off. Finance is engaged to pay the bill each month.

What does the CCoE do in this phase?

So essentially, they do the following:

- Design and build your cloud foundations.

- Create guiding principles for using and architecting on Google Cloud.

- Automate the requests they receive to provision Google Cloud products.

- Produce repeatable patterns to simplify subsequent requests and improve consistency and alignment with the standards.

- Put feedback loops in place to capture lessons learned.

Do not let the CCoE become a single point of failure. If you channel all requests through a single team, at some point, they will become blockers. Only through establishing key performance indicators (KPIs) and measuring them can you aim to predict when the tipping point will be likely. I'll cover more on those KPIs later in this chapter.

Who should be in the CCoE for tactical adoption? And what does the team structure look like?

At this point, you need those cloud champions/rockstars, the ones who enjoy working on Google Cloud and, almost equally as important, enjoy talking to others about working on Google Cloud. In tactical adoption, the CCoE must understand the use cases for Google Cloud and the expected business benefits. They must evangelize Google Cloud and its benefits to the broader organization.

The tactical adoption CCoE needs the skills to cover the core Google Cloud product categories:

- Compute

- Data analytics

- Databases

- Networking

- Management tools

- Operations

- Security and identity

- Storage

- CI/CD

I've put data analytics in here because most Google Cloud customers I've worked with that are in the tactical phase have been attracted to first do proof of concepts or proof of value projects in data analytics given Google's lead in this area.

Also, note that while the Google Cloud product category called Operations is listed, I am not proposing that the CCoE performs business as usual-type operations of workloads running in Google Cloud. Instead, I am saying that the CCoE should have experience working with the products listed within the Operations product category.

A useful approach to filling your CCoE is to find out who used a cloud or Google Cloud as Shadow IT. They are your potential champions/rockstars. At a minimum, they are problem-solvers who take action and see the benefits the cloud brings, all of which are useful characteristics in the early phase of a CCoE.

The CCoE doesn't need to be a formal team during tactical adoption. I've worked with organizations guiding them at the start of their tactical Google Cloud adoption. While working with one customer, it became apparent that formalizing the CCoE would mean changing line management. There was talk of new performance objectives and job description updates which meant contract changes which needed HR and senior management approvals.

Instead, I proposed a solution: line management should not change at the start of tactical adoption. Instead, the CCoE can be a virtual team, focusing on the skills and characteristics needed to deliver against the requests that come their way while simultaneously building momentum through advocacy. I've taken this approach with subsequent customers and again saw a reduction in the time to implement a CCoE.

The virtual CCoE should still have a nominated leader of the capability. Having a person in this role ensures a holistic view of requests, successes, and blockers. They can establish feedback loops with other team leaders.

However, at a certain point in the tactical adoption phase, you will need to formalize the CCoE. This point comes when requests are coming faster than the virtual CCoE can deliver, KPIs you've put in place get breached, and quality is suffering, leading to a bad taste all around, thereby essentially making them a blocker to Google Cloud adoption, as mentioned earlier. It's where some people are critical about establishing a CCoE.

Strategic Adoption

In the strategic adoption phase, a planning process has likely been undertaken to develop a strategy. The strategy will have an executive sponsor, and the heads of various IT functions will be behind it. The business case will have been written and approved.

I've worked with some organizations that have skipped the tactical Google Cloud adoption phase. With no prior Google Cloud relationship or experience, they've gone straight to working with me on their business case to justify a strategic move to Google Cloud. Once approved, I've worked with them to put a strategy in motion for organization-wide adoption.

What Does the CCoE Do in This Phase?

Just because a strategy is in place doesn't mean that internal teams suddenly have the direction and skills to move forward.

If you skipped tactical adoption and therefore have no existing CCoE, then the CCoE will perform the same functions I described earlier under tactical adoption, then eventually evolving to assume more responsibilities.

If you are ready to build upon an existing CCoE, then in addition to the functions described earlier, they will also do the following:

- Enable others to do more through knowledge sharing, building an internal community, and hosting events like lunch and learns or hackathons.

- Formalized training sessions.

- Financial operations, focusing on being cost-efficient and making recommendations.

- Advise others on certification paths and benefits.

- Guide hiring manager on skills and characteristics they need to fill their teams.

- Guide leaders whose business units are lagging or appear disengaged.

Who Should Be in the Strategic Adoption Phase CCoE and What Does the Team Structure Look Like?

In strategic adoption, the skillset within the CCoE should be fully functional. By that, I mean the team needs the skills and experience to cater to all Google Cloud product categories over and above those I listed earlier. Additional product categories the CCoE needs to cover are as follows:

- AI and machine learning

- API management

- Containers

- Developer tools

- Hybrid and multicloud

- Internet of Things

- Migration

- Serverless computing

If your organization has skipped the tactical adoption phase, then it's likely you don't have a CCoE (virtual or formal). The CCoE needs a leader in strategic adoption, but the team size should still be around 8 to 12 maximum, which helps to keep lines of communication simple.

Strategic adoption is also where bringing in a Google Cloud partner can benefit you. An experienced partner will have the skills and knowledge required to accelerate your progress.

Organization Transformation

Organization transformation is about redefining the current state of your organization. It focuses not only on technology but also the business model, process, and culture, also referred to as digital transformation. The C-level of your organization will drive organizational transformation.

What Does the CCoE Do in This Phase?

It can depend if your organization's transformation is happening after you've already moved to Google Cloud or if the executive stakeholders see moving to Google Cloud as the organization transforms. While Google Cloud can be a catalyst, only moving workloads to Google Cloud is not an organization transformation.

In an organization transformation, the role of the CCoE should cover the tasks defined in tactical and strategic phases. It should also include the following:

- Guidance on DevOps/site reliability engineering.

- Advise on the technology alignment to business objectives.

- Guidance on innovation possibilities and evangelize technological innovation.

- Guidance on business process automation.

Who should be in the organization transformation phase CCoE and what does the team structure look like?

You'll need the team members and skills listed in the tactical and strategic adoption phases. In addition, having site and customer reliability engineers can help identify improvements and efficiencies. You'll generally want to ensure you have problem-solvers and out-of-the-box thinkers. This blend can help empower transformation through technology.

How Can You Mitigate the Risk of the CCoE Becoming a Blocker?

It's through the KPIs. You'll want to measure the following:

- Number of service requests (total)

- Number of service requests by Google Cloud product category

- Number of service requests by type of request

- Number of service requests by department/team/project/
  business unit

- Average time to complete a service request

- Resolution category of the service request (automation, employee
  enablement, CCoE improvement)

The outcomes of these types of KPIs are patterns that should yield insights to show time spent delivering the work and not enabling others to be self-sufficient. I've worked with customers implementing these or similar KPIs and gained good insights.

Such as the team's ability to promptly get through requests. Often velocity at the start can be slower, while processes are embedded (or still being formulated!). If the velocity never increases, then it could be that the standards are too high, which is a watch point I mentioned previously.

Summary

Establish a cloud office and clearly define and communicate its responsibilities. Plan to expect teams and their responsibilities to evolve, such as the infrastructure team becoming a platform team.

Identify any early adopters of Google Cloud within your organization, such as those who use it as Shadow IT. Understand their use cases and what's working well and what's not and what have they learned along the way.

Depending on your organization's cloud maturity, establish a virtual cross-functional CCoE team. If your organization is further along the journey, formalize that team. Consider putting those early adopters in the CCoE. They show problem-solving characteristics and see the value in Google Cloud. Put a person in charge of the CCoE capability. If it's a virtual CCoE, then they do not have to be a line manager of the team. If it is a formalized team, then it's likely line management would change. Put in place KPIs for the CCoE and measure them often to avoid the CCoE becoming a blocker.

PART IV

Migration Journey

In this part, I will discuss what you need to consider to execute a successful migration to Google Cloud. I'll cover how to quickly and effectively categorize and rationalize your workloads, so you'll be able to decide what needs to move and how and what should go first. I'll also cover Google Cloud's rapid assessment and migration program, which provides a framework covering process, planning, and tools, and, finally, I'll discuss container migrations. First, let's look back on what we've covered so far.

Progress recap

From Part 2, you now have an understanding on

- Four approaches to cloud adoption

- How to build a business case for Google Cloud

- How to create a cloud strategy

- How to define your cloud operating model

- What migration strategies and approaches to take

- How to define your modernization strategy

- How Google Cloud partner accelerates you

- Working with your IT outsourcer

And from Part 3, you should have an understanding on

- Cultural changes required during a cloud adoption state

- How to use Google's Cloud Adoption Framework

- How to prepare for your organization and teams for a cloud operating model

- How to get the skills in the organization that are needed to succeed

- Cloud adoption teams (Cloud Office and Cloud Centre of Excellence)

- The roles and responsibilities of the Cloud Office and CCoE during the different phases of cloud adoption

You now have a more holistic view of cloud adoption. However, for a cloud adoption checklist, including tasks and activities from the rest of the book, visit my website: infrastructureleader.com.

Each cloud provider has its view on how you should migrate to their cloud. Having guided organizations with migrations to AWS, Azure, and Google Cloud, I can inform you that it's a fairly similar process across the three. I've also found that while having a defined migration journey is useful, enabling people and adapting processes are key to a successful migration. For migrations to Google Cloud, I advocate following Google Cloud's migration journey. It's split into four phases:

Assess - Discovering your IT estate and workloads and any additional information that you can use to help define the migration type and effort

Plan – Defining a workload's migration order and scheduling migrations

Migrate – Moving the workloads using the defined migration paths

Optimize – Making efficiency gains through performance tweaks and modernization to Google Cloud managed services

Let's look at what each of these phases entails.

CHAPTER 15

Assess

In this chapter, I will cover the Assess phase of the migration journey and who you should engage during this phase, the assessment tools you need, how to categorize your workload and define their migration approach, and then how to define what your first-mover workloads are.

As mentioned earlier, the Assess phase covers discovery and assessing what you've discovered. Discovery is all about getting data on your current IT assets. And to discover what IT assets (a precursor to identifying workloads) you have within your estate, you want to use an automated discovery tool. It's important to know what IT assets you have so you have visibility into what to migrate. Without a definitive list of IT assets, you would likely miss some.

Larger organizations will probably have a Configuration Management Database (CMDB), which will contain some or most of your IT assets. However, in my experience, these quickly fall out of date and rely all too often on manual updates, which means they are not solely a source to base your discovery on. They also haven't been designed with cloud migration in mind. So the analytics you get from them isn't useful for deciding on a migration approach. If you have one, use it to enrich any data that an automated tool discovers. If your organization doesn't have a CMDB, you might find you have security tooling deployed across the estate with assets reporting in. Again while this isn't a data source I'd base my entire discovery around, it can be a helpful reference.

Application Owners

Most organizations I work with have the notion of a business application owner. This is typically a person who leads a team that uses the application or is a person who has responsibility for a business unit that consumes the application. Often they have a technical peer who'll sit within the IT function and ensure the application is available, recoverable, secure, and updated.

169

© Jeremy Lloyd 2023
J. Lloyd, *Infrastructure Leader's Guide to Google Cloud*, https://doi.org/10.1007/978-1-4842-8820-7_15

I've found that proactive application owners who engage in a cloud adoption program are valuable allies to make. Often their desire to be a first mover or an early adopter outweighs the risks as they see them. Ensure they are adequately aware of the risks, and ensure you understand if their application fits your first-mover criteria.

In the context of this book and migrations to Google Cloud, I typically refer to applications as workloads because while the application binaries are installed on servers, there are additional components you must consider when migrating it to Google Cloud, such as the data storage, databases, and the underlying infrastructure like VLANS, firewalls, and load balancers.

Application owners do have the potential to derail a migration. They'll have authority over the application, and if they aren't ready or convinced about migration, you'll have to escalate to your stakeholders. It's a situation I've seen play out several times, unfortunately. Of course, in the end, it's possible to resolve the issues and migrate the application, but it'll cause delays in planning and scheduling.

So I'd advise you to identify the application owners early in the cloud adoption process. They may already be known and documented, so spend the time now to verify that list is correct. Identify who is suffering from challenges or pain around their current implementation so that you can align to how Google Cloud could solve the problem. Again the earlier to uncover this, the more useful this information is for building momentum and backing for migration to Google Cloud.

And as I mentioned earlier, failure to work with application owners can leave you with an adoption and migration strategy being too infrastructure-focused, which may lead to a slow or stalled adoption.

Assessment Tools

What is Google's approach to automated discovery and assessment?

Google acquired Stratozone in 2020, thereby making Stratozone Google's answer to performing automated discovery and assessment of your IT assets. Stratozone has a virtual appliance (the StratoProbe) that you install in your data center(s). Depending on how disparate your organization is across the globe and how segmented your network is, you might need to install more than one StratoProbe. It's to overcome logically separate networks or subnets such as DMZs. The StratoProbe is the data collector; you configure it via a GUI on the virtual machine it's running on. Give the probe the CIDR ranges you want to scan and the credentials to access the servers, and it will start collecting data.

StratoProbe sends data back to Google Cloud, which is analyzed and made available in the Stratozone portal. Currently, this is a separate portal to Google Cloud, however a more integrated experience has recently been announced called the Migration Centre. Back to Stratozone, three security levels define the collected data sent from the probe to Google Cloud for analysis. I recommend leaving the default option of security level one configured, which sends all information that StratoProbe has collected.

In the Stratozone portal, you can group your servers under an application. Give them a name that reflects what the application/workload is known as to the organization. Once you group servers into Stratozone applications, you can look at a dependency map. This helps to de-risk a migration, as you can analyze the critical and noncritical dependencies that the application has before any actual migration.

You can produce several automated reports from Stratozone, from Google Cloud cost model reports, that allow you to get the cost of one of your servers, an application group, a data center, or every asset discovered. You can model that against the different options on Google Cloud for hosting servers. Stratozone will also let you export the raw data in CSV format for server inventory, running services, or processes.

Stratozone isn't a complicated tool to install and configure. There are guides to help you. Google will also be able to assist through a Customer Engineer (CE) should you need it and likewise a Google Cloud partner with the migration specialization.

Third parties also create other automated discovery tools. Some of these tools have strengths that might make them more suitable for your organization's needs. Cloudscape, a tool Flexera acquired, is one worth calling out for its discovery strengths. Created by Risc Networks, Cloudscape is now part of the Flexera One platform. This discovery tool provides excellent dependency mapping in an interactive graphical form. You can also easily group workloads and filter them out, clearly visualizing the critical dependencies you'll need to plan for.

Remember that if you decide to use a third-party discovery tool, you will have to pay for the license costs.

Now, unfortunately, your data gathering isn't over just yet. There are additional data points that need to be collected.

Assessment Tools

If your migration strategy focuses on understanding modernization opportunities instead of defaulting to lift and shift for everything, to know what can/can't modernize, you need to use tools that provide insights to help you make decisions. I recommend three tools in this space to my customers.

Google's Migrate to Containers can perform a container fit assessment against workloads and gives you a container fit report. This report details issues to be addressed before migration to containers is possible. It provides an overall fit assessment with scores that range from "excellent fit" to "needs major work" or "no fit" and "insufficient data." The fit assessment rules are on the Google Cloud Migrate to Containers documentation page. It's worth reading through these to understand what it's looking for.

More recently, the tool's assessment report provides recommendations on a lift and shift to Compute Engine. It's useful as it can provide insights into areas you may need to fix pre- or post-migration.

Uniquely this tool can also perform automated containerization of the VMs to containers as you migrate into GKE, GKE Autopilot, or Cloud Run. Keep an eye on this tool's roadmap and release notes as it continues to expand and improve.

CAST Software

The next two tools are third-party products by CAST Software. The first CAST Highlight provides Cloud Readiness Insights by assessing the workloads against 100s of known cloud migration patterns. It provides effort estimates, blockers, container fit insights, and a dependency map. It then provides recommendations for each against the Gartner R's style approach. In this instance, the terms are Rehost, Refactor, Rearchitect, Rebuild, and Retire.

CAST Highlight also provides Software Composition Analysis, which details the use of open source software, security vulnerabilities, and a prioritized list of security recommendations. It provides Software Health Insights, which recommend resiliency and maintenance issues stemming from known code patterns. Finally, it provides Private Data Detection, which looks for keyword patterns within the workload, such as identity data like passport, driver's license, etc. It then provides a score derived from the type of data held (given a weighted value), the number of occurrences, and the number of files.

It works by performing static code analysis on the workload through an agent. This code scan executes locally, so your source code doesn't leave your on-prem environment.

Next is CAST Imaging, whose strapline is "Google Maps for your architecture" (CAST). CAST Imaging gives you the next level of detail that Highlight doesn't, from database structures and code components to interdependencies, all down to low levels, such as an individual DLL. CAST Imaging presents the detail in interactive visuals that CAST calls the architecture blueprints.

Overall, CAST Highlight helps you quickly understand a likely direction for a workload and the estimated complexity to modernize. You can run CAST Imaging against those modernization candidates you decide to progress with. It'll help you form the backlog of items that a modernization team and workload-specific subject matter experts need to modernize on Google Cloud.

Workload Categorization

Does your organization have a database that details every workload within the organization? No? Why would they?

Well, all workloads have a shelf life, no matter how critical to an organization. Maintaining such a database of workloads is often referred to as Application Portfolio Management (APM). Sometimes this comes in the form of a dedicated tool, or it's likely an extension to a CMDB tool. ServiceNow offers precisely this type of extension. APMs provide additional context to help organizations see the costs, lifetime, duplication, usage, and business value of those workloads and provide dashboards with scores to help you see priorities. APMs will hold data such as but not limited to the following:

- The correlation to IT assets (servers, storage, etc.) in use by the workload

- The end user usage by business unit, location

- The volume of incidents or tickets

- A categorization, priority, or another unit of measure that identifies its criticality to the organization

APM done properly can highlight costly workloads the organization isn't utilizing well, which can help make strategic decisions about the future of the workload. If you have an APM tool or extension to your CMDB, can you rely on that data to be accurate enough to build a migration and modernization strategy? If you don't have an APM but have a CMDB, it's likely to have outdated records and poor data quality. It's also unlikely to correlate IT assets to actual workload names.

So, you will need another approach, one that gets you the information you require and then combines that with an approach to categorize each workload. It's why I recommend using Stratozone.

Once you have that list of workloads, you will need to categorize them in order of their importance to the business. After all, a single server with only a few dependencies and a few outbound HTTPS connections might appear like a potential first mover in your migration wave, until you realize that this server is part of your payroll system as it is deemed critical.

Often when I work with customers on categorizing their workloads, I run an exercise with the business and technical application/workload owners based on a simple quadrant as shown in Figure 15-1. I arrange an application interview with them and ask them to categorize each application/workload they are responsible for based on its criticality and value to the organization.

Figure 15-1. *Categorizing workloads by value and criticality*

To help understand what high value and critical are vs. low value and noncritical requires you to ask a set of questions against each workload. I define a critical workload as one that has a significant business impact in terms of revenue and reputation.

To define a workload as critical, ask the business and technical application owners the following questions:

- Do a high percentage of your total customers interact and transact through this workload?

- Do a significant number of your employees interact with this workload?

- Is this workload (or data) dependent on other critical workloads?

- Is this workload strategic to your organization in terms of revenue and market share?

- Would any downtime to this workload have a financial impact?

This list is by no means exhaustive. I've kept the list short to get to the answer quickly and hopefully simply too. You can add your additional questions to cater for more specific scenarios. For example, a manufacturing customer added a question related to the workload's link with their manufacturing production lines. If the workload is down and a manufacturing process stops, it ultimately impacts revenue. If the workload is down, but manufacturing can continue as the workload is linked to the process but is not directly controlling the equipment used, then there is no financial impact.

If you add additional questions, ensure you write them in the same format, which is answering yes to any of these questions means that workload is critical, and everything that was a no is noncritical. That leaves you with an understanding of the workload's value to the organization.

I define value by the type of data held within the workload. I do that because the data holds value to your organization. A customer feedback app with no data inside doesn't have much value, compared with a feedback app that has 5 years' worth of data. With that data, you can extract valuable insights to inform business decisions. To define a workload as high value, ask these questions:

- Is the data within this workload used to grow revenue and/or market share?

- Does the workload contain data related to your customers?

- Is their proprietary data held within this workload?

- Can the workload data help us be more efficient (reduce costs)?

Answering yes to any of these questions means the workload is of high value, and answering with a no means it's low value. Again you might be able to add additional questions to this list that align with your organization's goals and outcomes, such as if reducing costs and being more operationally efficient is a high priority; you might ask, can the data within the workload be used to improve operational efficiency?

Use an application interview to capture other useful qualitative information that might help you understand how and when or if you should migrate the workload. For example, consider getting the following details:

- The workload lifecycle/roadmap

- Planned or required upgrades and maintenance windows

- Specific security, compliance, or regulatory requirements

- Third-party license considerations

- Any other specific infrastructure or architecture requirements

I also use the application interview as a chance to explain to the business application owner the process and different migration approaches. More often than not, they aren't familiar with this process, unlike their technical counterparts. Ensure you allow time for them to raise any questions and concerns they may have. Either provide answers then and there if you can, or ensure you take action to follow up with them.

Assessing the Migration Approach

Earlier in the book, I discussed migration strategies in the form of the Gartner Rs and Google's take on them. Having those defined and written down combined with your workload categorization doesn't fully answer the question of how a workload should migrate. For example, should all critical but low-value workloads be a lift and shift or replaced with a SaaS product?

Outside factors might drive the answer to this question, such as a compelling event, like a contract renewal on a colocation facility or a pledge to shareholders to be "in the cloud" by a certain time. Factors like that would indicate that speed is required; therefore, you might default to a lift and shift/rehost approach for all workloads.

If your organization isn't driven entirely by such factors, you need a lens to help set each workload's direction. How will you know if you should replace a workload with a SaaS product? Or which workloads should you transform?

To figure that out, you need to perform two steps. Step 1 is to assign a migration complexity or effort rating to the workload. I use a scale of simple, medium, or complex. Step 2 is to identify if the workload competitively differentiates you. Use the data points you've uncovered with the automated discovery tool and application interviews to assess each workload.

Table 15-1 shows how I advise you to define the migration complexity or effort rating.

Table 15-1. *Assigning a complexity rating to a workload's migration*

Criteria	Simple	Medium	Complex
Discovery supported with automated tooling	Yes	Yes	No
OS is supported by migration tooling	Yes	Yes	No
Third-party license changes required	No	No	Yes
Critical external dependencies (such as external storage or a database or another component of this workload)	No	Yes	Yes

If any of the criteria for medium or complex is met, that is the label you give that workload, and then move onto the next workload; rinse and repeat.

I've used various criteria with customers over the years. Some want to be more verbose by adding additional criteria such as external dependencies or the network complexities around load balancing and firewall rules. Experience has taught me that this can lead to analysis paralysis.

For example, you end up in a situation where a single criterion has led the workload to be classified as complex when under all the others, it's simple. This then can lead to weighted scores against each criterion. And while there might be merit in this granularity and accuracy, the reality is you need to quickly know if that workload's migration is simple, medium, or complex. And use that data point to make an informed decision on how you will migrate the workload.

Step 2 – you classify whether each workload is a competitive differentiator or a commodity. Using the example workloads from earlier, does your HR app make you stand out against competitors? Is it the reason customers choose you? Probably not; therefore, that is a commodity and should be replaced with a SaaS product. And in the customer feedback app, while the data within it holds much value to the business, the feedback app itself doesn't differentiate you, as your competitors may use the same. The ecommerce platform, however, does differentiate you or at least it can.

The overall aim here is that for workloads that differentiate your organization, you want to be able to move fast and innovate by using cloud-native products and services. However, as the general migration complexity of the workload increases, so will the time and cost to achieve that. Therefore, consider time boxing the first approach I recommend and try the alternative method afterward. If that still fails, default to lift and shift/rehost, and consider a post-migration modernization strategy.

Table 15-2 summarizes the complexity/differentiation of the proposed migration approaches.

Table 15-2. *Migration complexity alignment with a migration approach*

Migration complexity/differentiation	Migration approach
Simple/high differentiation	Refactor to cloud-native[1]
Simple/medium differentiation	Time boxed Replatform; otherwise, Rehost
Simple/low differentiation	Replace if unable and then Rehost
Medium/High differentiation	Replatform
Medium/medium differentiation	Rehost
Medium/low differentiation	Replace if unable and then Rehost
Complex/high differentiation	Time boxed Replatform; otherwise, Rehost[2]
Complex / Medium differentiation	Rehost
Complex / Low differentiation	Replace if unable and then Rehost

[1]*See Part 5 cloud-native development for guidance*

[2]*The temptation is to transform workloads in these categories; if the goal is to move to Google Cloud, then focus on getting the workload there. You can transform it once in Google Cloud. Stick to my guidelines laid out in Part 2, modernization strategies*

First Movers

If you are undertaking a migration to Google Cloud, a workload, or several, will have to go first. They are known as first movers. How do you select the first movers from your identified workloads? There are several different approaches.

Low-Hanging Fruit

This approach aims to identify the simplest workloads to move. Typically they will have the following characteristics:

- Simple workloads (as per criteria previously detailed).

- Are not business-critical and preferably non-production.

- Managed by central teams.

- Are not edge cases or outliers (not unique in terms of OS, licensing, stack used, architecture; and therefore present a good learning opportunity).

- The workload's business owner is supportive of a migration.

- Do not contain vast amounts of data.

- Can afford a cutover window (as in can incur some scheduled downtime).

Cross Representation

Identify workloads from across your organization's business units; these are typically a mix of different complexities and use cases. Where this approach differs from low-hanging fruit, the aim is to learn lessons that might be unique to a specific business unit or country. And in attempting to achieve that, you don't limit yourself to a small number of simple workloads. You remain open that any workload from a business unit, country, or another delineating form provides a learning opportunity.

Highest Priority

It is the most urgent need due to constraints (scaling or availability issues, end-of-life hardware). This approach is also open to any workload, but that workload is likely suffering from performance or time-bound problems, meaning it needs to move first. You will learn valuable migration lessons, but given the possible time-sensitive nature of this approach, how applicable those lessons are to other migrations depends on how you migrate the workload and if that method follows your anticipated standard migration patterns and tools.

Summary

In the Assess phase of a migration to Google Cloud, deploy Stratozone to discover your data center servers. Engage application owners early to reduce likely delays later on. Categorize your workloads. Define each workload's migration approach. Define your first-mover criteria and then agree on your first movers.

CHAPTER 16

Plan

This chapter will cover the essential tasks required to progress through the migration journey, from putting the correct prerequisites in place through to undertaking pilot migrations.

The Plan phase entails much more than you automatically think it would. And because of that, it's essential to ensure that your teams and stakeholders understand. It's planning and preparing across

- Tools and prerequisites

- Cloud foundations and a migration landing zone

- Communication and engagement

- Migration wave grouping and scheduling

- Implementation of the organizational readiness plans

- Pilot migration

Let's look at each of these in more detail.

Tools and Prerequisites

Now that you have a good understanding of your workloads and their migration paths, you'll need to evaluate, select, install, and configure the migration tools you require to get your workloads into Google Cloud.

You should undertake tool evaluation and selection during the Plan phase. However, I often find that the engineers working closely with the workloads during the Assess phase already have opinions on the required tools. Don't discount them. Instead, evaluate their selections against these key considerations:

181

© Jeremy Lloyd 2023
J. Lloyd, *Infrastructure Leader's Guide to Google Cloud*, https://doi.org/10.1007/978-1-4842-8820-7_16

- What skills are required to use the tool? And do we currently have them?

- What is the tool's cost and ease of procuring it (does the tool vendor need to be on a preferred supplier list)?

- Does this tool support all of the migration scenarios our organization has?

- Where does the tool need to be deployed, and how many required instances?

- How is data being transferred to Google Cloud, and what is the encryption used?

- Does the tool require any configuration on the source VMs before migration?

Within this phase, you'll want to complete any prerequisites that the tools need, be that an on-prem migration connector, firewalls rules, or configuration to source VMs if required. If you have many sites to migrate, then prioritize the sites that contain the first movers and those that'll contain the next wave of migrations.

Cloud Foundations and a Migration Landing Zone

Within the Plan phase, you'll need to design and deploy your Google Cloud cloud foundations and a migration landing zone. What are they?

The cloud foundations are Google Cloud products and services that are pillars upon which you can build and deploy your workloads. I cover cloud foundations in Part 6 in more detail, but they cover areas such as identity access management (IAM) and your Google Cloud organization hierarchy, which defines how you logically organize your resources. During the Plan phase, ensure you design the cloud foundations and how you will deploy them. And then actually build and deploy them. Your migration landing zone builds on your cloud foundations, which Figure 16-1 illustrates.

Figure 16-1. *Cloud foundations and migration landing zone structure*

Expanding on the migration landing zone, it's the configuration of Google Cloud products and services that forms the location where you will move the VMs during the cutover process. And depending on what migration tooling you use, you might need a virtual appliance deployed in Google Cloud to control the migration process. Any such appliance would form part of your migration landing zone. As shown in Figure 16-2, you must configure a host Google Cloud project for Migrate for Compute Engine (more on this tool shortly). Figure 16-2 also shows two Google Cloud target projects where the migrated VMs will reside. You may need more or less than that, depending on your requirements.

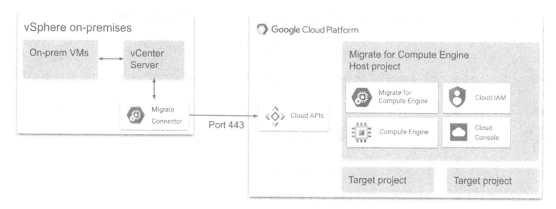

Figure 16-2. *Resource and structure of a migration landing zone*[1]
Copyright Google Cloud

Key considerations for your migration landing zone

- Bandwidth requirements between your on-prem sites and
  Google Cloud.

- The data path between on-prem source VMs and the Google Cloud
  destination, does your organization allow the data to route over the
  Internet, or does it need to route through a VPN or interconnect? (I'll
  cover more on networking later.)

- How many Google Cloud folders and projects do you require?
  Primarily this is driven by the environments you'll be supporting
  (sandbox, dev, pre-prod, prod, etc.) and how they will be separated,
  by folder, by a project?

- Subnet sizes and layout, for example, will all production sit within
  one subnet? Or will you require subnets for web-facing production
  VMs and separate subnets for databases?

---

[1]This image was created by Google Cloud, and is used according to the terms described in the
Creative Common Attribution 4.0 License. Source: https://cloud.google.com/migrate/
virtual-machines/docs/5.0/concepts/architecture.

Communication and Engagement

The earlier you inform the organization that you are moving to Google Cloud, the better. Communication should be clear on what is happening and why, who the stakeholders are, and the calls to action required by the organization. This may start with simply responding to the migration team's requests for information. Make it easy for anyone within the organization to contact the cloud office.

Migration Wave Grouping and Scheduling

A migration wave is simply a collection of workloads to be migrated during a single 2-week migration sprint. You'll want to group workloads into waves within the Plan phase. The first wave is simple, as it's your first movers per your criteria. Subsequent waves should be grouped based on the workload category. The Migration Center appears like it will, in the future, offer you the ability to catalog and group servers into migration waves, keep an eye on its roadmap.

You should also schedule the migration waves. Doing this enables you to inform business and technical application owners of the potential dates and times you could move their workloads. Give them enough time to ensure they can align the migration team with any team members they have that can provide application-specific knowledge.

Without the correct stakeholder sponsorship, communication with the business and technical application owners, and preparation by the application and migration teams, workloads will slip from their assigned wave into later waves. I've seen this happen time and time again.

The most common reason for this occurring is when you don't have approval for the migration of that specific workload, be it one person or several who've blocked it. You have to plan and prepare for that scenario. It'll often be down to the risk, and not everyone feels comfortable. On the one hand, prepare in advance who can block the workload migration. Engage them, understand their concerns, and work to alleviate them well in advance. Continually give them a channel to voice any new concerns as the Discovery, Assess, and Plan phases occur. And plan your migration waves to spare some additional capacity so that if a workload does slip, you can more easily schedule it into a later wave without pushing other workloads further down the order.

You'll only know if the team has any spare capacity if they create a migration backlog and estimate the effort to complete the tasks in the backlog. I usually suggest that the migration program has a scrum master-type role for this purpose. They act as a guide for the teams, primarily helping them to prioritize the migration backlog and estimate the effort to complete tasks.

Implementing Organizational Readiness Plans

In Part 3, I discussed organizational readiness and what is required to ensure your organization is ready for change. In the Plan phase, you need to implement those changes and monitor them to ensure progress is moving forward.

Specifically, I am talking about the following:

- Cloud operating model

- Learning paths

- Security controls

- Governance controls

Pilot Migration

Some organizations might require that you undertake pilot migration. Use the pilot to test the end-to-end migration and rollback processes if this is required. I recommend piloting with a new VM created specifically for testing. It should have just an OS. You can delete the VM once the tests are complete.

Summary

Agree on the migration tools you will use to start with. Lay cloud foundations and your migration landing zone. Enact your comms and engagement plan. Group workloads into migration waves, and start to schedule the first few waves. Start to deliver on the rest of your organizational readiness plan. Pilot a migration with a test VM.

CHAPTER 17

Migrate

In this chapter, I cover the Migration phase, specifically the migration life cycle, feedback loops, and operational handover. Let's look at each of these in more detail.

Migration Tools

Within the Migration phase, each server will go through the migration life cycle, which is the act of taking the server from the source location to the destination with some steps in between. This process uses specific migration tools, and I will discuss the Google Cloud tools available at no additional cost.

Server Migration Tools

In 2018, Google acquired a multicloud migration tooling organization called Velostrata. Out of that acquisition, Google has now released two tools: Migrate for Compute Engine (M4CE), also known as Migrate for Compute or Migrate to Virtual Machines, and Migrate for Anthos (M4A), now known as Migrate to Containers. It would appear that there will be some workflow integration with these tools and the new Migration Center.

For now, let's focus on Migrate for Compute Engine. M4CE is a virtual appliance that enables you to replicate a server from a source location (your on-prem data centers) to Google Cloud. It does this without needing an agent installed on each server. Instead, you install a migration connector in your on-prem data center with outbound HTTPS access to Google Cloud APIs.

A handy feature is once a server's initial replication has taken place, M4CE lets you deploy a test clone in Google Cloud on Google Compute Engine (GCE). This enables you to ensure the server will boot up in Google Cloud and gives you a chance to perform some basic tests to gain assurance for the cutover. The complete M4CE server migration life cycle is shown in Figure 17-1.

© Jeremy Lloyd 2023
J. Lloyd, *Infrastructure Leader's Guide to Google Cloud*, https://doi.org/10.1007/978-1-4842-8820-7_17

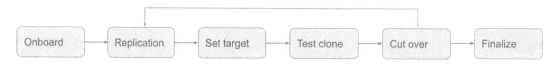

Figure 17-1. *Migration for Compute Engine's VM migration life cycle*[1]
Copyright Google Cloud, VM Migration Lifecycle

Another feature is the ability to upgrade certain Windows Server 2008 R2 servers to Windows Server 2012R during a migration. While this might seem like a risky approach, at a minimum, you can use the previously mentioned test-clone feature in conjunction with the OS upgrade feature to check if it will work without affecting the original Windows 2008 R2 server on-prem. If you have one or two servers to upgrade, it might be easier to do it manually (but what has stopped you from doing it years ago?). If you have hundreds to thousands, then automation is the only realistic way.

Also, if you'd rather not do an OS upgrade during the migration or if your Windows Server version is already Server 2012 R2, see the modernization strategies chapter for another method to help you.

Currently, M4CE only supports the VMware hypervisor. Other third-party tools support non-VMware hypervisors, such as Sureline by Persistent Systems.

VMware's Hybrid Cloud Extension (HCX) and NSX-T

Google Cloud VMware Engine (GCVE) is VMware-as-a-Service running in Google Cloud. I will discuss it more and its use cases later in Part 6. If you have VMware on-prem and are going to use GCVE, then you can migrate servers using VMware's HCX capability.

HCX offers zero downtime migrations through vMotion. And high-throughput as HCX is working at networking Layer 2. Offline and bulk migrations are also possible.

Another VMware capability that you can use to migrate servers from an on-prem VMware environment to GCVE is NSX-T. NSX-T again operates at Layer 2.

Both methods require different forms of an appliance/connector to be deployed on-prem. Although if you use NSX-T overlay networks on-prem, then you don't need the NSX-T Autonomous Edge appliance.

---

[1]This image was created by Google Cloud, and is used according to the terms described in the Creative Common Attribution 4.0 License. Source: https://cloud.google.com/migrate/virtual-machines/docs/5.0/concepts/lifecycle.

HCX requires a Cloud Interconnect, which is a way of connecting directly or via a Partner Interconnect to Google's network backbone (I discuss in more detail in day 2 operations), while NSX-T only requires a VPN.

Custom Image Import

If your organization has standard template VM images for on-prem deployments, then you can import those into Google Cloud. Doing so will allow you to build GCE instances from your existing images, which can be helpful in bringing your own license (BYOL) and bring your own subscription (BYOS) scenarios. It supports VMDK, VHD, and other formats.

Container Migration Tools

Previously, I've mentioned Migrate to Containers in the modernization strategies chapter in the context of modernizing suitable VM-based workloads into containers. Those source VMs can currently be in VMware, AWS, Azure, or Compute Engine in Google Cloud. The targets for those modernized containers can be GKE, GKE Autopilot, Cloud Run, Anthos on Google Cloud, and Anthos clusters on VMware, AWS, or bare metal.

It'll work with Windows and Linux operating systems, but those Windows servers will need to have been migrated into Compute Engine on Google Cloud beforehand. Use one of the server migrations methods discussed previously to achieve that, and then you can turn it into a container.

Migrate to Containers has a workflow that starts with creating a processing cluster from which the Migrate to Container components can run, as shown in Figure 17-2.

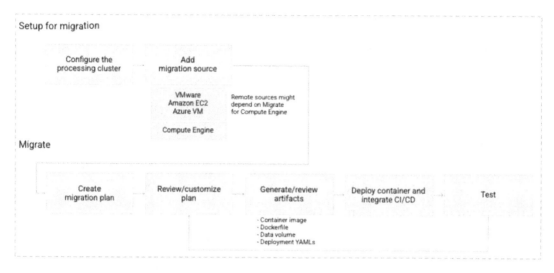

Figure 17-2. *Migrate to Containers workflow*[2]
Copyright Google Cloud

Database Migration Tools

Google Cloud has a product called the Database Migration Service (DMS). DMS is used to assist with DB migrations to Google Cloud CloudSQL. It supports migrations from self-managed instances of MySQL, PostgreSQL, SQL Server, or Oracle running on-prem or in other clouds. It also supports migrations from AWS's RDS and Aurora-managed DB instances.

This is a serverless product that is accessible via the Google Cloud console. You have the option for one-time or continuous replication.

An alternative third-party product for DB migrations to CloudSQL is Striim. Striim can also ingest data into BigQuery, Cloud Spanner, Cloud Pub/Sub, and Cloud Storage. Striim also has some helpful monitoring and alerting capabilities, as well as the ability to filter, transform, enrich, and correlate data during the ingestion. What I like most about Striim is while it is available to deploy from the Google Cloud Marketplace, you get access to Striim's team, who care deeply about making your migrations a success.

---

[2]This image was created by Google Cloud, and is used according to the terms described in the Creative Common Attribution 4.0 License. Source: `https://cloud.google.com/migrate/` `containers/docs/migration-journey`.

Data Migration Tools

Storage Transfer Service enables you to transfer data from on-prem Azure and AWS or across Google Cloud regions into Cloud Storage. The service has an agent that resides inside a container you deploy on-prem. This approach means you can simply add more agents to increase your transfer performance, enabling you to scale to transfer hundreds of TBs if needed. Your available bandwidth will likely become your bottleneck. The transfer service can set bandwidth limits to ensure you don't impact other workloads.

There is also the transfer appliance, a physical appliance you can request to have delivered to your data center. You can load your data onto it and ship it back to Google Cloud, where the data uploads into Cloud Storage in a region you've chosen. For large-scale data transfer, the transfer appliance method removes your bandwidth from being the bottleneck. There are two appliances, one with a capacity of 40TB and the other 300TB.

Feedback Loops

I'm sure you know what feedback loops are by now, applicable in many different development and operations frameworks such as SRE as a mechanism to capture improvements to increase performance. Having formalized feedback loops from the teams performing migrations is critical to increasing the number of migrations and shortening the time a migration takes. How can you establish a feedback loop?

As I mentioned before, migration waves are 2 weeks' sprints. So having a sprint retrospective to capture what went well and what can be improved is the simplest way to implement the feedback loop.

I previously mentioned using a Scrum Master. Another of their functions would be to run the sprint retrospective and then help estimate the effort to implement the identified improvements.

Operational Handover

It doesn't stop once servers cut over to Google Cloud. There must be a well-defined handover process to any business as usual (BAU) teams who will pick up the operational side once servers run in Google Cloud. I advise that it is another team who picks up the operational activities and that it doesn't become the responsibility of the migration teams. This remains the case even if you have only tens to low hundreds of servers to move. Placing an operational burden on a migration team will slow progress down.

The handover process will take place within the migration phase, so both teams need to be in regular communication with each other. The BAU teams must be aware of each migration wave's scheduled workloads. The BAU teams might have previous knowledge of these workloads, as they may have had operational responsibility for them on-prem.

If the BAU team hasn't previously supported the workload, you'll need to plan how to bridge the gap in advance. The best way to do this is to get the team currently responsible for the workload to hand over their knowledge and leave it to the team looking after workloads in Google Cloud to apply what is relevant once the workload is in Google Cloud.

Summary

Deploy and configure migration tools. Implement feedback loops for migration teams, so they can learn and improve. Ensure migration and BAU teams have established and formalized handover processes.

CHAPTER 18

Optimize

The term optimize in a cloud context often refers to cost reduction, such as rightsizing servers to smaller instance types to meet the server's performance needs without paying for more CPU/RAM than it needs. In the Google Cloud migration journey, the Optimize phase has a wider scope. Treat it as a continual optimization loop. It takes on some Site Reliability Engineering (SRE) principles and concepts.

It starts with defining your optimization requirements and then creating measurable goals to meet them. To define your requirements, you ask questions about the quality characteristics of the workload. I advise that you use existing quality standards that your organization may already use, such as the ISO/IEC 25000 series. The ISO has a product quality model that divides quality into eight characteristics.

- Functional suitability
- Performance efficiency
- Compatibility
- Usability
- Reliability
- Security
- Maintainability
- Portability

Within each characteristic, some sub-characteristics help you further define your requirements.

For example, two questions that align with the reliability characteristic are "Can your infrastructure and its components scale vertically or horizontally? Does your infrastructure support rolling back changes without manual intervention?" *(Migration to Google Cloud: Optimizing Your Environment | Cloud Architecture Center)*. You should aim to have questions defined against each characteristic.

193

© Jeremy Lloyd 2023
J. Lloyd, *Infrastructure Leader's Guide to Google Cloud*, https://doi.org/10.1007/978-1-4842-8820-7_18

Let's continue by answering the two example questions with the following answers:

- Not every infrastructure component can scale horizontally.

- Undoing infrastructure changes does require manual intervention.

With our answers, you can now form requirements such as the following:

- Increase the [specific components] availability.

- Increase infrastructure automation to remove manual intervention.

Now you can define your goals based on the SRE approach of service-level indicators (SLIs), which are quantitative measures, and service-level objectives (SLOs), which are target values for a service level. A single goal may cover one or many requirements. A single goal will cover both the example requirements:

- Provide 99.9% availability for [specific components].

With your goals defined, you then assess your environment, teams, and the optimization loop itself for optimization improvements. Then you measure the environment, teams, and the optimization loop by implementing monitoring. Then you analyze the monitoring data you've collected against your defined SLIs and SLOs and finally prioritize and implement the optimizations.

It is a complex but more encompassing approach that would still cover activities like rightsizing servers. For example, you cover cost management activities under the performance efficiency characteristic.

The optimize loop also covers the team performing the optimizations. As the infrastructure leader, you should continually assess if the team has the required skills to make optimizations. The skills and optimization activities performed on servers shortly after the cutover to Google Cloud won't be the same skills and activities required to optimize a workload that has been running in Google Cloud for months or years.

Finally, there's assessing the optimization loop itself. The approach to optimizing workloads should be consistent, clearly documented, and performed in a sprint-based approach. It will give you data points you can analyze afterward to identify blockers and improve optimization loop performance.

Summary

Treat the Optimize phase as a continuous loop. It doesn't simply end after VMs are rightsized. Use industry standards for multidimensional optimizations, such as ISO 25000 series, to help define your optimization requirements. Document your optimization process and loop for ways you can improve the process itself.

PART V

Cloud-Native

Part 5 discusses the key considerations that, as an infrastructure leader, you must be aware of when your organization is doing cloud-native development. I'll explain the advantages that cloud-native development brings and the functions that an infrastructure team should pick up to find a balance between complete developer freedom and controls that are too restrictive.

CHAPTER 19

Cloud-Native Development

In this chapter, I will discuss cloud-native advantages and architectural considerations, before expanding into what your development teams need from you and how Google views cloud-native security.

Cloud-Native Advantages

When discussing cloud-native architecture with development or infrastructure teams, I frame it in the context of the business benefits/outcomes it enables. Typical benefits/outcomes of cloud-native architectures are as follows:

- **Improve customer experience and loyalty.**

  - By reducing time-to-value

  - By increasing your software delivery performance and reliability to make stable releases to production more frequently

  - By providing better availability and resilience, with deployments spanning multiregions and automatic self-healing

- **Grow market share** with greater agility to enter new markets.

  - By quickly deploying to new regions faster than your competitors

  - By being flexible to react to global trends and threats immediately

  - By attracting talent by being at the forefront of cloud-native

- **Increase revenue and profit per customer.**

  - By being operationally efficient and scaling up and down and lowering operating costs

© Jeremy Lloyd 2023
J. Lloyd, *Infrastructure Leader's Guide to Google Cloud*, https://doi.org/10.1007/978-1-4842-8820-7_19

- **Improve sustainability**.

  - By employing Green IT or Green Coding principles

What about practical technology advantages to cloud-native architectures that are responsible for helping to deliver those business benefits/outcomes? At a high level, they are as follows:

- **Simplified development and operations**

  - Developers can spend more time on writing code.

  - Infrastructure teams can spend more time focusing on observability and optimizations to improve operational efficiency.

- **Greater integrations**

  - With tools such as Cloud Build and other open source software.

  - Improve the speed, security, and quality of software delivery performance.

  - Reducing lock-in, as Google often builds on existing open source software or open sources their internal software.

Most other practical benefits come under these two, such as being more cost-efficient, which is under simplified operations by making optimizations.

Integrated Development Environment

Integrated development environments (IDEs) provide developers with a single location to write and edit code. IDEs also enable developers to perform debugging, compile executables, and use syntax highlighting and autocomplete. Essentially an IDE helps developers to develop faster with fewer mistakes.

Google Cloud has three products to help make development faster and deployment simpler. The first is Cloud Code, a plug-in for popular IDEs such as Visual Studio Code (VS Code) and IntelliJ IDEA.

Cloud Code provides developers with a streamlined experience in developing software that will run on Kubernetes or Cloud Run. It does this by providing run-ready code and out-of-the-box configuration examples. Integration with Google Cloud products and services enables functionality like simplified GKE cluster creation, browsing Cloud Storage buckets and blobs, and access to Google Cloud Client Libraries which provides you with the recommended ways of calling Google Cloud APIs.

The second product is Cloud Shell Editor, which is Google Cloud's browser IDE based on the open source Eclipse Theia IDE. Cloud Shell Editor brings together the integrations developers need when developing workloads that run on Google Cloud. It also integrates with Cloud Code, bringing the advantages I've previously mentioned, as well as the ability to perform debugging, integrate with source control, work efficiently with multiple projects, and use Cloud Shell for command lines.

Cloud Shell Editor provides developers with a more unified experience, bringing together the integrations a developer needs to reduce the need for switching between different tabs and tools.

Why do these IDEs matter to an infrastructure leader?

Ensure that your development teams have the right tools to set them up for success with cloud-native development, and guide and advise them of the advantages these products provide. If the developers use a specific IDE and getting them to switch to Cloud Shell Editor isn't likely to happen or can't happen because they require functionality not offered by Cloud Shell Editor, then start with the Cloud Code plug-in.

Secondly, developers can test their code either locally or remotely. If they are developing for containers, then this means they have the option to deploy to a local Kubernetes cluster on their workstation using a tool like Minikube. Or they can deploy to a remote cluster which could be GKE running on-prem or in Google Cloud.

As an infrastructure team, you'll have less control over a local Minikube environment, but ensure you follow best practices for privileged access management, the security of the physical workstation (secure boot, encryption), and the security of the OS. Failure to correctly restrict, secure, and monitor these areas could lead to vulnerabilities in the software supply chain, as I previously discussed. Which is why the third product exists, called Cloud Workstations. It provides a centrally managed development environment that you can customise, secure and access from a web browser or a local IDE.

Cloud-Native Architecture

At some point in your organization's Google Cloud adoption journey, a person, team, or business unit will want to use Google Cloud to build and deploy workloads that use cloud-native architectures. You design, build, deploy, and maintain cloud-native architectures with the cloud in mind. What exactly do I mean by that?

It's an architecture that takes advantage of the cloud-native products and services and the flexibility they provide in scaling up and down and only paying for what you use. Cloud-native architectures use modern software development approaches such as microservices and containers. Infrastructure creation is in code, and testing and deployment are automated.

This combination enables cloud-native architectures to achieve advantages that aren't possible with traditional on-prem infrastructure, such as a database management system (DBMS) that can scale to meet peak demand but where you don't need to maintain the underlying OS.

In Google Cloud, there are two paths cloud-native development can take.

- Serverless

- Kubernetes

If having a higher degree of control over the operating environment is important, you'll likely go down the Kubernetes route. If focusing on the business logic is the priority, you'd go down a serverless route.

Regardless of the route, you should design cloud-native applications with the universally used 12 factors or, more recently, the 15 factors. I advise you to visit 12factor.net and also read the ebook for the 15 factors. Knowing them will give you the ability to understand better what your development teams are writing and provide you with the ability to shape the design.

Establishing cloud-native design principles for your organization is highly advised. A few common principles continually recur as good practices. These are the following:

- Use Google Cloud managed services.

- Automate, automate, automate.

- Be smart with state.

- Privacy by design.

- Security by design/shift-left on security.

- Loosely coupled architecture.

- Streamline change processes.

- Use open and flexible instrumentation.

What is the role of the infrastructure leader in cloud-native development?

While I will provide you with the key considerations, I highly recommend that you engage with the development team leader(s) to understand their needs. What jobs are they doing? What is slowing them down and causing them toil? Knowing answers to these questions will help you put the right processes and controls to enable development to flourish.

Given the on-demand nature of the cloud, you want to encourage and empower development teams to experiment. Of course, you should do this in environments away from production. It's often typical for organizations to require business cases to justify the time and effort required to test an idea. As the infrastructure leader, challenge this with your development team counterparts. Experimentation will lead to value creation, and the faster your organization can unlock that hidden value, the better.

Regardless of the stage of Google Cloud adoption, the needs of development teams are reasonably consistent. The adoption approach gives you an indication of when development teams may look at cloud-native development. Developers using Google Cloud need

- Access to Google Cloud projects to provision new resources to experiment

- An integrated development environment (IDE) upon which to write code and improve code quality

- A location to store their code and artifacts in source control

- The ability to monitor, log, and alert on production workloads

- To be able to test and debug efficiently

- The skills to use Google Cloud-native products and services

- To be able to select the right tools for the job

- The knowledge of designing cloud architectures

- To design with security in mind (shift-left on security)

- To be able to get to production efficiently

- A stable infrastructure upon which to build and deploy

- Supportive leadership

So how can the infrastructure leader empower development teams to use Google Cloud for cloud-native development? Let's take our list of developer needs and, under each, define the activities you can control for each.

Access to Google Cloud Projects to Provision New Resources to Experiment

- A Cloud Identity group with the roles required to enable developers to experiment. Try and stick to using predefined roles.

- A Google Cloud organization hierarchy (folders and projects) that provides developers with Google Cloud project(s) where they can experiment and apply lightweight governance standards such as the following:

  - Limit access to specific IAM groups.

  - Agree on a budget and set budget alerts to notify the development team and someone outside of the development team of the spend.

  - Labels such as environment, owner, requestor, expiration date, purpose, or experiment name.

- Create a standard infrastructure-as-code pattern for the experimentation Google Cloud project with the lightweight governance standards built-in. Use Terraform or YAML if you want to use Google Cloud's Deployment Manager for deployments.

- Create a simple deployment method for developers to invoke the IaC used to create Google Cloud projects for experimentation. Use Deployment Manager or Cloud Build.

- Implement measures (ideally automated) that will delete experimentation projects on a schedule based on their expiration date label. Developers won't love you for this, but it's an excellent way to prevent something in experimentation from becoming production, and it forces the developers to automate and streamline their processes. It also reduces risks associated with activities such as integrations with production systems/data or a lack of regard for security standards. I usually explain that this is the trade-off of having complete freedom to experiment, while ensuring the risk to the organization remains low.

An Integrated Development Environment (IDE) upon Which to Write Code and Improve Code Quality

- Educate them on the use of Cloud Code, Cloud Shell Editor, and Cloud Workstations the integrations and benefits these tools provide.

A Location to Store Their Code and Artifacts in Source Control

- Inform them about Cloud Source Repositories.

- If they want to continue using an existing source code repo, then assist them with any authentication and authorization requirements to get the repos securely connected with Google Cloud

The Ability to Monitor, Log, and Alert on Production Workloads

- Use Google's Cloud Monitoring product and gain familiarity and confidence with the product to be able to provide assistance to efficiently diagnose infrastructure problems and interactions between services.

- Ensure Cloud Monitoring is set up to provide insights into the workload's overall health, not just one specific area.

- Use the same familiarity and confidence in Cloud Monitoring to enable the development teams.

- Onboard and enable the development teams to use Cloud Monitoring, and ensure the teams have access to any other tools and data to perform troubleshooting.

- Advise developers to adopt the OpenTelemetry tracing package. Google is transitioning their client libraries to this standard.

To Be Able to Test and Debug Efficiently

- Advice on automated testing.

- Understand their current approach to managing test data and what controls you need to put in place in Google Cloud.

- Again, educate them on the use of Cloud Code and Cloud Shell Editor.

- Guide them in the use of local Kubernetes environments such as Minikube so that they can quickly, simply, and securely stand up on their workstation.

- Combine a local Kubernetes environment with Skaffold (open source tool by Google). Skaffold helps automate local Kubernetes deployments.

The Skills to Use Google Cloud-Native Products and Services

- Foster a community-type spirit; get your infrastructure team members who are skilled in Google Cloud to help others learn.

- Understand where the development teams skills gaps; use the Likert scale approach that I previously explained in Part 3.

- Propose a learning and enablement plan, and include Google Cloud certifications in that.

To Be Able to Select the Right Tools for the Job

- If you prevent the devs from getting access to the Google Cloud marketplace, you could impact their ability to select tools which could improve their software delivery performance.

- Ensure you are aware of the tooling the development teams are using. If your organization has multiple development teams, ensure they communicate on what tools they use. You might even think about establishing a baseline of tools once cloud-native development has been taking place for 3–6 months.

- Ensure an item in a sprint retrospective is the current product and services used to build, deploy, and run workloads.

The Knowledge of Designing Cloud Architectures

- Cocreate with the development team(s) cloud-native architecture design principles.

- Create architecture patterns to solve common scenarios you've identified.

- Document and store in a central location the lessons learned on cloud architecture, from what you should do through to what not to do and why.

To Design with Security in Mind (Shift-Left on Security)

- Have your cloud guiding principles guide developers to design with security in mind.

- Shifting left on security requires that an information security (InfoSec) function has the access required to be involved in the earlier stages of development and testing.

- Create a Cloud Identity group and associate it with the required predefined roles.

- Allow the InfoSec team also to experiment; they can use the same mechanism mentioned earlier for the developers, which allows them to identify tools that could benefit the development life cycle and review libraries that they can approve for use.

- Have InfoSec review and preapprove modules of IaC your team has created.

Be Able to Get to Production Efficiently

- Modules of IaC to provision resources such as a new project through to a VPC, storage bucket, and beyond. All in alignment with the approved governance standards.

- Work with testers to automate the testing of the Google Cloud infrastructure resources. This task is effective if you use standardized modules of IaC.

- Automated Google Cloud infrastructure deployments.

- Provide continuous integration and continuous deployment tools and pipelines.

- An efficient change management process.

A Stable Infrastructure upon Which to Build and Deploy

- Write infrastructure-as-code modules and store them in source control.

- Automated Google Cloud infrastructure deployments.

- Work with the workloads owner to define service-level objectives (SLOs).

- Schedule and perform disaster recovery tests; see Google's guidance on this (https://cloud.google.com/blog/products/management-tools/shrinking-the-time-to-mitigate-production-incidents).

- Understand how the workload will respond to failure using controlled failure injection.

Supportive Leadership

- Aligned stakeholders, proactively engaged in supporting improvements to the development process

- Providing vision, inspirational comms, intellectual stimulation, personal recognition

As an infrastructure leader, you should attend sprint retrospectives. You can continue to uncover the blockers and challenges the development teams are facing and understand how your team can assist them.

At some point, when IT is providing core services to enable wider adoption of Google Cloud, the infrastructure leader will need to empower development teams to use Google Cloud while ensuring standards are maintained.

Google's Approach to Cloud-Native Security

I mentioned earlier in the book how Google designs its infrastructure to enable its products and services to run as microservices in containers, with Borg being their cluster management system. This means Google products and services are cloud-native by design, giving Google years of experience securing distributed microservices at scale. This has led to a security implementation known as BeyondProd, which Google uses to secure their internal and external products and services.

Google has written a whitepaper describing its approach, available at `https://cloud.google.com/docs/security/beyondprod`. Within it, they detail the critical considerations for cloud-native security. They give their security principles upon which they use to guide product development. And they detail their internal approach and tools that piece it together.

When it comes to securing microservices-based cloud-native workloads, the traditional methods do not stand. Advise your security team to review the BeyondProd whitepaper and document the takeaways and architectural principles they'd want your organization to adhere to.

Summary

Understand cloud-native's business and technical benefits/outcomes, and champion these among your development team leaders. Understand what the developers need from Google Cloud to be able to thrive, and then provide them with that environment and the guardrails. And understand how Google is seeing cloud-native security, and be able to confidently guide a conversation with your development and security teams.

CHAPTER 20

Containers

In this chapter, I will cover what containers are and how to overcome some of the challenges they bring and Google's answer to on-prem and multicloud container management.

What are containers?

Containers are essentially packages of software. They contain the application code, configuration files, binaries, and libraries required to run in a self-contained state. Containers don't contain an operating system. Instead, they share the OS kernel and associated resources such as CPU and memory.

What are the benefits of containers?

- **Portability** – containers are lightweight and highly portable between environments such as on-prem to cloud or cloud to cloud.

- **Efficiency** – they are more efficient to run as they share the OS kernel and associated resources, so you can increase the density.

- **Consistency** – drive up consistency in the standards of your operation tasks through automation by design, such as a pipeline to build and deploy container images.

- **Microservices** – fit perfectly into a microservices architecture approach. As you want self-sufficient components.

- **Scalability** – containers can scale up and down quickly and offer the flexibility to scale just the required individual components.

While using containers provides numerous benefits, they do introduce some challenges. However, given Google's use of containers, it should be no surprise that they have answers to help you overcome them.

© Jeremy Lloyd 2023
J. Lloyd, *Infrastructure Leader's Guide to Google Cloud*, https://doi.org/10.1007/978-1-4842-8820-7_20

In no particular priority order, those challenges are across the following areas:

- Management of hundreds to thousands of containers and multiple nodes

- Maintaining container image integrity and software security

- Managing legacy workloads

- Unfamiliarity and lack of container skills

To help solve the developer's container challenges and to be able to support them proactively, your team needs the required skills to manage container infrastructure on Google Cloud.

You can do this by aligning Google Cloud's products and services to help streamline the software delivery process and ongoing management. Containers and the products and services created by Google and third parties to help you build, deploy, and manage require new skills for both the developers and infrastructure teams.

When I speak to infrastructure teams about their current experience and use of containers, it's limited, with some having experience in running small container environments inside VMs.

The default position of most appears to be to wait until the demand for containers comes from the development teams. Instead of waiting, isn't it much better if you've been experimenting with containers and the supporting products in Google Cloud already? Doing so will accelerate your organization's ability to adopt the technology.

I'll discuss specific container day 2 operations in Part 6. Let's take each challenge and discuss how Google Cloud's products and services can solve them. As an infrastructure leader, you must understand the challenges within this area and the needs of the developers so that you can align appropriate tooling, governance, security, ways of working, and skills.

Management of Hundreds to Thousands of Containers and Multiple Nodes

Running a handful of Docker containers across a couple of nodes with little to no automation and orchestration is a manageable task. Still, it does come with risks of human error. However, unless your microservices architecture is for a small, simple, and largely static workload, you'll find tens of Docker containers can quickly scale with new features and functionality added to the workload and, hopefully, an increase in demand. When tens of containers become hundreds and possibly beyond, those simple manual operational tasks become complex at scale.

It's why Kubernetes (K8s) was created. "Kubernetes, also known as K8s, is an open source system for automating deployment, scaling, and management of containerized applications" (Kubernetes.io).

As mentioned, K8s was created by Google based on their experiences of running containers at scale. K8s has a control plane and worker nodes. This is known as the Kubernetes cluster. K8s can be deployed and run anywhere, sometimes called DIY Kubernetes.

In DIY mode, K8s can be deployed in an on-prem data center or to any cloud provider. Doing so in this manner will require additional management effort, though, from provisioning the control plane and worker nodes to ensuring the availability and reliability of the physical infrastructure if installing K8s on-prem.

If deploying DIY mode K8s within Google Cloud, you can configure the K8s control plane and the worker nodes to run on Compute Engine instances. Or there is a more straightforward way. You could use Google Kubernetes Engine (GKE), where Google has dramatically simplified the deployment, configuration, and maintenance of a K8s environment. This is giving you K8s as-a-service. Kubernetes is now the default standard for container orchestration, and Azure and AWS also provide K8s as-a-service options with the Azure Kubernetes Service (AKS) and Elastic Kubernetes Service (EKS).

Given that this book is about Google Cloud, I wouldn't advise you to spend time and effort deploying Kubernetes in DIY mode unless necessary. And if you are only now starting to use containers, then you won't have the burden of any incompatibilities that might have occurred if you were going from an old version of Kubernetes in DIY mode to a newer version GKE will run. GKE simplifies the deployment and ongoing maintenance of your Kubernetes clusters.

GKE comes in two modes, standard and autopilot.

Standard mode – Kubernetes gives you control over the nodes. It requires you to ensure the right amount of compute capacity available to fulfill the demands of the containerized workloads. The trade-off is that you get more flexibility in configuring your cluster and its nodes.

For example, GKE nodes provide the compute (CPU, memory) that ultimately is where your containers run. These nodes require a host OS. On GKE, the default host OS comes from a node image called container-optimized OS, created by Google, locked down by default, and ready to run containers out of the box. You can implement further recommended security configuration using the CIS benchmark for container-optimized OS. However, you can also use Ubuntu or Windows Server node images with GKE nodes.

Standard mode allows you to create node pools using Spot VMs and Preemptible instances. These provide compute at a lower price and fit certain workload use cases. I will cover Spot VMs and Preemptible instances in Part 6. And in standard mode, you are charged on a per node basis.

Overall standard mode provides you with the ability to define the configuration across the following areas:

- The cluster type

- The size and number of nodes and node pools

- Provisioning resources

- The node image

- Security

- Networking

- Upgrade, repair, and maintenance

- Authentication credentials

- Scaling

- Logging

- Monitoring

- Routing

- Cluster add-ons

Autopilot mode – GKE doesn't require you to do any tasks with the underlying infrastructure. Autopilot mode provides a production-ready configuration that follows all the GKE best practices. You still get access to the Kubernetes API, tools, and the wider ecosystem.

Autopilot mode can greatly accelerate your organization's use of containers, especially if your organization hasn't got existing Kubernetes experience. Being aware of the trade-offs is key to being able to run production workloads. Autopilot mode is Google

Cloud's opinionated view on how GKE should be configured and managed securely. In Autopilot mode, the configuration is locked down completely in areas such as the following:

- Node image

- Provisioning resources

- Upgrade, repairs, maintenance

- Authentication credentials

A few important points, autopilot mode also doesn't support binary authorization, which is a useful feature that I will discuss in more detail later. And in autopilot mode, you are charged on a per pod basis. Once you've chosen an operating mode, you cannot change it. Instead, you'd need to create a new GKE cluster in the desired mode and redeploy your containers.

Maintaining Container Image Integrity and Software Security

Containers provide many security advantages over VMs, such as the following:

- A reduced attack surface due to the host OS's minimal footprint. As you package dependencies into the container, not the host OS.

- A defined life cycle; a container, once deployed, doesn't run forever. When changes are required, you don't make those changes on a deployed container. You make the changes in code and build and then deploy a new container.

- Containers are running services to perform specific tasks. You can significantly restrict the access permissions to the required levels of service-to-service communication.

- Process and resource isolation using the Linux kernels namespace and control group features. Process isolation using a namespace helps in reducing the blast radius should a security incident occur, and resource isolation using control groups helps you control performance for a single or group of processes which could help limit blast radius again.

While containers do provide security advantages, they also bring some different security-related challenges that you must deal with. Some of these security challenges are because containers allow you to make more releases to production. So code is compiled more often, albeit limited to a specific service, and updates get to production faster. This increases an attacker's chances of activating a malicious piece of code.

In the microservices and container approach, you must ask yourself questions such as how do you ensure the container's image is trusted and isn't compromised? Do the dependencies contain any vulnerabilities? Have credentials ever been leaked?

Unfortunately, in 2020 and 2021, there have been several high-profile cyberattacks on organizations such as Solarwinds and Codecov. Both are targets because they are used by government agencies in the United States and other countries worldwide. These attacks infiltrated those organizations' software supply chains by leveraging undetected vulnerabilities. Open source software vendors faced a 650% year-on-year increase in cyberattacks (*Sonatype's 2021 State of the Software Supply Chain*).

Enter the concept of securing the software supply chain. This concept requires that you know every component in use in your software, including open source and third-party dependencies and any other artifacts and then validating their provenance.

A short digression but a partly related subject, Google, in collaboration with OpenSSF, has proposed a standardized approach to securing the supply chain, known as the supply-chain level for software artifacts (SLSA) which is the evolution of Google's internal processes to secure the supply chain. SLSA has four levels, with level 1 starting with basic protection and level 4 being maximum protection. The levels are incremental, and the SLSA website (slsa.dev) provides plenty of actionable tasks to help you progress through the levels. SLSA aligns with the software development life cycle. Figure 20-1 gives you a high-level view of the development cycles and the goal of securing the supply chain.

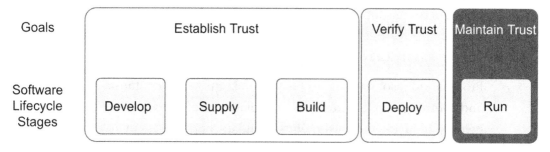

Figure 20-1. *Securing the software supply chain*

In Google's internal development process, they have been using what they classify as an "internal deploy-time enforcement check" (Google Cloud) known as binary authorization for Borg (BAB). BAB's role is to minimize insider risk by ensuring that Google's software meets defined standards and is properly reviewed and authorized.

Back to the original challenge of ensuring container image integrity and the software's security, when developing using containers, you must start with a base image.

On top of that, you'll add the configuration files, binaries, and any libraries required to fulfill that service's need. Those supporting artifacts should be under artifact management using Google Cloud's Artifact Registry. Within the Artifact Registry, you can store your artifacts in private or public repositories, and it integrates with other essential products such as container analysis, which I will discuss later.

To further help you secure your supply chain, Google has created an Assured Open Source Software service. This service is essentially Google verifying OSS packages on your behalf and making them available as secured and protected by Google. It's how Google serves their internal development teams. And given Google identified over 36,000 vulnerabilities across the top 550 OSS projects, this will prove to be an invaluable service in protecting your software supply chain.

So, how do you ensure the base image you start with is secure and has no vulnerabilities?

There are two parts to answering that. First, you need to get the base image from a trusted source, not randomly off the Internet via a growing number of downstream repackagers. Google Cloud maintains some container images for popular Linux distributions. These are known as managed base images. Google uses these same images to perform their internal development and performs vulnerability scanning on them. You can easily consume these images via the Google Cloud Marketplace.

The second part of this answer takes us back to the evolution of Google's binary authorization for Borg (BAB). BAB has provided us with a product in Google Cloud known as binary authorization, which works with GKE or Cloud Run. Binary authorization enables us to define policies to restrict container images to only those trusted authorities have signed (establish trust) and then enforce validation that only verified images are used in the build and deployment process (verify trust). Then use a feature of binary authorization known as continuous validation to perform periodic checks of container images being used within your GKE clusters (maintain trust).

With your base image trusted, you need a build process that pulls together the configuration files, binaries, and libraries required into the container. For this build process, Google Cloud has Cloud Build.

Cloud Build is Google Cloud's Continuous Integration and Continuous Deployment (CI/CD) product. It allows you to automate your build pipeline while generating provenance metadata such as built images, input source location, build arguments, and build duration.

Cloud Build also creates what is known as an attestation. Think of it as signing an image done at build time. The image is signed with a private key either manually or as part of an automated build process, with the corresponding public key stored in an attestor. This attestation enables Google Cloud's binary authorization to control deployments to trusted images by verifying the public and private key pairs.

However, before you get binary authorization to verify the container is trusted and deployable, there is an additional step, container analysis. Container analysis allows us to manually or automatically perform vulnerability scans on images stored in a Google Cloud Artifact or Container Registry. The scans are against packages publicly monitored for security vulnerabilities from locations such as the National Vulnerability Database, which is maintained by the National Institute of Standards and Technology (NIST) and Linux distribution sources such as Debian, Ubuntu, Alpine, Red Hat Enterprise Linux, and CentOS. After a scan, it produces metadata and stores it within container analysis.

You can also manually or automatically add additional metadata to container analysis. Figure 20-2 shows this as metadata is being added from the source code repository, the CI and CD stages, and the target. All the metadata is available to query through an API, enabling you to use it as part of your CI/CD pipeline to verify trust before deployment.

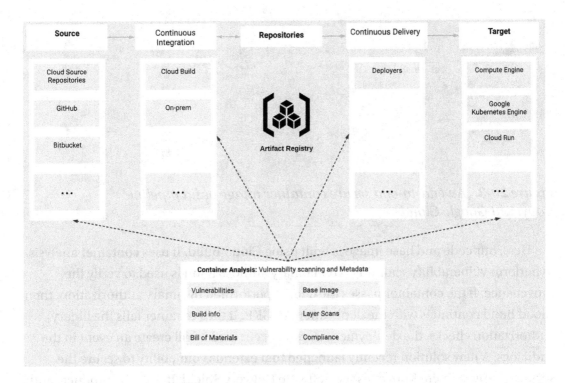

Figure 20-2. *Container analysis adding metadata across the container life cycle*[1]
Copyright Google Cloud

So piecing it together, a secure container build and deployment pipeline using the described Google Cloud products looks like Figure 20-3.

---

[1] This image was created by Google Cloud, and is used according to the terms described in the Creative Common Attribution 4.0 License. Source: https://cloud.google.com/ container-registry/docs/container-analysis.

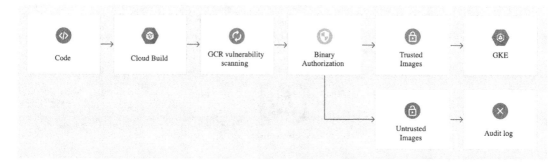

Figure 20-3. *An end-to-end secure container image build pipeline[2]*
Copyright Google Cloud

Here, our code and base image is built using Cloud Build. It uses container analysis to perform vulnerability scanning. Then binary authorization is used to verify the provenance. If the container passes the checks performed by binary authorization, then Cloud Build continues with the deployment to GKE. If the container fails the binary authorization checks, the deployment doesn't occur, and it will create an event in the audit logs. A new solution recently launched that extends your ability to secure the software supply chain. Known as the Software Delivery Shield. It uses the products and services discussed here plus additional components and seamless integrations.

Your role as infrastructure leader is to inform the developers of the processes and tools to ensure that your product's software supply chain is secure. There are a lot of new tools and ways of working here; don't take for granted that the developers will know what the best practices are within this space; instead, guide them through creating a secure CI/CD pipeline.

Managing Legacy Workloads

Containers by design provide you with a radically different approach to maintaining and managing them compared with virtual machines. With VMs, you have an OS that you secure by applying hardening policies. You have to keep the OS up to date with security patches. You can log in to the OS and make manual changes or manual installations of new software. You can grant local administrative access. You can store data locally through mounted drives.

---

[2]This image was created by Google Cloud, and is used according to the terms described in the Creative Common Attribution 4.0 License. Source: https://cloud.google.com/architecture/binary-auth-with-cloud-build-and-gke.

In the container world, you don't do that. The way of working completely changes. You perform operations and installations programmatically. The OS is an image maintained by a vendor and stored in a container or artifact registry. And you do not log in to it to make post-deployment configuration changes.

So as an infrastructure leader, how do you deal with two different operating models?

Part of that answer lies in assessing legacy VM-based workloads for their container fit. Google Cloud's Migrate to Containers provides precisely this ability. Taking some of your legacy workloads and managing them as containers will reduce some of the legacy burdens. Google Cloud's Migrate for Containers will also enable you to migrate suitable workloads directly into containers you can run and operate on GKE.

For VMs that you cannot easily containerize, Google Cloud's Anthos for Virtual Machines will enable you to run VMs using Kubernetes and standardize your operating model and tools. I will discuss Anthos as a product offering in more detail later. Anthos for Virtual Machines provides two methods for managing VMs. The first option is for those who currently use vSphere. Anthos will enable you to connect your vSphere to the Anthos control plane and perform your operations and monitoring through Anthos. The second option is to shift those VMs to a Kubernetes cluster with KubeVirt, an open source virtualization API for K8s.

Using these approaches should leave you with only a few outliers that can't, or that you've strategically decided not to manage as containers. Overall it should enable you to standardize your operating model to an Anthos/Kubernetes approach and continue with a more legacy approach for those outlier VMs. Of course, you can perform modernizations against those outlier VMs to streamline operations. For information on how to approach that, see the modernization strategies section in Part 2.

Unfamiliarity and Lack of Container Skills

If your development teams haven't used microservices and containers, then there are a lot of new products, processes, and skills to learn. Likewise, it's the same situation if your infrastructure team hasn't had to manage any container workloads.

Where and how do you start?

To better understand the terminology, concepts, and technology, I suggest you start with the structured learning paths that lead to Google Cloud certifications. For developers, they'll want to follow the Professional Cloud Developer track. For infrastructure team members, they should follow the Associate Cloud Engineer track.

For the infrastructure teams getting hands-on, there are several tutorials that you can access from the Google Kubernetes Engine docs webpage. Become familiar with K8s manifest files by editing example files and deploying them to understand the changes.

Then if you are in the process or planning on migrating to Google Cloud, select low-risk and non-production workloads. Run the container fit assessment and see if you have some workloads you could move into containers with little effort.

If your development teams are building cloud-native workloads from the ground up, then ensure they follow best practices around the software development life cycle, specifically that they have non-production environments. Use those non-production environments to accelerate your infrastructure team's skill set before a production container workload goes live.

These approaches provide real experience and will accelerate the learning and ways of working before your teams have the confidence to tackle a production workload. They'll allow you to ensure you can establish build and deployment pipelines and that those workloads will have monitoring, logging, and alerting setup.

While learning and testing non-production workloads, consider using GKE in autopilot mode. It'll ease the path to deployment and still provide ample learning opportunities. Ensure you are aware of the limitations, some of which I discussed previously.

Products to Centralize Management/Operations

Anthos

Everything I've mentioned within Part 5 has been focused on cloud-native development. What if you need to maintain some workloads on-prem or your organization has a multicloud strategy and you need to deploy and manage workloads across multiple clouds? That's where Anthos comes into play, with the ability to manage Kubernetes clusters on VMware on-prem, bare metal, and Kubernetes clusters on Google Cloud alongside AWS and Azure.

What exactly is Anthos?

Anthos is a container orchestration and management service. It's made up of several different components that, when combined, enable you to provide secure and consistent operations across your entire environment.

At a high level, those components are as follows:

- **Anthos Config Management** – deploy version-controlled policies consistently across environments.

- **Anthos Identity Service** – which provides integration with your existing identity providers to enable authentication of organization credentials to access Anthos clusters.

- **Anthos Service Mesh** – manage, observe, and secure services; a managed service based on Istio.

- **Binary Authorization** – provides validation that only trusted and verified container images are deployed.

- **Cloud Logging and Cloud Monitoring for Anthos system components** – monitor and logging managed service with integration to monitor Anthos Clusters on VMware and Google Cloud.

- **Cloud Run for Anthos** – a fully managed serverless platform built on Kubernetes using Knative.

- **Migrate to Containers** – convert VMs into containers.

- **Multi-Cluster Ingress** – Google Cloud hosted HTTP(S) load balancer that supports multi-cluster and multiregion deployments.

Why does Anthos matter to the infrastructure leader?

For the infrastructure leader, Anthos provides your teams with the tools they need to manage container complexity across multiple environments and at scale. I cover day 2 operations for Anthos later in the book. It also helps provide developers with standards and patterns to design against, which ultimately can lead to more reliable and scalable workloads.

Summary

Invest time now to build container and Kubernetes skills within the infrastructure team. Use Google Cloud products and services to help you secure your software supply chain. Understand how you can use Anthos to manage outliers or multicloud.

CHAPTER 21

Serverless

In this chapter, I'll cover Google Cloud's serverless products and services and their benefits.

At the start of this part, I mentioned that cloud-native development in Google Cloud has two paths, serverless and Kubernetes. I've discussed Kubernetes, so now let's look at serverless.

Firstly, what is serverless?

Serverless products and services provide a higher level of abstraction from the underlying infrastructure, meaning developers can focus more on business logic than infrastructure configuration. Of course, under the hood, Google Cloud's serverless products still run on physical infrastructure.

Cloud Run

Cloud Run allows you to run containers without worrying about the underlying infrastructure. It sounds remarkably similar to GKE autopilot, and it is. Except with Cloud Run, the abstraction isn't just from the underlying infrastructure. It's also from Kubernetes itself. I previously mentioned the complexity of Kubernetes and Google's attempts to make it easier with GKE standard and autopilot modes. Cloud Run completely removes the need to learn Kubernetes.

Cloud Run provides developers with a fast and simple way of deploying a container, pledging that you can go from a container to a URL within seconds, built on top of the open source Knative Kubernetes-based platform, which, incidentally, Google created and still heavily contributes to, being based on open source software and Kubernetes, which runs anywhere. This means you have no lock-in risk when you deploy your services to it.

© Jeremy Lloyd 2023
J. Lloyd, *Infrastructure Leader's Guide to Google Cloud*, https://doi.org/10.1007/978-1-4842-8820-7_21

One of the straplines of Cloud Run is its ability to run any language, library, and binary. You only pay when your code is run, which makes it cost beneficial for services that don't continuously run.

Cloud Run provides monitoring integration with Cloud Monitoring out of the box. Autoscaling is completely taken care of by Cloud Run. It scales as required to handle the incoming requests and also considers CPU utilization and settings that you can configure, such as how many requests can be simultaneously processed by a container and the minimum and the maximum number of containers.

Cloud Run also works with Anthos, which provides the benefits of Anthos's centralized management and ability to run on-prem via GKE on-prem.

At the time of writing, there are a couple of disadvantages, namely, a lack of configuration of security settings, and it doesn't support stateful applications.

From an infrastructure team perspective, there isn't much that needs to do. Ensure developers have a location to experiment with Cloud Run and that any Cloud Run managed containers running in production have Cloud Monitoring views and reports created.

Cloud Functions

In cloud-native architecture, actions must be performed in response to events occurring. Sometimes this is referred to as event-driven architecture. These events can be cases such as file creation in Cloud Storage, an HTTP request coming from a third-party source, or the creation of a VM. To take action against an event, you must have a trigger that is listening for that event. Then you need a function to execute code that performs a single action.

In Google Cloud, the product that enables this is called Cloud Functions, which provides Functions-as-a-Service (FaaS) meaning there is no underlying server infrastructure to manage. In Cloud Functions, you create triggers and bind them to functions that perform actions. A single trigger can be bound to many functions, but you can only bind a function to a single trigger. Cloud Functions supports the following:

- HTTP functions

- Background functions

- CloudEvent functions

Google has created an accelerator to help you create well-written functions, called the Functions Framework, which is open source.

Functions are charged based on how long they run, how many times they run, and how many resources they require.

What are the considerations from an infrastructure perspective?

Cloud Functions, by design, are abstracted away from the underlying infrastructure. Day 2 operations tend to focus on monitoring and alerting, be that for a service to service communication, security events, or performance events. Cloud Functions integrates with Cloud Monitoring by default. So ensure your team has dashboards and views set up to understand the overall architecture health and has the knowledge to troubleshoot. Ensure development teams have access to Cloud Monitoring and can also perform troubleshooting.

App Engine

Another serverless product from Google Cloud is App Engine, which was Google Cloud's first serverless product released in 2008. App Engine provides developers with a product where they can host web applications written in one of the supported languages. App Engine supports the most popular languages but specific versions of them. If you need to run a version that isn't supported or if your developers write code in a language that isn't supported, then App Engine has a solution.

That leads us to the two different types of App Engine, the standard environment and the flexible environment.

The standard environment supports specific versions of popular languages like Go, .Net, Java, and Node.js, among others. The applications deployed to standard run in a secure sandboxed environment that can go from a cold-start to operational in seconds. This enables the application to scale easily and rapidly across multiple servers, which defines the type of applications that I'd suggest should use App Engine standard. Standard is a good fit for applications that encounter sudden traffic spikes, but you can scale back to zero or the free tier when possible.

Google introduced the flexible environment later to provide more, you guessed it, flexibility. Flexible runs the application instances inside a Docker container on a Compute Engine VM and allows you to run applications developed in other languages. The cold-start time is minutes due to the requirement of a Compute Engine VM. A useful advantage of the flexible environment is integrating with other services running on the same VPC.

What are the considerations from an infrastructure perspective?

Both App Engine environments have minimal management of underlying infrastructure. The flexible environment uses Compute Engine, but it's more of a managed Compute Engine. With auto-patching and restarts weekly, predefined health checks with auto-healing is required. And remember, the services are running within a container, so the underlying VM is replaceable.

Workflows

Google Cloud helps to enable an automation-first approach to build, deploy, and manage your workloads. What if you aren't trying to automate just a single task? What if an automated task must run in a sequence as part of an end-to-end process or workflow, and it needs to make calls to other Google Cloud products and services?

Typically that's when you'll want a workflow orchestration tool that can execute many steps across multiple products and services until the process or workflow is complete.

Google Cloud Workflows is Google Cloud's answer to that, a serverless orchestration tool that provides the ability to execute steps in a defined order. Workflows integrate with other Google Cloud products such as Cloud Functions, Cloud Run, BigQuery, or even any HTTP-based API.

What are the considerations from an infrastructure perspective?

Since its introduction, I've seen a mix of development and infrastructure teams create and own workflows. With many possible use cases, it's best to ensure that the team has experience with Workflows so they can easily create process automation.

Serverless Data Products

Google Cloud also has several options for serverless managed database products. So let's briefly look at them.

Firestore is a NoSQL document database, aimed at making the development of mobile and web applications more effortless, with iOS and Android and Web SDKs and live synchronization and offline modes for real-time applications.

Firestore is part of the Firebase development platform, which provides a suite of products to make mobile and web application development, build, test, and deployment easier. Under the hood, a Firebase project is a Google Cloud project and is visible from within the Google Cloud console and the Firebase console.

CloudSQL is a managed relational database service for MySQL, PostgreSQL, and SQL Server. It offers easier integrations with other Google Cloud products and services such as Compute Engine and GKE. It can scale horizontally (via read replicas) and vertically within a matter of minutes and offers 99.95% availability.

I mentioned the Database Migration Service (DMS) product previously. DMS enables you to migrate your databases into CloudSQL with minimal downtime.

Cloud Spanner is a managed relational database service that can boast industry-leading 99.999% availability for multiregion instances and unlimited scale. With that in mind, while you can start with small sizes and scale as required, Cloud Spanner is for large-scale databases.

The multiregional configuration provides two read-write regions; within each region, there are two read-write replicas, while regional contains three read-write replicas.

Cloud Bigtable is a managed NoSQL database that can handle petabyte-scale, designed to provide 99.999% availability in multi-cluster mode and able to meet sub-10ms latency. It has easy integrations with the broader Google Cloud data products such as BigQuery, Dataflow, and Dataproc. Dynamically scale additional nodes as required and without downtime.

BigQuery is a serverless data warehouse that provides multicloud data analysis of large datasets in sub-seconds. It enables you to create machine learning models with SQL queries.

AlloyDB for PostgreSQL is a managed PostgreSQL database service offering full PostgreSQL compatibility and blazing fast transactional processing performance compared with standard PostgreSQL. It's been designed for your most demanding workloads and comes with a 99.99% availability SLA. It has simplified operations that use machine learning.

Summary

Ensure development teams have the correct access. Provide a place where experimentation can take place. Put guardrails in place using a combination of opinionated views of the configuration options and ways of working (documented). Understand the value proposition of each serverless Google Cloud product.

PART VI

Day 2 Operations

Improving daily work is even more important than doing daily work.

—Gene Kim, The Phoenix Project

In this part, I will guide you through the key day 2 pillars and give you information on Google Cloud products and services that you can make use of to simplify and improve your day 2 operations. I aim to provide you with the information you need to consider when designing your day 2 operations.

This section is still relevant for those who primarily manage commercial off-the-shelf software. As unless your software vendor is deploying and managing the workload for you, there will still be decisions that you need to make on how to build, deploy, and run and securely maintain that workload. Using the "days" concept helps to position the operational challenges you might face.

CHAPTER 22

Day 2 Operations Explained

In this chapter, I will focus on what day 2 operations are and the common antipatterns to watch out for.

What are day 2 operations?

Day 2 operations is a term used within DevOps to describe everything you need to do to keep a workload running until the end of that workload's life. This means people, processes, and technology. It's part of the development life cycle, with day 0 being the design stage and day 1 the development, build, deployment, and configuration stage. With that context, you'll see that day 2 operations don't refer to the second day a workload is operational.

The reason for this "days" concept is to bring the day 2 operations into the design (day 0) stage, essentially shifting left the operations to ensure you design workloads to meet reliability, availability, security, and data management requirements, rather than designing and building a workload and trying to get it to meet those requirements after you've designed and deployed.

Day 2 Cloud Challenges

The challenges of day 2 operations in a cloud environment relates at a high level to consistency, observability, security, and optimization. These high-level areas are interlinked, as shown in Figure 22-1. This section of the book will cover how to handle day 2 challenges in greater detail.

© Jeremy Lloyd 2023
J. Lloyd, *Infrastructure Leader's Guide to Google Cloud*, https://doi.org/10.1007/978-1-4842-8820-7_22

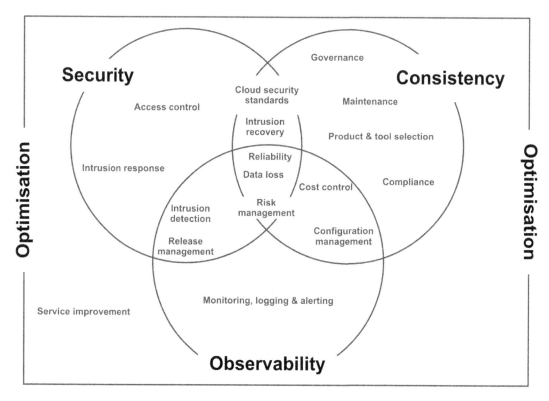

Figure 22-1. *Day 2 challenges*

Optimization is around all of this. Making service improvements to simplify your day 2 challenges requires continual investment, ensuring you have the skills to understand and see the improvements and the time to deliver them. Treat optimization as a cyclical process to tackle the challenges instead of being a separate function.

How can Google Cloud help with day 2 operations?

Google Cloud assists you with your day 2 operations in many ways, from the many products and services you can use to build and run your workloads with clearly defined SLAs, to REST APIs and verbose logging to create automated workflows around everyday operations.

With Google Cloud, you can also put the controls and auditing capabilities in place to make difficult those behaviors you want to change. Of course, this comes with ensuring you make it easy for people to start or keep doing the right behaviors.

Day 2 Antipatterns

Where do people commonly go wrong in day 2 operations? Within day 2 operations, there are antipatterns which you should plan to avoid.

Extend Existing On-Prem Tools for Use Within Your Google Cloud Environment

This common antipattern sees existing on-prem focused tools used for Google Cloud. This ranges from server management and security tools to tools designed for software deployments. While some tools may fit your initial requirements, there is a good chance that your needs will change as you mature and grow your Google Cloud footprint, and tools not built to service cloud/Google Cloud will become a blocker and slow you down.

Manual Changes to Google Cloud Resources

Google Cloud provides an intuitive console upon which you can easily change resources. Doing so in this manner can cause several issues. You introduce human error, and your change might have unintended consequences. The more activities and tasks are done manually within the Google Cloud console by numerous teams, the more the likelihood of something breaking and no one knowing what or why.

If you make manual changes in an environment that you deploy using Infrastructure-as-Code, and with CI/CD in place, you break the integration, which might not become immediately apparent until the next person deploys a change through the correct CI/CD pipeline and overwrites your change unbeknownst to them. If that manual change was a security fix, guess what? You've just reopened the vulnerability.

Incorrect Use of Service Model

There is often more than one product to satisfy your requirement. However, starting with a default to VM-based approach is common because of unfamiliarity with managed service equivalents.

Your Google Cloud champions/CCoE need to ensure they gain familiarity with managed services that you feel will be commonly required, such as databases, GKE, and Functions. Keep aware of those early deployments and understand the use cases. It might offer the ability to steer team members toward managed services, save some operations pain, and rework down the line.

Alerts for Everything

Every Google Cloud product and service can produce logs. It can lead directly to creating too many alerts, which results in alert fatigue and people ignoring them. This is a risky position to be in.

Instead, focus on the key metrics that matter most, the ones that will ultimately affect the workload's performance and impact the users. From the SRE book, these are the four golden signals: latency, traffic, errors, and saturation.

Defaulting to Stability and Making No Improvements

Historically, in operations, the focus was on stability which led to lengthy and complex change control processes. I often see that approach applied to Google Cloud environments. It means day 2 optimizations (improvements) are missed or are slow to be implemented.

Instead, put the ways of working in place to focus on SLI and SLOs. It gives you an error budget upon which you can make improvements on a more regular basis. Google Cloud allows you to easily create non-production environments that replicate your production. It allows you to test those changes in advance and gain confidence that you can make the change in production without issues.

Loss of Alignment to the Business

I've mentioned throughout the book that aligning your cloud strategy with the business's outcomes is key. Putting it down on paper ahead of a lengthy migration can often leave it neglected. Over time how you make decisions often defaults back to the status quo. Continually focus on the business outcomes you are driving. Ensure you report on them to the stakeholders.

Lack of Health Checks

Telemetry data from your workloads is what you use to ensure that it's operating as expected. If you have no health checks reporting status, you find yourself devising means to ascertain the workload's health through a combination of data. Work with developers to ensure they design ways that their services report their health status. For off-the-shelf software, request the vendor to inform you how you report service health.

Summary

Introduce the concept of day 2 operations within your organization. Work closely with development teams to design what day 2 operations will look like. Understand the antipatterns and try to avoid them.

CHAPTER 23

Cloud Foundations and Landing Zones

In this chapter, I will cover what cloud foundations and landing zones are.

What are cloud foundations?

To answer that, let's look at the self-service Google Cloud onboarding process. You sign up for Google Cloud, access the Google Cloud console, and can deploy any Google Cloud product and service available. Each product and service has configuration settings you can make before deploying it. Common items across all products and services will be a name for the resource, region, and zone to deploy into.

However, what if your organization can't have data outside of the EU? And will you allow people to use their personal emails to sign into Google Cloud? You can't prevent those things from happening with no guardrails in place. Instead, you must rely on that no one will do it, even by mistake. And these are just two examples of many important considerations. You can align all of these core considerations to some pillars:

- Organization hierarchy
- Identity and access management
- Networking
- Security tooling
- Logging, monitoring, and audit
- Billing and cost management
- Shared services

The core pillars are what are known as the cloud foundations as shown in Figure 23-1. Within these pillars, you have specific functions such as privileged access management or data leakage prevention.

239

J. Lloyd, *Infrastructure Leader's Guide to Google Cloud*, https://doi.org/10.1007/978-1-4842-8820-7_23

Cloud Foundations

Networking   Shared Services   Billing & Cost
                                             Management

              Organisation Hierarchy

Identity & Access   Logging, Monitoring &   Security Tooling
Management   Audit

Figure 23-1. *The pillars of cloud foundation*

Under each function will be one or more products or services you configure
to ensure they meet your standards. What standards? Well, you need to form an
opinionated view on how you will configure each function and its underlying products
and services.

What are the considerations for cloud foundations in a day 2 operations context?

You can configure cloud foundations in several ways, just like any Google Cloud
product and service.

Firstly let's start with manual configuration through the Google Cloud console,
often referred to as ClickOps. You use the Google Cloud console to configure the
required products and services manually. This approach is quick but does have several
downsides. With this approach, there is no repeatability. If the same configuration
is needed again, you'll have to rely on the original engineer to have made adequate
documentation and perform the same steps again. Auditing the configuration is more
challenging, such as tracking changes that will happen over time.

Within the Google Cloud console, another option involves using a command-line
interface (CLI) known as Cloud Shell and a command-line tool known as gcloud. Gcloud
can be used to configure your cloud foundations by writing the individual command
lines or scripts with your required configuration within them and running those
command lines or scripts within Cloud Shell.

Using gcloud does mean that the configuration is repeatable, but you must store
those command lines and scripts within source control. Else it's highly likely that they
will become outdated. If a Google Cloud console user makes a manual change to a
setting that your script configured, then the script is no longer valid. In fact, reusing that
script could remove that change which might have an impact on your environment.

Another method involves writing your configuration declaratively, commonly referred to as infrastructure-as-code (IaC). Using code, you write the desired state for those Google Cloud products and services. In Google Cloud, you use the declarative configuration language YAML or Hashicorp's Terraform, which is an open source cloud-agnostic language that Google Cloud endorses.

The advantages of this approach are that the code is humanly readable, meaning if a key employee did leave, someone else proficient in YAML or Terraform will be able to understand the configuration. You must store the YAML or Terraform configuration files in source control. They should also be used with products and services to enable continuous integration and continuous deployment (CI/CD), such as Google Cloud's Cloud Build. Provisioning your cloud foundations in this manner will reduce human error and improve the consistency and security of your foundations. You can also use this method to provision Google Cloud products and services that form a workload landing zone, which we will discuss later.

A disadvantage of this method is if your team isn't skilled in IaC, there is a learning curve. Then add in the changes to ways of working when using CI/CD pipelines, and you can find a simple configuration change that you could do via the console in seconds, which can take longer.

However, this is the preferred method for the reasons previously mentioned. YAML and Terraform are common methods, so the skills exist. And hiring someone with experience who can upskill the team would be one way to accelerate the ability to provision through IaC. Another method would be to use a Google Cloud partner who will have deployed cloud foundations for many customers.

The final option would be to use the publicly accessible Google Cloud REST APIs. This method involves using a programming language such as Go, Java, .Net, Node.js, and many others to perform HTTP requests to a resource's unique URI through Google's client libraries. These libraries provide benefits such as better integrations and improved security. The other way to invoke the APIs would be by sending the HTTP requests and parsing the responses. The APIs return data in JSON (JavaScript object notation) format.

This approach provides an automated way to provision but can become overly complex, and the languages used are likely unfamiliar to infrastructure engineers. Again the code should be stored in source control. I wouldn't recommend this method for cloud foundations.

To help you create your cloud foundations through IaC, Google Cloud has published a set of public GitHub repositories known as the Cloud Foundation Toolkit (CFT). Use them to accelerate the development of your cloud foundations. They provide a great reference point when you need an opinionated view on a configuration setting but have nothing to base your decision on. These repositories align with Google Cloud's best practices. The modules are available in YAML and Terraform languages.

Building on the CFT GitHub repository, Google has created secure variants of those foundation modules, known as the Security Foundations Blueprint (SFBP), which focuses on secure Google Cloud adoption. An accompanying whitepaper and web documentation show the thinking and opinionated views that SFBP brings. There is no doubt this is an incredibly useful accelerator. However, if your team is new to Google Cloud and IaC, then it'll take some time for them to understand the code and how to make changes to it in the future. It's when it's helpful to engage a Google Cloud partner to assist you in deploying CFT or SFBP. They can make it work for your organization and provide you with the knowledge and skills as part of a handover.

Any learning and effort is worth it, as research conducted into software delivery performance and published in the book *Accelerate* shows that "Keeping system and application configuration in version control, was more highly correlated with software delivery performance than keeping application code in version control" (Forsgren et al., 2018).

Landing Zones

What are landing zones? This is a common question that I get asked. People are confused about why a landing zone isn't part of foundations or vice versa and where the line of delineation is.

The concept of a landing zone is having an environment ready for production workloads to run in. You must consider what Google Cloud's products and services you'll need and how they should be configured and integrated before your workload can land. It's the workload's landing zone. However, note that it's good practice not to have a 1:1 ratio of workload to the landing zone. Instead, you design a landing zone to enable several workloads to use it. I advise grouping workloads together that consume similar Google Cloud services or operate similarly in the same landing zone.

So a bottom-up view in the order of what you deploy first. You have cloud foundations and the bottom, then you deploy the landing zones built on top of them, and finally, you deploy your workloads built to run on your landing zones as shown in Figure 23-2.

Figure 23-2. *A holistic view of cloud foundations and landing zones and how they correlate*

Going back to the previous landscape gardener analogy, the cloud foundations are the concrete that gets poured before you can lay your paving on. It's the hole for your pond that gets dug before you can put a liner down. The landing zone would be the paving slabs and pots for plants and the soil. And the workload would be your plants and shrubs, with some planted together, some in isolation.

Landing zone examples would be a migration landing zone for Compute Engine virtual machines. Where migrated, servers can securely run in production and have the governance controls in place. Other examples would be a landing zone for an application development environment, a modern data platform, or a container environment. You'll likely have several landing zones catering to those specific use cases. There will be integration points between the landing zones for observability and analytics/business intelligence.

Back to day 2 operations, a key consideration is to delineate configuration code related to your cloud foundations vs. the configuration code for a landing zone. It means you can more easily make changes to a landing zone as/when required without it affecting all your workloads and any other landing zones.

Summary

Cloud Foundations contains the key pillars you'll need to configure before putting workloads in Google Cloud. Landing Zones provide a production-ready location where you can migrate or build a cloud-first workload on top of, such as GKE or Compute Engine.

Understand if you have the in-house skills to use IaC to deploy your foundations and landing zones. Have a plan on how to get those skills if you don't have them, either through hiring or partnering. Use the open source Google Cloud GitHub repositories to accelerate you. Start to think about what landing zones you need based on who has the immediate demand for Google Cloud.

CHAPTER 24

Compute

In this chapter, I will cover the different options for hosting servers, ensuring you know when to use each option to meet your security and compliance requirements while being able to balance the performance vs. the cost of running.

Server Hosting Options

Google Cloud has different hosting options for your servers. I will explain each of these. Be aware that quotas and limits apply to Google Cloud products and services; therefore, you should always check the quotas and limits for the regions you need.

Compute Engine

First launched into preview in Google Cloud in July 2012, Google Compute Engine (GCE) enables you to create new virtual machines that run within a Google Cloud region. GCE provides pre-built images to build Windows or Linux virtual machines. Google or third-party vendors maintain these public images. Some public images come with an additional cost for the licence to use the image. These are premium images from vendors such as SUSE, Red Hat, and Microsoft. You can create custom virtual machine images and upload them for future deployments, more on that shortly.

GCE Machine Configuration allows you to configure the region, zone, CPU/memory, security, disks, network, and management settings. All of this can be defined, in the GUI, by the GCloud command line or via the REST APIs. Regarding the processor/hardware configuration, GCE provides different Machine Families that cater for different use cases as shown in Table 24-1.

© Jeremy Lloyd 2023
J. Lloyd, *Infrastructure Leader's Guide to Google Cloud*, https://doi.org/10.1007/978-1-4842-8820-7_24

Table 24-1. *The GCE Machine Families and suitable use cases*

Machine family	Description	Suitable for
General-purpose	Optimized for cost and flexibility	• Web servers • Mobile games • Small to medium databases • Back-office workloads
Compute-optimized	Highest-performance CPUs	• High-performance web servers • Game servers • Scientific modelling
Memory-optimized	Memory-intensive workloads	• In-memory databases • Large relational databases (SQL server) • Real-time analytics
Accelerator-optimized	High-performance computing and machine learning workloads requiring GPUs	• High-performance computing • Massively parallelized computation • Visualization and computational graph

Within each Machine Family is the Series, which defines the CPU type by generation. Newer processors are second generation and known as N2. And older CPUs, being first generation, are known as N1.

Then finally, the Machine Type defines different CPU to Memory configurations. These are known as predefined machine shapes. You can also provision VMs with GPUs (Graphics Processing Units), suited for graphics-intensive workloads.

GCE also offers Custom Machine Types (CMT), which allows you to select the CPU Series you need and then make a custom configuration of CPU and Memory. GCE still requires a certain ratio of CPU to Memory. However, you can select an option to extend the memory. Doing that can have an effect when it comes to using Committed Use Discounts, more on that shortly.

You can provision GCE VMs as on-demand, preemptible, and spot instances. I will explain each of these.

On-Demand

On-demand is when you provision a GCE instance (predefined or CMT) and receive a bill at the end of the month for the number of hours it was running.

Why should you consider on-demand instances?

Provisioning a predefined or CMT instance in an on-demand method means there is an immediate need for the compute to satisfy a particular requirement. While on-demand VM instances are charged per second, it's an efficient way to access compute immediately. You can terminate the VM instances as soon as you no longer require them, and you won't incur further costs. However, on-demand VM instances are the most expensive way of running VMs on Compute Engine.

If you require a considerable amount of compute in a specific zone with a specific CPU or GPU, you might consider making what is known as a Reservation. Reservations assure you that the capacity is there when you need to burst your workloads. You will pay for the compute you reserve while you have it reserved, but the charges will stop as soon as you delete the reservation. Reservations also qualify for sustained and committed use discounts which I cover in a later section.

Consider an online retailer whose online platform uses a maximum of 300 vCPUs. However, in capacity planning ahead of Black Friday, they expect their traffic spike to be three times greater than any other period. They might create a reservation of another 600 vCPUs in advance of the event, allowing auto-scaling to consume those reservations as needed. After the event, they can delete that reservation.

Preemptible VM Instances

Preemptible VM instances provide a temporary VM that runs on Google Cloud. While still available for use, note there is a successor of preemptible VMs, called Spot VMs, which I will discuss later.

Why should you consider Preemptible instances?

Google Cloud's preemptible VM instances are VMs that cost much less (60-91%) than on-demand VMs but come with a caveat that they might stop (be preempted) at any point. This is because they use excess capacity within a Google Cloud zone/region. They are therefore subject to availability, and if you require a large amount of preemptible compute, you may have to use multiple regions.

Preemptible VMs are suitable for workloads that need to burst to serve the demand promptly and can handle fault tolerance, such as a typical batch processing job. Preemptible VM instances have a maximum life of 24 hours, and because of that, they do not support live migration. Instead, Google will simply terminate them.

Given the burst nature of workloads that use preemptible VM instances, it's very important to check your quotas and limits in advance and submit a request for the limits to be raised as required.

Spot VMs

Similar to preemptible VMs but a newer product by Google Cloud, Spot VM can be preempted (terminated) at an uncertain time. This is because Spot VMs also use the excess Compute Engine capacity. However, Spot VMs do not have a maximum runtime. Another reason to consider Spot VMs is the considerable cost reduction (60-91%) over standard predefined VMs.

Spot VMs do not have an SLA and don't offer the live migration capability I've previously mentioned standard VMs use. They support a shutdown script, so ensure you write one suitable to how your workload needs to handle the termination. The same quota considerations apply, as in check you have sufficient quota available to your Google Cloud projects ahead of time.

Cloud Tensor Processing Units

A differentiator for Google Cloud is its application-specific integrated circuits (ASICs), known in Google Cloud as Tensor Processing Units (TPUs) or Cloud TPUs. TPUs are designed specifically for the demands of machine learning applications.

Why should you consider Cloud TPUs?

Optimized for TPUs machine learning applications, they offer you the ability to train models faster and simultaneously reduce costs. With performance scaling up to 100 petaflops, that's 100 quadrillion floating-point operations per second. Putting that into context, what one petaflop can calculate in one second would take us 31,688,765 years if we performed one calculation every second (University Information Technology Services, 2021). Google's offering 100 times that performance!

Check the TPUs are available in the region you require. Secondly, there are two pricing models. One is for a single device based on the cost for a single TPU. The other is a TPU Pod model, in which you purchase 1- or 3-year commitments to enable you to access multiple TPUs connected together via a dedicated high-speed network.

Google Cloud VMware Engine

Google Cloud VMware Engine (GCVE) is a product that provides you with an on-prem VMware capability but inside a Google Cloud region. A huge advantage of GCVE is that it reduces your need to procure, licence, refresh, and maintain the physical infrastructure required to run VMware. Google will take care of all that for you, leaving you a fully managed software-defined data center.

GCVE enables organizations with on-prem VMware implementations to extend into Google Cloud without re-skilling. You can manage GCVE through vCenter like it's another on-prem location with some resources available.

Why should you consider using GCVE?

GCVE serves several different use cases. Let's briefly look at each.

Data Center Exit

You can migrate on-prem VMware virtual machines to GCVE over HCX. HCX is VMware's latest proprietary technology to enable migration and business continuity across multiple sites and clouds.

Data Center expansion

You might need additional capacity but don't have the time, space, or budget required to build that on-prem.

Disaster Recovery

Your current DR solution for your on-prem VMware environment might not be fit for purpose. And the cost of provisioning a DR environment within another data center might not make it a viable solution.

Virtual Desktop Infrastructure

You might need to extend an existing VMware Horizons or Citrix environment with additional capacity or provide a new virtual desktop infrastructure service.

Application Modernization

Moving existing VMware-hosted workloads to GCVE offers easy integration with other Google Cloud products and services. This can enable you to modernize your current workloads.

What other considerations are there for GCVE?

Each GCVE private cloud must contain a minimum of 3 nodes, while the maximum is 64.

Your on-prem VMware environment will have backups by tools like Veeam, Rubrik, Commvault, and others. GCVE private clouds also integrate with those providers and more. Google Cloud purchased the Actifio backup product in 2020. This product enables you to back up your GCVE private clouds and any Compute Engine instances.

To join your on-prem and your GCVE private cloud networks together, you'll need to have a VPN or a Cloud Interconnect. I'll discuss more of those options later in this section. You'll need to ensure that your VMs have access to DHCP and DNS. Don't rely on DHCP and DNS coming from services running on-prem. Ensure the GCVE private cloud has the capabilities locally on it.

If you currently use vRealize Operations Manager for your on-prem VMware environment, then you'll know the benefits of this tool. You can connect your GCVE private cloud to an externally hosted instance of vRealize.

Sole-Tenant Nodes

By default, Google Cloud's data centers are for multi-tenancy. However, you may have requirements that mean you cannot run workloads on multi-tenant infrastructure. Sole-tenant nodes give you exclusive access to a physical host within the data center. Sole-tenant nodes enable your VMs to run on the same physical host, as shown in Figure 24-1.

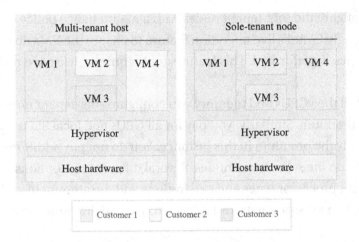

Figure 24-1. *VMs on a multi-tenant host vs. VMs on a sole-tenant node[1]*
Copyright Google Cloud

Why Should You Consider Using Sole-Tenant Nodes?

You might have specific compliance or security requirements that lead you down this route. Or you might temporarily need to move a VM from a multi-tenant node to a sole-tenant node to perform some debugging or performance tests. Google Cloud supports moving from one to the other and back again. You might have Microsoft Windows workloads that must meet specific licence requirements around core counts. Your workloads might have specific performance requirements, such as a high volume of input/output operations per second (IOPS).

Sole-tenant node groups can contain zero or more nodes. For example, you may provision two nodes in a group for a short specific purpose; afterward, you can reduce the number of nodes to zero. Node groups are bound to a particular zone within a Google Cloud region. Node groups also support auto-scaling with two modes, scale-out and scale-in or only scale-out.

VMs that reside on sole-tenant nodes must have a minimum of two vCPUs. Sole-tenant nodes do support overcommitting of VM CPUs, which essentially enables the sharing of spare CPU cycles with other VMs. This can help to reduce the number of cores you may need to licence if you plan to run workloads with per-core BYOL licences.

---

[1]This image was created by Google Cloud, and is used according to the terms described in the Creative Common Attribution 4.0 License. Source: `https://cloud.google.com/compute/docs/nodes/sole-tenant-nodes`.

You can configure the sole-tenant nodes with a maintenance policy to enable the nodes to use Google Cloud's live migration feature to ensure the VMs do not go down while maintenance is performed. This feature does require at least two nodes in the node group.

You pay for all the vCPUs and memory you configure sole-tenant nodes with, plus an additional 10% premium. Similarly, you pay for all GPUs and local SSDs if you add them, but you do not pay the premium in this instance. You do not pay additional charges for the VMs that run on the sole-tenant nodes. Several different size options are available based on different processor types and generations and the amount of vCPU and RAM required on each node. Sustained use and committed use discounts do apply to sole-tenant nodes.

Provisioning Sole-Tenant Nodes

You provision sole-tenant nodes by first creating a sole-tenant node template. This template specifies properties for all the sole-tenant nodes that will reside in a group. You can create the template in the Google Cloud console (during the group creation process) or via the gcloud CLI or directly through the API. Once you have created your template, you create the group using that template. Finally, you can provision your VMs to reside within the sole-tenant node group.

Regional Extensions and Bare Metal Servers

Regional Extensions are essentially colocation data centers that Google Cloud Partners own, in which "Google Cloud provides and manages the core infrastructure, the network, the physical and network security and hardware monitoring capabilities" (Google Cloud, 2021). Bare Metal Servers (BMS) are physical servers that reside within those Regional Extensions, which you can provision to run your workloads.

Why Should You Consider Using Bare Metal Servers?

It's for specialised workloads such as those that require third-party virtualisation software. Or workloads that require direct, low-level access to the server, such as Oracle. The BMS hardware has been certified by Oracle.

With the Regional Extension connected to a Google data center through a Cloud Interconnect, you'll find less than 2ms latency.

There is a list of customer responsibilities for Bare Metal Servers. At a high level, you are responsible for operating system and hypervisor, software, data, licences, security, logging and monitoring, backups, and more. See the Bare Metal Server planning page for a full list.

If you need to use a BMS close to a Google Cloud region that will host your other workloads, then ensure you check for availability. As BMS isn't available in all regions, Google Cloud has data centers.

There is a lead time for a BMS to provision. That time can vary depending on the region, but do plan accordingly and don't expect it to be as quick as provisioning a GCE VM instance. Contact your Google Cloud sales rep to go through the process of having the environment made available to you through the Regional Extension. You must connect a VPC network to the Regional Extension using a VLAN attachment.

Summary

Understand the different compute options Google Cloud has for your workloads. Be aware of quotas and limits that apply to your usage within each region. Understand any limitations to be aware of when selecting one product over another.

CHAPTER 25

Containers and Serverless

In this chapter, I will cover what day 2 operation activities you need to be aware of when your developers are using containers and serverless products and services.

Containers

If your development teams are experimenting with cloud-native architectures, then it's likely that containers will feature somewhere. Developers don't want to manage container environments. And the infrastructure team will typically not have the experience and skills required to manage containers or know and understand the supporting tools and ways of working. Suppose your organization hasn't yet switched to operating in a more DevOps/SRE approach. In that case, there is a good chance that responsibility for managing the containers will fall on the infrastructure team.

This lack of experience is where I commonly see blockers to organizations making real progress with containers. And if your teams suffer from a mindset that shows a reluctance to change and learn, then it can leave the infrastructure team with limited involvement and understanding of your organization's use of containers. Worst case, it can silo them into just looking after the legacy environments. It's a situation that, as an infrastructure leader, you must steer your teams away from.

Ensure your teams view the organization's container adoption as a chance to evolve your team from an infrastructure team to a platform team, where the team not only manages and controls changes to the infrastructure but also controls the release of new versions of application/services into production.

And to address the skills gap, back in Part 3, I discussed the learning paths available for infrastructure engineers. If you urgently need container skills within the team, consider hiring a new team member who can share knowledge among the wider team as they do their job. You might also look to a Google Cloud partner to accelerate you in this space.

© Jeremy Lloyd 2023
J. Lloyd, *Infrastructure Leader's Guide to Google Cloud*, https://doi.org/10.1007/978-1-4842-8820-7_25

So what does your team need to know?

In a day 2 operations context, tasks and activities related to containers revolve around the following areas:

- Container Images life cycle; build and secure; update; deploy, release, and test; terminate and delete; rollbacks.

- Container compliance.

- Container operations, debugging, logging, monitoring, and alerting.

- Container orchestration with GKE.

Ensure the terminology used by the development and infrastructure teams is consistent. Everyone should know what a release means to your organization. They should also understand what CI/CD and continuous delivery mean and know the difference between them.

Google Cloud can support Windows and Linux containers. However, it doesn't mean you should mix your container environments just because Google Cloud can. I find developers select the operating system they have experience with. When this is Windows, you'll find your container environment will become Windows, while following the path of least resistance is a good way to accelerate development early on. In day 2 operations, Windows containers do have some limitations.

Some of these limitations come from Kubernetes itself, and then other limitations are within GKE. For example, Windows containers running in Kubernetes must run Process Isolation and not Hyper-V Isolation. Process Isolation sees a shared kernel among the containers, whereas Hyper-V Isolation sees each container run inside a VM with its own kernel. See the respective pages on the Kubernetes and GKE sites for a full list of Windows limitations.

Challenge the development team leads around the Linux skills within the teams. Advise them on learning paths and available learning material. Inform them of the Windows containers' limitations when using Kubernetes and GKE.

Container Images

Switching to managing and updating images and not logging in and configuring VMs is one of the bigger changes the infrastructure team has to adapt to. Early on, establish what container images your development teams will use. As mentioned earlier, if they want to use Windows, ensure you are familiar with the limitations and the impact these will have on your day 2 operations. Aim to use a minimal number of images with as few libraries as possible. This will reduce your overall attack footprint and keep the container image small for faster cold starts.

For VMs that you've turned into containerized workloads with Migrate to Containers, there will come a time that you'll need to apply updates, patches, or configuration changes. In these instances, you can continue to use the Migrate to Containers generated Dockerfile that Google has designed specifically with day 2 operations in mind.

Designing the Dockerfile to use multistage builds keeps the image size small by leaving behind anything you don't want from the previous stage. As Figure 25-1 shows, it can be used as part of your CI/CD pipeline and ease your day 2 operations for VMs you have migrated to containers.

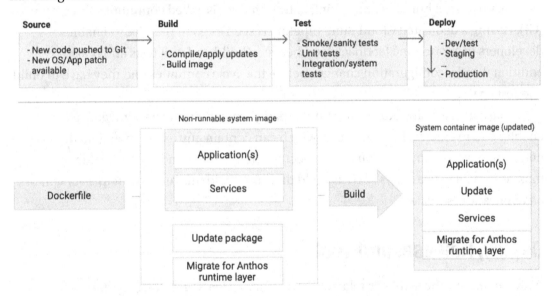

Figure 25-1. *Using the Migrate to Containers generated Dockerfile as part of your ongoing CI/CD pipeline[1]*
Copyright Google Cloud

---

[1]This image was created by Google Cloud, and is used according to the terms described in the Creative Common Attribution 4.0 License. Source: `https://cloud.google.com/migrate/containers/docs/post-migration-image-updates`.

Build and Unit Tests

The guidance in Part 5 on securing your software supply chain is highly relevant to ensuring that only trusted and verified images are built and deployed and that any vulnerabilities are easily detected during the process. This involves creating your container images, which will require you to set up an automated pipeline using Cloud Build.

Treat containers as immutable. In other words, you don't modify them after deployment. Any updates in the form of configuration, patching vulnerabilities, or a newer version of an application/service will require you to create a new container image and perform unit tests against the code and other changes. This task will often happen, so automating your container image creation process is time well spent.

The process of building and testing in this manner is called continuous integration (CI). Having a dedicated Cloud Build pipeline is seen as good practice. It enables developers to shorten the feedback loop between build and unit tests and make additional code/configuration changes before the cycle continues and they have to build and test again.

I'd also advise using labels/tags functionality when building new images. This enables you to create a key/value pair which can contain any useful metadata that will help with day 2 operations. You can inspect the metadata to find the key/value pair making it ideal to use labels such as build date and build image or link it to a version of an application/service.

Deploy, Release, and Test

With containers, the activities related to deploying, releasing, testing (performance, quality assurance, integration), terminating, and deleting are closely related. It's why the term continuous deployment (CD) exists. Continuous deployment and continuous delivery are not the same. In Google's eyes, they define continuous delivery as "the capability of releasing code at any time" (Kubernetes and the Challenges of Continuous Software Delivery | Cloud Architecture Center, 2020). Continuous deployment builds on continuous delivery to allow you to automatically release new versions of your application/service straight to production.

Again you can use Cloud Build for this purpose. Consider having a centralized Cloud Build instance, certainly for deployments into production. It makes it easier to secure access, audit usage, and report changes.

It's where container orchestration tools such as Kubernetes or Google Cloud's product Google Kubernetes Engine (GKE) come into play. GKE can greatly simplify day 2 operations, especially when you compare it with running containers inside VMs. It enables you to use several patterns to deploy, release, and test your containerized workloads.

Using GKE, you can deploy your containers in the following ways:

- Recreate.

- Rolling update.

- Blue/green.

Let's briefly cover each of these. With the recreate pattern, you tear down the existing application/service and recreate it with the new version. This pattern does mean there will be downtime. Understand your service-level objectives and agreements to ensure you don't breach them if you use the recreate pattern.

The rolling update pattern sees the new version deployed on an instance-by-instance basis. So when you deploy an instance with the new version, an instance with the old version is terminated. This process continues until no instances with the old version are left.

The rolling update pattern means there is no downtime, but you must consider how you'll handle running two versions of the application/service for the rollout.

Blue/green means you deploy each required instance twice: a blue version and a green version. Only one version will be serving user requests and therefore live. When you need to deploy a new version, you deploy it to the version that isn't live. Once testing is complete, you make the version available to serve user requests. You repeat the process for the next version.

Blue/green also offers no downtime but essentially duplicates your running costs. It also offers the benefit of instantly rolling back if needed, unlike the previous two patterns.

With the updated containers deployed, you can perform testing in the following ways:

- Canary

- Shadow

- A/B

Canary – which involves filtering a subset of users to a new release, enabling you to observe in production the behaviors of the new release. Once ready, you roll it out to the rest of the users.

Shadow uses real production traffic from the current release and mirrors it against the new release without impact.

A/B – similar to canary, you deploy the new release and make it available to a subset of users. However, that subset of users is targeted based on factors such as their location, browser, or other useful identifiers you can filter traffic on. You use it to test the effects of a change on the users and the market, whether the change is positively or negatively received.

Terminate and Delete

Healthy running containers will be terminated for several reasons, from a new release or draining a node to remove it from the node pool to freeing up node resources when a node hits resource constraints. You also need to work with the development teams to ensure that running services within a container can shutdown gracefully once it receives the termination instruction.

Rollback

Again, this is where Kubernetes simplifies operations for you. It has a built-in rollback mechanism. A Deployment in Kubernetes creates what is known as a ReplicaSet. The ReplicaSet creates the Pods. The ReplicaSet also enables you to define the number of Pods instances you want running in the cluster.

After an update, the previous ReplicaSet still exists but with zero replicas inside it. This means if your new update has broken production, you can now easily roll back to the previous working version. By default, Kubernetes keeps the last ten ReplicaSets.

Container Compliance

As your organization's Google Cloud container estate grows from tens to hundreds or thousands of running services. The challenge of maintaining compliance increases too. I've previously mentioned the industry agnostic security standards you should adopt for your entire Google Cloud operation. NIST, CIS, PCI DSS, and even GDPR publish container-specific security standards upon which you can benchmark. I'll cover tools to assist you with container compliance in the security chapter later.

As the infrastructure leader, understand the security standards your organization will require for containers. And then understand what controls can be put in place to assess compliance.

Container Operations

The need to observe what is happening with your containerized workload is critical. By design, they are highly distributed, and understanding that all services are healthy is key. Again Google Cloud is helping to make this simpler.

Logging, Monitoring, and Alerting

GKE integrates with Google Cloud's Cloud Operations suite (Cloud Logging and Cloud Monitoring), often referred to in documentation as Cloud Operations for GKE. This integration allows you to select system and workload (application) logs and metrics to be collected. This integration also creates a monitoring dashboard called GKE. The dashboard gives you high-level visibility into alerts, container restarts, error logs, and CPU and Memory utilization broken down by clusters, namespaces, and nodes.

Prometheus is an open source monitoring tool that's gained a huge user base for monitoring Kubernetes. Google Cloud has a managed Prometheus, saving you from deploying, scaling, and maintaining the underlying infrastructure typically required to run Prometheus. Collectors can be managed or self-deployed. You can use managed Prometheus to collect data from any data source that standard Prometheus supports. Managed Prometheus gives you scale. It uses the same data store backend that Google uses internally.

Grafana is an open source tool used to compose dashboards. It offers ease of use combined with it being highly flexible. It led to Grafana becoming a popular choice for many developers. It integrates well with Google Cloud and Prometheus.

Health Checks

Yet again, Kubernetes is making your life easier regarding container operations. Kubernetes has three types of health checks: readiness, liveness, and startup. You can use each probe with Command, HTTP, or TCP. Each health check has a setting to define an initial delay in seconds. Tuning this to your services is key to ensuring optimal performance. Readiness probes inform Kubernetes when the pod is ready to serve requests.

The liveness probe continually checks if pods are alive or dead. If dead, it can instruct Kubernetes to restart it. The liveness probe also supports the gRPC health check protocol. It's important to get the initial delay setting right; it'll take some testing to get this balance right. Too short, and Kubernetes will restart the pod before it's had a chance to start, causing a loop.

The startup probe lets you define a startup threshold to cater for a service that takes time to become operational. It's useful for workloads that you've migrated into containers from VMs. Those types of workloads don't start with the typical speed of a cloud-native service. It also means you don't need to lengthen the readiness and liveness probes just to cater for a slow starting service.

Container Orchestration with GKE

As mentioned earlier in the book, GKE presents a new way of working for many. GKE standard mode provides many configuration options that require knowledge and understanding. I have seen many customers simply using the default GKE configuration in production environments. While that might work fine, you'll need to ensure that configuration meets your security and compliance requirements.

CIS publish a GKE-specific benchmark, as well as a general Kubernetes benchmark, both located on their website (`www.cisecurity.org/cis-benchmarks`). I would advise that you review that and use it as your benchmark for a securely configured GKE. If you don't use the CIS GKE benchmark, then the following are some areas you'll need to consider what configuration you decide upon.

Release channels – Kubernetes will release newer versions that contain bug and security fixes or new features. These newer versions are made available to your GKE environments at different cadences. You subscribe to a release channel on a per-cluster basis. The channels are as follows:

- Rapid – new releases available several weeks after the upstream open source general availability

- Regular (default) – is every 2–3 months after the rapid release

- Stable – 2–3 months after the regular release

There is a trade-off between number and frequency of updates and new features you want to make use of or bug/security fixes that you want to implement. Google assesses each rapid release for stability before promoting it to the Regular channel.

There is also an option to select no channel. Doing so means you must deploy the newer versions to the control plane and nodes. You must still comply with Google's supported Kubernetes versions as per their publicly stated policy. You can't simply stay on a static version forever.

If you want to test the latest features without affecting your production clusters, then you can always create a GKE Alpha cluster. As the name suggests, this gives you access to all the current Kubernetes alpha features.

Maintenance and exclusion windows allow you to control when cluster maintenance can and cannot occur. Automatic maintenance tasks in GKE include deploying newer versions of Kubernetes to auto-upgrade enabled clusters and nodes. It also includes configuration changes that cause nodes to recreate or that change the cluster's internal network topology.

Regional clusters have replicas of the control plane, meaning you can still perform operations even when maintenance occurs. For zonal clusters, you can't as there is a single control plane in a single region. Note that Google does reserve the right to override maintenance policies for critical security vulnerabilities. You can disable auto-upgrade, but again you must comply with the supported version as previously mentioned.

GKE private cluster – a private cluster is one that only supports internal IP addresses. It supports outbound connectivity through a NAT gateway such as Cloud NAT. The cluster's control plane does still have an internal and external IP address, but you can disable its external IP. Doing so means the control plane is not accessible externally. So you then need to ensure you can reach it through a Cloud VPN or Cloud Interconnect.

Cluster access control – there are two partially overlapping services when it comes to assigning and controlling access. There is Google Cloud's Identity and Access Management and the native Kubernetes Role-Based Access Control (RBAC).

Kubernetes RBAC provides fine-grained roles that can be scoped down to Kubernetes object level. These roles only exist within the cluster and are assigned on a cluster and namespace level.

Google Cloud's IAM in the context of GKE has predefined GKE-specific roles that you can assign to users or groups. You assign these roles at the Google Cloud project level.

GKE Sandbox – the concept of a sandbox in IT that has existed for many years; an isolated test environment which enables developers to deploy and test code without affecting other environments

The GKE Sandbox is the same concept enabled at a GKE node pool level. The GKE Sandbox uses the open source gVisor product. GKE Sandbox doesn't work currently with Windows Server node pools.

Pod and Node Scaling

To keep your operating costs as low as possible, GKE has two autoscaling concepts: horizontal Pod autoscaling and vertical Pod autoscaling.

Put simply, horizontal Pod autoscaling enables you to define thresholds and, when met, will automatically add more Pods. Vertical Pod autoscaling allows you to define thresholds that will change the Pod size (CPUs and memory).

From the node's side, you have Cluster autoscaler and Node Auto-Provisioning. Cluster autoscaler enables you to define when the numbers of nodes should be increased or decreased based on thresholds.

Use Node Auto-Provisioning in conjunction with Cluster autoscaler, and when enabled, it means that Cluster autoscaler can extend node pools available CPU and memory.

Remember, I previously mentioned that GKE has two modes of operation, standard and autopilot. Autopilot is handling those autoscaling performance calculations for you. And it automatically provides your services with the required compute to be performant and healthy.

Anthos

In Part 5, I introduced you to Anthos, Google Cloud's on-prem and multicloud Kubernetes management product. If you think about Anthos's purpose, it exists to simplify operations. It does this by allowing you to manage, secure, and deploy consistently across heterogeneous environments.

There are, of course, still day 2 operations tasks and activities to cover. They fall into the following areas:

- Cluster management

- GKE maintenance

- Resource and security management

- Storage/networking

- Observability

Cluster Management

Anthos clusters fit into two categories:

- Anthos attached clusters

- Anthos clusters on (cloud provider)

Anthos attached clusters support AWS's Elastic Kubernetes Service (EKS), the Azure Kubernetes Service (AKS), Redhat's OpenShift, and SUSE's Ranchers Kubernetes Engine (RKE). In fact, Anthos attached clusters support any other Kubernetes variants, as long as that variant conforms to the Cloud Native Computing Foundations (CNCF) standards as shown on their website.

Anthos attached clusters can be provisioned through the respective cloud providers console and securely and simply be attached to become managed via Anthos.

Anthos clusters on are either Anthos provisioned Google managed Kubernetes clusters running on AWS or Azure, or they are on-prem using GKE for VMware or run on Google Cloud's Bare Metal solution, but let's pick those two scenarios later.

You can provision Anthos clusters on AWS or Azure through a multicloud API that provides a consistent provisioning experience. Clusters running on AWS or Azure will integrate with cloud-native storage, load balancing, and key management services.

What does cluster management entail?

Creation, deletion, and ongoing management of all your Anthos managed clusters. Anthos has a dashboard view to let you easily see what you are managing. And regardless of where the Anthos managed clusters reside, this dashboard provides you with a single pane of glass view.

To get existing clusters visible and managed by Anthos, you need to use the Connect gateway feature. The gateway also enables you to run commands consistently and securely against Anthos managed clusters regardless of where you host them.

You can group your Anthos managed Kubernetes clusters into fleets. Think of fleets as logical groupings of fleet-aware resources with a lot of service-to-service communication. Not every Anthos component and, therefore, not all Anthos resources are fleet-aware. Refer to the Anthos documentation for the latest on what is.

Access mgmt.

I previously introduced the Anthos Identity Service in Part 5. As part of cluster management, you must ensure people can authenticate and access the required clusters to perform tasks. Consider how you will do this, for example, integrating with OpenID Connect or Lightweight Directory Access Protocol providers.

Maintenance

Anthos and the variants of Kubernetes all have security patching requirements. Google Cloud publishes an Anthos shared responsibility model that clearly defines responsibilities against each hosting scenario, such as on Google Cloud, AWS, Azure, or VMware.

I won't go into each specific responsibility against each hosting scenario. However, at a high level and consistent across each scenario, Google Cloud is taking care of elements such as maintaining and distributing the required software packages, product integrations, container vulnerability scanning, and providing audit logs.

Your responsibility falls into the areas such as maintaining your workloads components such as application code, containers images, and access management. You are also responsible for system administration for the clusters themselves. This covers configuration and upgrades to ensure your Anthos managed clusters run on supported versions.

Resource and Security Management

Anthos Config Management

Your next resource and security challenge is having the means to put governance controls and policies in place. Security standards will need to be defined, such as using the CIS Kubernetes Benchmark I mentioned previously. But with standards defined, how do you put governance controls in place to ensure resources are compliant and that your heterogeneous environments are consistent?

The answer to that question is through Anthos Config Management, which has three independent components to solve those specific challenges. The components are Policy Controller, Config Sync, and Config Controller.

The Policy Controller enables you to create fully customizable policies that specify and enforce your desired configuration against any field of a Kubernetes object. Config Sync's role is to ensure that your defined cluster configuration doesn't drift. It does this by continuously polling those clusters and reconciling any drift.

Finally, the Config Controller provides an API endpoint that enables you to provision and manage 120 other Google Cloud products and services in the same declarative way you manage your Kubernetes clusters.

Together they allow you to define, apply, and audit your desired security policies consistently and continuously across on-prem, Google Cloud, AWS, and Azure Kubernetes clusters. Then have continuous monitoring for configuration drift across those environments and any other supported resources provisioned in this way, as shown in Figure 25-2.

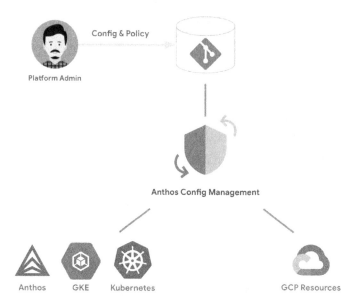

Figure 25-2. *Shows config and policy getting applied to Google Cloud resources and container-based resources with Anthos Config Management*[2]
Copyright Google Cloud

Binary Authorization

Another component that assists with your security posture is binary authorization. I previously discussed this in Part 5. I will discuss its use in relation to those day 2 operation tasks and activities that a platform team would undertake. Please note that binary authorization is only available for GKE, Cloud Run, Anthos clusters on VMware, and Anthos Service Mesh at the time of writing.

Remember I said that the platform team (an evolution of a traditional infrastructure team) is responsible for releases into production. This requires deploying containers. When binary authorization is enabled, the commands are the same. However, you have to reference the image's unique identifier, the image digest, instead of just using tags to identify the image and version.

---

[2]This image was created by Google Cloud, and is used according to the terms described in the Creative Common Attribution 4.0 License. Source: `https://cloud.google.com/anthos-config-management/docs/overview`.

Binary authorization requires policies. A policy contains deployment rules and any exempt images. You apply one policy to each Google Cloud project. It is possible to create a centralized Google Cloud project containing the policy you wish to use on more than one Google Cloud project and its subordinate resources, attestors, and attestations.

An attestation is essentially the process of signing an image using a private key from a key pair. An attestor is a Google Cloud resource that contains the public key. Binary authorization uses it to verify the attestation.

When your organization starts experimenting with containers, I strongly recommend you enable binary authorization. Doing so means you have the best practice ways of working at the start of your container journey. If you haven't done that, it's still not too late.

Binary authorization has a dry-run mode. It enables you to continue deploying all container images, but dry-run mode will log the image's compliance against your policies. Therefore you can monitor for a period of days to weeks. This gives you time to engage those users who are using images that would be blocked and have them put remediation steps in place before you enforce policies that could cause a production issue.

And if binary authorization is blocking an image, you can use breakglass mode, which enables you to deploy a blocked container image. It logs an auditable event at the time of deployment. It's for emergency use only and should not become a standard way of working. Instead, engage the user of blocked images and help them to understand the steps required to ensure they use an image that meets the enforced policies.

As you can see, much of binary authorization's focus is validation at the time of deployment. What if you want to validate running container images against policy changes you've made after deployment? Or what if a container image deployed using breakglass mode needs to be regularly validated against your policies?

Enter a new feature called Continuous Validation (CV), which is pre-GA at the time of writing. So there might be some minor changes or additions before it goes into GA. CV does precisely as the name suggests and performs binary authorization checks of your running containers at least once every 24 hours. Identified policy violations get logged.

Storage/Networking

When it comes to networking with Anthos across heterogeneous environments, things become more complex. And that's because the network integrations enable your workloads to communicate with each other and the outside world.

Load Balancers

There are several load balancing options when using Anthos, depending on where those Anthos managed GKE clusters are running. For Anthos clusters on AWS or Azure, you can simply integrate with the native load balancing offered by each cloud.

For Anthos on-prem, there is a growing list of supported options from F5 BIG-IP and Citrix to open source projects such as MetalLB and Seesaw. Google developed the latter, and it's now open source.

For Anthos on Google Cloud, you have Cloud Load Balancer, which offers Layer 4 and 7. You can also run customer ingress controllers such as Nginx.

There's also the Multi-Cluster Ingress controller, which enables external HTTP(S) load balancing across multi-clusters and multiregional environments. Finally, a new tool, currently in alpha, was designed by the Kubernetes community as an evolution of the Multi-Cluster Ingress controller. It's called the GKE Gateway controller.

It is designed to work in a role-oriented resource model, offering fine-grained access controls while offering flexibility. It enables the user roles of developers and service owners to perform their respective tasks. Meanwhile, ensuring overall control and compliance with policy remains with a role they've identified as a Platform Admin, not the developers or service owners. The Gateway controller will make managing access control for ingress easier. I'd advise the Platform Admin role would sit within the infrastructure/platform team.

An important point to be aware of is all Ingress controller resources will be able to be converted to Gateway controller resources. There are no known issues running both services simultaneously. Google is alluding that over time the Gateway will deliver new functionality that the Ingress can't.

Dataplane V2

Continuing with networking, there's an improved dataplane for GKE and Anthos clusters, now using extended Berkeley Packet Filter (eBPF). This has simplified network policy enforcement and routing. eBPF allows sandboxed programs to run in the OS kernel without requiring changes to the kernel itself. The dataplane V2 uses eBPF in a networking context to decide how to route and process incoming packets using Kubernetes-specific metadata.

Currently, dataplane V2 isn't the default option unless you create a GKE auto-pilot cluster. Although Google has said it will become the default option. I'd advise any GKE clusters you create and do so with the dataplane V2 enabled.

Volumes and Persistent Volumes

It'll be highly likely that your organization's developers will decide how they use storage within your Kubernetes environments. Kubernetes provides two abstractions, Volumes and Persistent Volumes. Volumes do not persist after the Pod ceases to exist, so think of them as temporary storage. Persistent Volumes use Compute Engine persistent disks and will be available to the cluster after a container or Pod ceases to exist.

It's important to understand the storage options used for which containers. Appropriate monitoring will need to be put in place to ensure that storage is available.

Observability

Anthos Service Mesh

As your organization's use of containers grows over time, those microservice-based architectures become increasingly complex and fragmented. The Anthos Service Mesh, based on the open source project Istio, helps you manage and secure service-to-service communications.

It also provides service-level monitoring capabilities across three of the four SRE golden signals: latency, traffic, and errors. It does this through what is known as a sidecar proxy. Essentially the sidecar proxy is a separate container that runs in the same Pod as the workload.

The sidecar proxy approach intercepts all inbound and outbound HTTP traffic to the workload. A huge benefit of this is it saves the developers from writing lines of code to collect telemetry data. There are preconfigured dashboards, ensuring they satisfy your monitoring needs.

In day 2 operations, the sidecar proxy may also require some troubleshooting. This is identifiable when you see pods without sidecars or the sidecar exists but doesn't receive its configuration. The Google Cloud docs site has basic troubleshooting to assist with sidecar injection issues. There is integration with Cloud Logging to help with diagnosing issues.

Serverless

Serverless Google Cloud products and services have specifically been designed to abstract the underlying infrastructure away from you. Therefore, tasks and activities related to managing it in a day 2 context become more about observability than reliability, which in serverless products is largely taken care of by Google.

Your day 2 considerations should focus on understanding which teams use serverless products, ensuring that appropriate security controls are in place and that your infrastructure team understands the integrations between services and what to monitor and how to ensure they get the logs they need to create rules that will generate alerts. The team also needs to know the actions to take when alerts are triggered.

Other day 2 considerations are around the security of your deployment pipelines. The use of serverless products is an enabler in creating microservices services architectures. In a day 2 context, this means frequent releases and deployments to production.

From the infrastructure team's perspective, you need to be closer to the deployment process, whether being informed or undertaking the deployments. It means the team is aware of what has changed and can ensure appropriate monitoring is in place.

Summary

Understand the container life cycle, from image creation, deployment, rollback, and termination. Understand how Google Kubernetes Engine assists with container day 2 operations tasks. Know how to monitor distributed microservice container architectures. Understand how to secure your container environment. Understand the value that Anthos brings and how to use it for container environments across on-prem and other clouds. Know if developers are using serverless products and how you'll monitor them.

CHAPTER 26

Networking

Google Cloud's networking products help you connect, scale, secure, and optimize your networking infrastructure. Note that some of Google Cloud's networking products and services fit into more than one of those categories.

Connect

For connecting to Google Cloud, you have several options. For high-performance requirements, you have Dedicated or Partner Interconnect options. The former provides a direct physical connection between your on-prem and Google Cloud's network backbone. The Partner Interconnect connects your on-prem and Google Cloud through a support third-party service provider.

Then there is Cloud VPN, which is an IPsec VPN connection. It offers a quicker way to connect to your VPCs in Google Cloud. There were two modes offered, HA VPN and Classic VPN. However, Classic VPN, which was just a single connection, has been deprecated. Now the HA (high availability) mode is the default. HA VPN guarantees 99.99% SLA, but note only for the Google side of the connection.

For day 2 operation considerations, ensure you have logging enabled on both sides of either connection option you select. It's advisable to configure the Google Cloud side of the networking through IaC, stored in source control.

Google also has the ability for you to connect your external sites by using Google's network as a wide area network (WAN). You create a hub and spoke model with a Router appliance providing the hub and your sites being spokes. You manage all of this through a product known as the Network Connectivity Center.

© Jeremy Lloyd 2023
J. Lloyd, *Infrastructure Leader's Guide to Google Cloud*, https://doi.org/10.1007/978-1-4842-8820-7_26

Virtual Private Clouds (VPCs)

The VPCs are the destination your on-prem connectivity services route to. It's also where your VMs reside inside and are assigned internal IPv4 addresses. A VPC is a global resource in Google Cloud, and its subnets are regional. This means you can create a single VPC that will span all Google Cloud regions and have regionalized subnets, or subnetworks as Google calls them, where your workloads will run from. It means you don't need to create a VPC for each region. By default, all VMs within the VPC can communicate with each other.

As a VPC is a global resource, you can greatly simplify a global network topology and connectivity complexity. This is a differentiator when compared with AWS and Azure, primarily because AWS and Azure treat VPC as regional resources. So you need a VPC in each region and then connect them using VPC peering so VMs can communicate. Google Cloud also has a VPC peering concept. However, it's only for use cases that require you to have multiple VPCs.

There is a concept of a Shared VPC, enabling you to create a network hub and spoke model. The Shared VPC resides inside a Google Cloud project that has a setting enabled that turns that Google Cloud project into a host project. VMs then reside in what gets referred to as service projects. These VMs can easily connect and use the Shared VPC inside the host project. This decoupled roles and responsibilities. It enables service owners to build and deploy as required and allows a network admin to control policies and maintain compliance.

There are a couple of common patterns of deployment using Shared VPCs. They are as follows:

- Single host project, multiple service projects, single Shared VPC

- Multiple host projects, multiple service projects, multiple Shared VPCs

What your organization requires will depend on several factors, the number of workloads and servers you have, the organization structure (departments, business units, countries, etc.), and your desired cloud operating model (centralized, decentralized, or hybrid operations).

I would advise starting with a host project containing a Shared VPC and a service project containing your VMs. It's a clear delineation and allows you to alter scale as/when required.

And finally, you can also bring your own IP (BYOIP) to VPCs. This is for public IPv4 addresses that you own. It can make migrations easier if your current public IP addresses must be maintained. Google has the ability for you to control when routes are advertised, ensuring a seamless cutover.

Scale

Under scale, you have load balancers, designed to cater for use cases from a handful of users through to global scale web platforms.

Load Balancers

When it comes to load balancers, Google Cloud has several options to understand. All of Google Cloud's load balancers are managed services. They have easy integrations with Compute Engine, GKE, and other products, allowing you to route traffic without complex configuration.

There has been a recent refresh of their external Layer 7 HTTP(S) load balancers, now built on the open source Envoy proxy. The external load balancer has two modes of operation, Global and Regional. The Global load balancer is when you need to route traffic to more than one Google Cloud region. The Regional load balancer is where your traffic routes to a single Google Cloud region. There is also the internal Layer 7 HTTP(S) load balancer, which also uses the Envoy proxy.

Google Cloud has two options for network load balancing TCP/UDP traffic at Layer 4: an External Load Balancer that distributes traffic from the Internet to your VPC and an Internal Load Balancer that only distributes traffic within Google Cloud's network. Both support all the well-known TCP ports such as 25, 110, etc.

Secure

Networking products and services related to security help you to put perimeter controls in place to protect your workloads.

VPC Service Controls

To help you mitigate the risk of data exfiltration, Google Cloud provides you with VPC Service Controls (VPC SC). VPC SCs allow you to create a perimeter around resources and the resource data.

You enable VPC SC at the Google Cloud Organization, Folder, or Project level. VPC SCs enable you to grant context-based access control that builds on top of Cloud Identities identity-based access controls. Done by applying policies that can

- Prevent access from Google Cloud products and services outside of the perimeter.

- Deny access from untrusted locations.

From a day 2 operations perspective, carefully plan what resides inside the perimeter. Then implement it within a non-production environment and perform your tests. These controls are powerful and valuable to mitigate data exfiltration risks. Still, when poorly implemented due to lack of planning and testing, I've seen them be removed or the perimeters expanding to a point where it reduces any risk mitigation.

Cloud Armor

It is a web application firewall (WAF). It protects against common web attacks and Distributed Denial-of-Service (DDoS) attacks. It does this by filtering traffic at Layer 7 and blocking malicious traffic before it reaches your services. In June 2022, Cloud Armor blocked the largest ever DDoS attack. It peaked at 46 million requests per second. The Google Cloud customer subjected to the attack was able to stay online and continue to serve customers.

Optimize

The Optimize network products and services offer you the ability to get the network performance you need and provide you with monitoring capabilities to see connectivity issues.

Network Service Tiers

I've previously mentioned Google's leading innovation in the networking space. When it comes to ingress and egress over the Internet, Google Cloud offers a Premium tier that offers cold potato routing. This minimizes the distance travelled and the number of hops between the end user and Google Cloud. Then they offer a Standard tier that uses hot potato routing, a cheaper option, but the trade-off will be lower network quality. Given just how fast Google's network backbone is, don't be fooled by that statement.

I recommend testing the Standard tier, doing your performance testing, and switching to Premium if required. The premium tier offers other advantages, making it well-suited for workloads spanning multiple regions.

Network Intelligence Center

Anyone who's ever had to manage a network that spans a few or more locations knows that it becomes complex rather quickly, having to monitor connectivity and bandwidth and maintaining configuration state and adherence to security policies.

Add connectivity to and from Google Cloud and between VPCs within Google Cloud and, unfortunately, the same challenges you faced in the on-prem world become true in Google Cloud. However, it's why Google created the Network Intelligence Center.

It aims to help customers get visibility into their connectivity to identify connectivity issues quickly. It also provides real-time performance metrics that you can easily integrate with BigQuery for additional analysis. And it provides firewall and VPC monitoring to help you tighten rules and identify suboptimal and misconfiguration. VPCs will also detect and provide notifications of service and network issues and inform you of the root cause of the failure.

Summary

Define how you will connect with your Google Cloud VPCs. Define your VPC network topology, single or multiple host projects. Single or multiple shared VPCs? Agree on what perimeter security controls you need to implement. Test the network performance as per your requirements. Start using the Network Intelligence Center to give you monitoring and troubleshooting capabilities.

CHAPTER 27

Additional Workload Architectural Considerations

This chapter covers how you implement and provide consistency, observability, reliability, and security for your workloads in day 2 operations.

There are a few factors at play. First and foremost is how much you can control. Are your workloads made up of commercial off-the-shelf (COTS) software, or is the software developed internally? You'll likely have a mixed estate. For internally developed workloads, you can design your day 2 operations on day 0. With COTS, your options can be more limited.

Consistency

Google Cloud provides products and services that help you improve consistency in your day 2 operations. Let's look at them in more detail.

VM Manager

VM Manager is a suite of tools that make day 2 operations for VMs easier. It requires an agent that comes preinstalled on GCE images. And it's made up of configuration, patch, and inventory management tools.

OS Configuration Management allows you to specify software and packages to install or remove from VMs and define their instructions on how to install through software recipes. You control configuration drift through compliance checks every 10 minutes.

© Jeremy Lloyd 2023
J. Lloyd, *Infrastructure Leader's Guide to Google Cloud*, https://doi.org/10.1007/978-1-4842-8820-7_27

OS Patch Management enables you to flexibly schedule patch deployments and report compliance across Windows and Linux VMs. Patch deployment settings include targeting VMs by zone and filtering by names and labels. You can also run pre- and post-patch scripts, useful in cases where you may need to stop and start services gracefully.

OS Inventory Management collects data on VMs such as hostname, OS version and other metadata, as well as the data on Windows updates or installed package information from Linux package managers. The data serves the patch compliance reports and provides insight such as vulnerability scores.

OS Images

As previously mentioned, you can import disks and images to Google Cloud. Existing VM disks must be in VMDK or VHD format. You can also import Amazon Machine Images (AMIs) and existing virtual appliances in OVA or OVF format. Importing disks and images can be useful in BYOL scenarios.

You can create custom images from disks, public images, snapshots, or an existing imported image. Custom images can be useful when you have baseline configuration settings you want all your created VMs to use. You can restrict your user's ability to create and copy images by requiring them to use approved images.

Custom images can be created manually or through automation using tools like Packer. Consider setting up an automation pipeline if you regularly need to create custom images.

Managed Instance Groups (MIGs)

Before I explain what MIGs are, let's first cover the two types of Google Cloud instance groups, unmanaged and managed. Unmanaged allows you to load balance traffic across a group of VMs you individually manage. And managed instance groups are a collection of VMs managed as a single entity.

Why should you consider MIGs?

For use cases that require horizontal scaling, such as increasing the number of VMs running simultaneously, like a web frontend. It makes managing those VMs by reducing the time taken on typical operations functions.

Using MIGs also moves you toward a more automated approach to deploying and managing your workloads. With MIGs, you don't individually update and patch each running VM. Instead, you write startup scripts that pull in the required libraries, binaries, and configuration files. It helps you move toward a way of working that becomes essential if/when you work with containers.

The startup script should explicitly specify versions of libraries and binaries you are including. Failure to do so can result in VMs within the MIG running different versions and causing unexpected issues.

MIGs can work for stateful and stateless workloads. This works by preserving the state of each VM within the MIG using persistent disks and the instance metadata. This can be useful for workloads like ElasticSearch, Kafka, and databases like MySQL or PostgreSQL.

From a monitoring point of view, set up application-based health checks. It will create a log entry whenever a VM's health state changes when enabled. Based on these events, you can implement auto-healing of the instance after the health checks report a failure.

Assured Workloads

Assured workloads enable governments and other heavily regulated industries to use Google Cloud in a secure and compliant manner. Typically those types of organizations are restricted to using physically isolated services such as specific Google Cloud government cloud regions. Google Cloud has removed that need by using software-defined controls to offer the security and isolation required by some compliance standards.

Why Should You Consider Assured Workloads?

If your organization is a governmental body or is in a highly regulated industry and needs to meet strict compliance standards such as FedRAMP Moderate, FedRAMP High, CJIS, IL4, HIPAA, and HiTRUST, then you should consider assured workloads.

Unsurprisingly most considerations around assured workloads relate to security. You'll need to understand how you perform key management, control who can access the Assured Workloads, and migrate your data from its current location into the Assured Workload.

How Do You Provision Assured Workloads?

To provision Assured Workloads, you must fill out a Google form. Note that it can take up to 10 days for your request to be processed. Once approved, Assured Workloads are enabled at the folder level, and you can then create a Google Cloud project under that and begin deploying your workloads.

Live Migration

The physical hosts your virtual machines run on occasionally require maintenance. This is to replace failed hardware and apply security updates, BIOS upgrades, and other regular infrastructure maintenance tasks.

Those of you operating your own data centers will be familiar with the process, usually moving the running VMs to hosts with spare capacity. Then you patch a host and restart it before moving those running VMs back again. All of this is usually without interruption of any workloads. The sheer scale of doing that in the cloud has caused some cloud providers challenges. Typically the cloud providers notify customers of dates/times when their VMs might restart due to the cloud provider patching a host. It can lead to some issues or a requirement for making a workload highly available. In Google Cloud, they've enabled live migration of VMs from host to host. Meaning Google Cloud can patch the underlying hypervisor without interruption to you.

The entire reason Google Cloud has this functionality is to reduce any planning and effort related to you having to move your VMs to cater for physical host maintenance. However, live migration isn't available for every VM running on Google Cloud. Exceptions are as follows:

- Confidential VMs
- VMs with GPUs
- VMs with TPUs
- Preemptible VMs

Bring Your Own License

Bring your own license (BYOL) is when, outside of any agreement with a cloud provider, you purchase licenses that enable you to use a software product. That might be an application, or it might be an operating system. I'll cover BYOL scenarios that fit the cloud use case. If your license is related to hardware appliances, it's likely it won't work in a cloud scenario. Instead, consider replacing that hardware with a Google Cloud product, service, or marketplace product.

Why Should You Consider Bring Your Own License?

Depending on the size of your organization, you might receive a discount on licenses vs. what you'd have to pay if you were to purchase the license through Google Cloud. A good example of this would be SQL server. You can provision a VM with SQL Server running on a Windows Server in the Google Cloud console. In this instance, you will be charged for your SQL and Windows licenses by Google Cloud. Now, if you already had existing SQL server and Windows licenses and met all the license requirements, then you might find you pay less for your licenses. In this instance, you would want to BYOL to save on costs.

Another reason for considering BYOL is when there is no other option. The vendor might not have a version to purchase through the Google Cloud marketplace. And they might not have a SaaS version of their product. Or if they do, the SaaS version might lack functionality vs. the version deployed onto a virtual machine or container.

In some BYOL scenarios, your license is for a specific number of physical cores or processors. In these instances, you'll need to use sole-tenant nodes or Google Cloud VMware Engine (GCVE).

Microsoft made a change to their licensing term on October 1, 2019. This change means you can no longer use any Windows server volume license purchased after that date on a sole-tenant node or Google Cloud VMware Engine. You can use Windows licenses purchased before that date, but ensure you check your Product Terms.

If you are looking to migrate and BYOL for Microsoft applications such as Dynamics CRM, SharePoint Server, or SQL server, then check you have the Microsoft License Mobility benefit, which is part of the Software Assurance benefits in your Microsoft license agreement. If you do, you'll be able to run Microsoft applications on sole-tenant nodes and GCVE.

You should consider creating a custom image for Windows Server, Redhat Enterprise Linux (RHEL), or other operating systems that you might use in a BYOL method. Google fully supports this and provides instructions on how to do so.

How do you check you are in compliance?

Before you move workloads and BYOL, review your license agreements. If it's unclear, speak to your license reseller, who will likely have a specialist you could talk to. The responsibility for being in compliance and reporting to the vendor remains with you. Google Cloud has a tool that, among several other functions, helps you track and analyze usage. It's called the IAP Desktop, and it enables you to manage multiple Remote Desktop and SSH connections to VM instances on Google Cloud.

Observability and Optimization

I've already mentioned that day 2 operations are not just about keeping the lights on. It's also about making optimizations. These optimizations take various forms, from improving availability through using Google Cloud managed services to cost efficiencies.

Monitoring, Logging, and Alerting

How do you define what to log and when you should set alerts to trigger for your workloads? And what Google Cloud products and services should you use to help?

Of course, while your workloads are on-prem, they have monitoring and alerting configured. This may work well, and you see no reason to change. Moving to Google Cloud provides a good chance to revisit your existing monitoring strategy. You can take advantage of Google Cloud products and services designed to make it easier to monitor workloads in a cloud environment.

Moving to a platform where everything is available as-a-service means you can turn on logging with a click of a button, coupled with the fact you'll expand your usage of Google Cloud products and services that complement or improve your workloads, resulting in a large number of Google Cloud resources generating too much log data for your existing monitoring strategy.

Service-Level Indicators

With the monitoring, logging, and alerting, you aim to instantly know if something has changed that could affect the health of your workload and, in turn, impact your end users. To do that, you need to have the metrics defined, which indicate that your workload is healthy and performing as required. These are the service-level indicators (SLI) from Google's SRE approach.

Define SLIs for services that make up your workload. A service could, for example, be a load balancer, web front-end VM or container, a storage bucket, or a database. Typically an SLI is either based on metrics that provide availability or latency data.

An example of an availability SLI would be as follows:

- The ratio of successful responses vs. all responses

An example of a latency SLI would be as follows:

- The ratio of calls below a threshold vs. all calls

When defining your SLIs, focus on your end-user journeys. Have those journeys documented. Avoid the common issue of creating too many SLIs. Look for ways to target the services that are critical for the user journeys.

Google Cloud's Cloud Operations Suite contains Cloud Monitoring, which allows you to capture metrics for Google Cloud's products and services out of the box and create custom SLIs. You find all available metrics within the Cloud Monitoring pages of Google Cloud's website.

Service-Level Objectives

With SLIs defined for your services. You now need to define Service-Level Objectives (SLOs). In Google's SRE definitions, SLOs represent the statement of desired performance. Setting your service availability goals at 100% isn't realistic and would become cost-prohibitive. Set the SLO as low as possible while meeting your end user's expectations.

For every service you define an SLI, you need to define an SLO. An SLO consists of the SLI of the service, the desired performance goal, and a time period. For example, the service must be available 99.5% over a rolling 30-day period.

Experiment with your SLOs; they will need perfecting. If you often fail to meet the SLO, then perhaps reduce it to what is realistic and then focus additional effort on stabilizing your workload.

Once SLOs are defined, you can work out your error budget, which is vital within SRE. The error budget is the difference between your SLO and 100% uptime availability. For example, if our SLO is 99.5%, our 30-day error budget is 3 hours 36 minutes.

Within SRE, the aim is to use that error budget to ensure new releases can be performed and upgrades or maintenance to infrastructure. It helps set the mindset that you shouldn't just leave your workload in a state whereby it's running but never improves. Maintaining COTS means you aren't in control of when new software versions are available. However, you are in control of when you update your production environments.

Service-Level Agreements

With SLIs and SLOs defined, you can create your Service-Level Agreement (SLA). This is your commitment to your end users, often written into contracts that detail specifics such as each party's responsibilities, performance, times, locations, and any penalties for failing to meet them. You should set the SLA to allow you to maneuver against your SLO.

Based on my previous example of a 99.5% SLO, the SLA should be 99%. This gives you some additional and hopefully not required error budget before the end user can demand their penalties.

Cloud Monitoring in Google Cloud provides out-of-the-box integrations and metrics. There are other third-party tools that you may also want to consider. Products such as Datadog, Prometheus, Grafana, and InfluxDB can help you monitor and alert your workloads.

Active Assist

The Active Assist is a suite of tools that provide specific recommendations on how you can optimize your cloud operations. The recommendation value pillars include cost, security, performance, reliability, manageability, and sustainability.

Active Assist is continually analyzing your entire Google Cloud environment. The tools also provide you with the ability to apply the recommendations easily, as well as guidance on the impact of applying the recommendations, for example, reducing costs by a specific amount or improving your security posture.

Sustained Use Discounts

What are Sustained Use Discounts?

Sustained Use Discounts (SUDs) are a discount that gets automatically applied when you run certain GCE Machine Families. The discounts for vCPUs and memory use across each region and apply separately for each machine type.

The discounts are applied monthly and depend on different usage levels. There are four usage levels, broken down as the percentage of the month the VM is running for. The levels are as follows:

- 0–25%

- 25–50%

- 50–75%

- 75–100%

To get the total discount, you'd need to run or create a VM on the first day of the month and have it on for 100% of that month. You will get no discount if you run a VM for only 0-25% of a month. Figure 27-1 shows the percentage of time the VM is in use vs. the SUD you will receive.

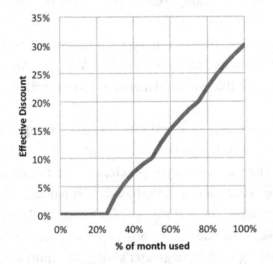

Figure 27-1. *The percentage of the discount applied against the time a VM runs over the month[1] Copyright Google Cloud*

N1 instances receive discounts of up to 30%, as shown above, and N2 and N2D instances receive discounts of up to 20%. SUDs do not apply for E2 and A2 machine types. They also don't apply to VMs created using App Engine flexible environments and dataflow.

---

[1]https://cloud.google.com/compute/docs/sustained-use-discounts

SUDs are automatically applied for applicable instances and appear on your bill at the end of a monthly billing cycle. You'll be able to identify them as they are separate line items within the statement.

Committed Use Discounts

A Committed Use Discount (CUD) is when you purchase a certain amount of CPU and Memory for either 1- or 3-year term, in return for discounts of up to 70%.

Why should you consider Committed Use Discounts?

CUDs are an excellent way to reduce costs for workloads with predictable or stable usage patterns. Google does not require upfront payment for this option. Instead, your CUD fee is split into monthly payments across the 1- or 3-year term. The CUDs are applied automatically to VMs used by GCE, Google Kubernetes Engine, and Dataproc and are visible on your monthly Google Cloud bill. CUDs are bound to a specific Google Cloud region.

CUDs are not available on all Machine Types, notably the small shared-core machines, preemptible VMs, and extended memory VMs. The latter is one reason you might decide not to use the extended memory option available in Custom Machine Types.

You will be charged for the CUD regardless of usage. If you agreed to purchase 1 year of 100 CPUs and 400GB Memory, but you are only using 90 CPUs and 360GB Memory, then you will still be charged for the amount you purchased, not the amount you are using.

You also cannot cancel CUDs once purchased. This typically leads organizations to purchase less than they need. The fear of over-purchasing leads to under-purchasing. This means that the risk of wasting money often costs organizations money when additional CUDs could be giving them greater savings. A report within the Google Cloud console shows how your CUD purchases align with CPU and Memory usage.

Large organizations that purchase CUDs on an ad hoc basis end up with two issues. One is having to manage multiple anniversary dates. This is something to be aware of, but the Billing section within the Google Cloud console does provide you with the ability to see all the CUDs and lists their term, start and end dates. CUDs do not renew, so ensure you put a process in place to monitor anniversaries.

The other issue is managing CUDs on a per-project basis. I've worked with several organizations with over 1500 Google Cloud projects, and this creates a management issue with CUDs, as you cannot centrally see what project does or doesn't have them in use. This results in some projects having CUDs but nearly enough.

There is a way to reduce the per-project CUD management overhead and reduce risk with under-purchasing or over-purchasing. It's to use a feature called commitment sharing. This gives you the ability to share CUDs across projects. The one caveat is the projects must share the same Billing Account. For example, if I have two Google Cloud projects, each using 125 CPUs, I can purchase a single CUD for 225 CPUs, and both projects will automatically use the available CUDs. The additional CPUs I use, 25 in this instance, will be billed at the on-demand pricing. CUD sharing across projects is useful no matter your organization's size.

The Active Assist discussed earlier will provide CUD recommendations for your environment. These recommendations are specific to your usage.

Reliability

Reliability can be defined as "The probability that [a system] will perform a required function without failure under stated conditions for a stated period of time" (Google - Site Reliability Engineering).

Therefore, availability objectives that I've previously discussed are one element that must be in place. In day 2 operations, you must understand the workload's recoverability from failures. That links directly with components and service's high availability. Let's look at those two characteristics in more detail.

Recoverability

While your workloads reside on-prem, you will back them up via several potential options, from legacy tape backups to online cloud backups. A common misconception is that once a VM runs in Google Cloud, you don't need to back it up. This is incorrect. Once you migrate those production workloads, you need to enable them for backups.

However, before you do that, migrating a workload to Google Cloud can be a great time to revisit each workload's disaster recovery plan. When it comes to recovery, Google's SRE approach to recovery is "The factors supporting successful recovery should drive your backup decisions, not the other way around" (*Google - Site Reliability Engineering*).

The principle that is trying to drive is a mindset that you shouldn't simply pick a Google Cloud or third-party product. Then standardize on your retention and frequency period and expect that it will solve all your backups and recovery requirements. Instead, understand the recovery scenarios for each workload that would lead you to need a backup to recover from.

You should create recovery plans for each workload that consider the following:

- What Recovery Time Objective (RTO) and Recovery Point Objective (RPO) are required to meet any defined SLOs for the workload

- The amount of time required to perform a recovery operation and detail any data points that can correlate how the time to recover (TTR) increases as the workload grows in size

- How and when you validate the integrity and completeness of the backups

- Any dependencies required to perform the recovery

- Prescriptive steps required to perform the recovery operation

- Post-recovery success validation and which team is required to confirm that

- Any post-recovery cleanup operations

With your workload's recovery scenarios and recovery plan defined, you must select what product(s) will perform your backups to meet the workload's recovery requirements. There are multiple Google Cloud products and services to consider.

For Compute Engine, you have

- **Machine Images** – a crash-consistent backup at the VM instance level. Machine images contain the configuration, metadata, permissions, and data. Machine images support multiple disks with data stored as differentials.

- **Persistent disk snapshots** – differential backups with support for single disk backups. You can share these global resources across projects.

- **Instance templates** – rather than a backup, use instance templates to create identically configured VMs to use within a Managed Instance Group. However, be aware of them during your recovery scenario.

- **Backup and DR** – Built on top of the Actifio GO product, which was an industry-leading backup and recovery product acquired by Google Cloud. Backup and DR has an agent and agentless modes. It'll backup Compute Engine and VMware Engine instances without requiring an agent. It's compatible with Nearline, Coldline, and Archive Cloud Storage. The agent provides additional capabilities such as being aware of databases (MS SQL, MongoDB, SAP HANA, and others) and file systems (NTFS, CIFS, NFS, XFS, and others). The agent mode also tracks block-level changes and is application aware for workloads such as SAP.

- **Google Marketplace third-party backup products** – in the same vein as Actifio GO, there are a host of other products created by third-party vendors, such as Rubrik, HYCU, Commvault, and many others.

High Availability

I previously mentioned defining availability service-level objectives. What your SLOs are for each workload will depend on what high availability (HA) options are required to meet them.

In a day 2 context, understanding when an SLI is not met and being able to guide and even resolve that through the configuration of current Google Cloud products and services to be made HA are key functions of the role.

You should also conduct tests to ensure the HA is working as desired. Design these tests to flush out antipatterns that will cause a breach of your SLOs. A good example would be a CloudSQL instance deployed to a single zone. A simple test would be to stop the instance literally.

Financial Operations

With the cloud's as-a-service-based model, you pay for what you use. The days of capital expenditure (CapEx) for new hardware every 5 to 7 years don't apply in the cloud. Cloud consumption is an operating expenditure (OpEx). The concept of financial operations is "the practice of bringing financial accountability to the variable spend model of the cloud, enabling distributed teams to make business trade-offs between speed, cost, and quality" (FinOps Foundation).

Who should be responsible for it?

The change from CAPEX to OpEx is a shift that can leave your finance team in the dark. Ensure you educate them on this fundamental change and what it will mean to the IT budget. The predictable spending patterns they've come to enjoy from IT won't be there anymore. If your organization has peak trading periods, start by explaining to the finance team how you'd expect your Google Cloud resource consumption to increase. And therefore, your end-of-month bill will too. I've seen finance teams put blockers on cloud migrations when costs increase rapidly, and the finance team has no context on why that happened and when or if the costs will plateau or reduce.

I recommend that FinOps be part of the cloud office during Google Cloud adoption and migration. And while every user of Google Cloud is responsible for being cost-efficient, the accountability should sit with the cloud office during adoption and migration. This enables them to monitor for the right behaviors and put controls in place where required. So remember, engage finance early, do not leave them in the dark, and get them trained. The FinOps Foundation has a mix of online self-paced and in-person training for technical and finance roles.

I previously mentioned that one of the guiding principles in the cloud strategy is making cost a forethought during design stages, not an afterthought. This does require cultural change. The teams using Google Cloud are responsible for the consumption, so ensure your principles drive the behaviors you want to see.

How to track when rising Google Cloud costs are a problem?

Spikes in Google Cloud costs are okay if that spike is related to increased use and revenue. To correlate the two data points, you must identify a business metric that you can use to correlate one dollar in Google Cloud spend to dollars created in revenue generation. Spotify correlates its Google Cloud spend to a cost per average daily user. This allows them to plot the trends and give the product teams optimization objectives. This helps to ensure that as Google Cloud costs increase, the cost per average daily user remains the same or decreases through optimization work (Backstage.io, 2020).

Apply that thinking on a workload by workload basis, and the business owner of the workload should be the one monitoring and reporting on this metric. As the infrastructure leader, you will need to help the business owner identify what business metric to use. And you can monitor the metric. It will likely take some effort to identify the metric and how to then report on it. So be prepared to adjust if it's not quite right.

In my experience, some workloads are easier than others to identify a metric. For example, it can be difficult on back-office workloads such as HR or holiday booking apps, but this type of workload should be fairly static and not have spikes in usage. Batch processing and high-performance compute (HPC) workloads can often lag between the Google Cloud cost and revenue generation. Take rendering a movie, for example. You will incur the Google Cloud cost, but it might be months to years before the release and revenue generated. However, you should capture that data to help better predict Google Cloud costs for the next movie.

Once you have the metric and how you can monitor it, consider creating a Google Cloud Data Studio dashboard for the business owners and train them on how to use it. Understanding the correlation between Google Cloud cost and business revenue for each workload will be worth understanding. Have your cloud stakeholder aware of the dashboard and ensure they understand it too.

If your organization is developing workloads that run on Google Cloud, then consider implementing the practice of a cost-saving sprint. Perform it quarterly to start with, and then move to a longer cadence. I've seen firsthand the incredible results of having a team focus solely on their operational efficiency for a sprint.

Prioritizing Cost Optimization Effort

A final method to help you orient teams in their cost optimizations is to show them visually the effort vs. the potential savings. Google Cloud estimates effort vs. cost savings as shown in Figure 27-2.

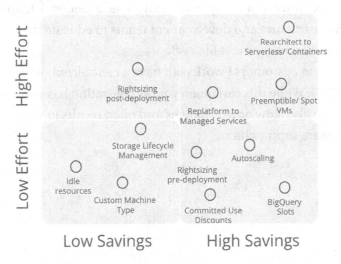

Figure 27-2. *The potential cost savings against the effort*

Security

The primary objective for implementing security controls across your infrastructure or the end-to-end software delivery life cycle is to prevent data loss and unauthorized access to your workloads.

Part 5 mentioned the concept of securing the software supply chain and that Google Cloud provides numerous products and services aligned to help you achieve that. These are primarily day 1 tools aimed at cloud-native architectures and containers.

So how do you approach day 2 security, also known as security operations, and ensure you have the proper security control for architectures that aren't cloud-native?

At the start of this book, I discussed Google's extensive background and approach to trust and security. Their continued investment in innovation and acquisitions in this space means there are numerous products and services to take advantage of in your day 2 operations.

During your early planning for Google Cloud adoption, I've already mentioned that if you have a Chief Information Security Officer (CISO) or security team, then engage them in conversation sooner than later. As I've previously mentioned, the cloud requires new ways of working, including the security function. As an infrastructure leader, you should objectively look at your organization's security culture. Behavioral changes will be required and may have to be led by the infrastructure team. Start with security reviews, set a regular cadence with the security team, and create a feedback loop of improvement. Work with your infrastructure and development teams to educate them that they must consider security at all development life cycle stages.

Typically, on-prem customers I work with have a centralized security function that looks like Figure 27-3. While this can mean your organization has consistent controls and standards, it can also slow down changes and often results in security being down at the end of the software supply chain.

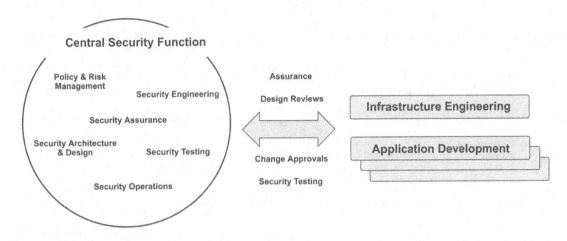

Figure 27-3. *A centralized security function*

Using Google Cloud allows you to shift left on security. If you decentralize your security functions to coexist within infrastructure and development teams, as shown in Figure 27-4, you can ensure that security is part of day 0 and day 1 activities and increases the team's ability to get to production faster.

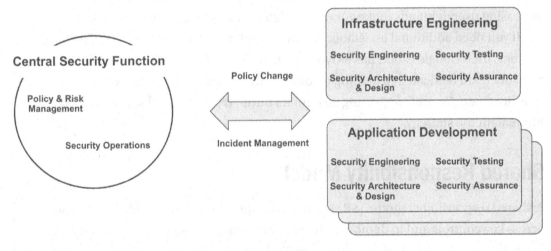

Figure 27-4. *A decentralized security function*

Depending on the size of your organization and the complexity of the workloads you are developing, there is also a hybrid approach. In the hybrid approach, a centralized security function still exists, but you also have a dedicated security resource within the infrastructure and development teams, as shown in Figure 27-5. Teams working on a workload that requires the agility of the decentralized model are empowered to assume more security functions to meet their needs.

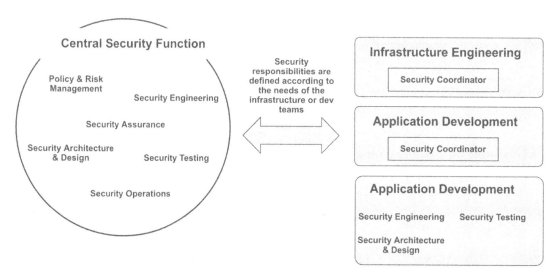

Figure 27-5. *A hybrid security function*

As an infrastructure leader, understand your organization's alignment with one of those approaches. Knowing the workloads your organization develops will help identify what approach you need. Workloads that need frequent releases to meet the ever-increasing user demands make good candidates for a hybrid security function.

If you need additional assistance before formulating your Google Cloud security strategy, then Google Cloud has a Cybersecurity Action Team (GCAT). This is an advisory team dedicated to helping Google Cloud customers with the creation of security strategies and supporting customers through professional services as they implement the strategy.

Shared Responsibility Model

A shared responsibility model (SRM) aims to define who is responsible for security across key controls and to demonstrate how this changes from on-prem through to Software-as-a-Service, as shown in Figure 27-6.

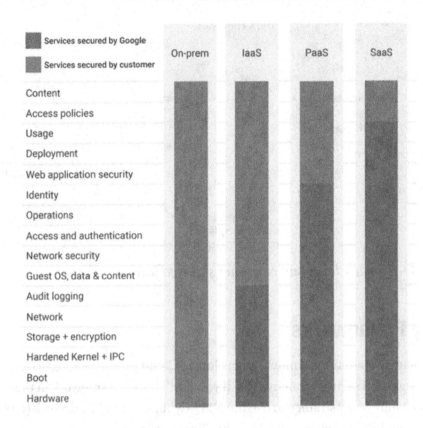

Figure 27-6. *The Google Cloud shared responsibility model[2]*
Copyright Google Cloud, Responsibility chart

The responsibility chart shows a massive shift from how security controls are managed on-prem to what you control once you migrate workloads to Google Cloud. As an infrastructure leader, ensure you work with your security teams to adjust existing security standards to fit the service models you will use in Google Cloud.

However, Google Cloud often uses the term shared fate to describe better how they view the relationship between themselves and their customers. They are not trying to leave gaps within those key controls that require you to solve creatively. Instead, they aim to provide you with the products and services that simplify your ability to secure your workloads, hence the shared fate. As shown in Figure 27-7, Google Cloud sees this as a cyclical process that works for you and Google Cloud.

---

[2]This image was created by Google Cloud, and is used according to the terms described in the Creative Common Attribution 4.0 License. Source: `https://cloud.google.com/docs/security/incident-response`

Figure 27-7. *Google Cloud and customer's shared fate*

Security Frameworks

In a day 2 security operations context, align Google Cloud products and services to fit industry-standard security frameworks. If you don't have a framework in place, I mentioned aligning your strategy to use the NIST Cybersecurity Framework (NIST CSF) earlier in the book. To recap, the NIST CSF has five functions:

- Identify.

- Protect.

- Detect.

- Respond.

- Recover.

For definitions, see Part 2. Many Google Cloud products and services serve one or more of the five NIST CSF functions. See Table 27-1 for alignment.

Table 27-1. *Aligning Google Cloud products and services to the five NIST functions*

Google Cloud product or service	Identify	Protect	Detect	Respond	Recover
Cloud Identity and Access Management	✓	✓	✓	✓	
Google Admin Console	✓	✓		✓	
Cloud Security Command Center	✓	✓	✓	✓	
Cloud Private Catalog	✓	✓			
Cloud Data Catalog	✓	✓			
Cloud IDS	✓				
Cloud Resource Manager	✓	✓			
Identity Platform (customer identity management)	✓	✓	✓	✓	
Policy Intelligence	✓	✓	✓		
Cloud Asset Inventory	✓				
Container Registry Vulnerability Scanner	✓		✓	✓	
Cloud Security Scanner	✓		✓	✓	
Cloud Armor	✓	✓	✓	✓	
Phishing Protection	✓	✓		✓	
Google Workspace Security Center	✓		✓	✓	
Cloud Operations Suite	✓		✓	✓	
VPC Service Controls		✓	✓		
Cloud Identity Aware Proxy		✓			
Cloud VPN		✓			
Context Aware Access		✓			

(continued)

Table 27-1. (*continued*)

Google Cloud product or service	Identify	Protect	Detect	Respond	Recover
Google Encryption at Rest		✓			
Google Encryption in Transit		✓			
Cloud Key Management Service		✓			
Customer Supplied Encryption Keys		✓			
Cloud HSM		✓			
Google Cloud Quotas		✓			
Autoscaling		✓			✓
Cloud Data Loss Prevention		✓			
Access Approval API		✓			
Titan Security Key		✓			
Shielded VMs		✓			
Assured Workloads		✓			
reCAPTCHA Enterprise		✓			
Binary Authorization		✓			
GKE Sandbox		✓			
Cloud Deployment Manager		✓			✓
Google Cloud Storage		✓			
Google Cloud Data Deletion		✓			

(*continued*)

Table 27-1. (*continued*)

Google Cloud product or service	Identify	Protect	Detect	Respond	Recover
Google Workspace Security Assessment		✓			
Incident Response Management		✓	✓	✓	
Google Cloud Disaster Recovery Planning Guide		✓			✓
Global, Regional, Zonal Resources		✓			✓
Google Cloud Load Balancing		✓			✓
Cloud CDN		✓			✓
Cloud VPC			✓		
Traffic Director			✓		
Advanced Phishing and Malware Protection			✓		
Network Telemetry			✓		
Android Enterprise			✓		
Cloud Pub/Sub			✓		
Cloud Functions			✓		
Log Exports				✓	
BigQuery				✓	✓
Contact Center AI					✓
Backup and DR					✓
Google Cloud Status Dashboards					✓

From this table, you can quickly understand how a product or service can align to meet your requirements within the framework. For example, it's easy to see how Cloud Identity and Access Management, Cloud Security Command Center, and Cloud Armor and Identity Platform (if you require business-to-consumer identity management) are essential in a day 2 operations context.

Shielded VMs

Shielded VMs provide additional protection through security features that guard your workload against threats such as malicious insiders in your organization, kernel- or boot-level malware or rootkits, and malicious guest firmware such as processor vulnerabilities like Meltdown and Spectre that became public knowledge in 2018.

Shielded VMs use specific security measures to do that. Shielded VMs use secure and measured boot, virtual trusted platform module (vTPM), UEFI firmware, and integrity monitoring.

Why should you consider using shielded VMs?

In the case where a workload requires additional checks to validate the underlying VM's integrity, Google Cloud provides shielded VMs. Use cases are when the workload might be subject to compliance or regulatory standards, the criticality of the workload, the sensitivity and classification of data, or all three.

If you need to create a custom shielded image for your workload, you must ensure you meet specific disk and certificate requirements. Disks require two partitions, one for the EFI System Partition (ESP), which should be 100MB and the other for the OS partition, which can be any size you require.

Four certificates are needed to enable secure boot. For full details of the certificates and how to generate them, see the creating shielded images pages on the Google Cloud documentation site.

You can use Cloud Monitoring to monitor the integrity and Cloud Logging to review the details of any events.

Shielded VMs can be deployed with one click and also enabled on existing VMs, providing that the VMs' image supports the additional security features that most modern operating system images do.

Shielded GKE Nodes are built on top of Shielded VMs. They improve your security posture by providing enhanced cryptographic verification to ensure the integrity of your nodes. And they also check that Kubelet is issued a certificate for the node upon which it's running. This prevents attackers from being able to impersonate a node in the cluster by gaining access to bootstrapping credentials.

The CIS GKE benchmark recommends Shielded GKE nodes. There is no additional cost to run Shielded GKE nodes.

Confidential Computing

Confidential computing encrypts data processed in memory without a significant performance impact. A dedicated key gets generated on a per-VM basis during the VM creation process. The keys are generated by AMD's Platform Security Processor (PSP) and reside solely within the processor. Google doesn't have access to the encryption keys. Google Cloud views confidential computing as adding a "third pillar" to its end-to-end encryption story. The other two pillars are encryption of data in transit and at rest.

Why should you consider using confidential computing?

For workloads that make use of a lot of memory, are compute-intensive, require high throughput, and need to encrypt data in memory, Google Cloud has confidential computing, built around the N2D instance types, which use AMD's second generation Epyc processors. Confidential computing is for organizations that must adhere to increased compliance and regulatory standards to protect data privacy and sovereignty. Privacy-enhancing computation has made Gartner's list of technology trends for 2021. Confidential computing allows organizations to meet those standards for their most intensive workloads.

Confidential computing doesn't support Google Cloud's live migration capability. When the underlying physical infrastructure needs maintenance, the confidential VMs must stop and receive a restart instruction. You will get a 60-second advance notice, which isn't a lot. You'll only find out about the advance notice if you query a maintenance-event metadata key. The value of this key changes 60 seconds before the maintenance event.

Confidential computing can be enabled with one click during the VM's deployment process through the Google Cloud console, or you can use the gcloud CLI or the REST APIs. Terraform also supports the creation of confidential VMs.

Confidential GKE Nodes

Building on top of confidential VMs, you can have confidential GKE nodes, enabled at either a cluster level or node level. Confidential GKE nodes leverage Shielded GKE nodes. They provide you with the ability to encrypt data in-use. Combined with encryption at rest and in motion, it enables you to have end-to-end encryption of your data. You can mix confidential node pools and nonconfidential node pools.

Automating Security Operations

Security orchestration, automation, and response (SOAR) tools allow you to collect inputs from various sources and then perform analysis and respond to security events with or without human intervention. Gartner's definition is "SOAR tools allow an organization to define incident analysis and response procedures in a digital workflow format" (Gartner).

A SOAR tool will collect data from sources such as a vulnerability management tool or a Cloud Security Posture Management tool (more on this later), as well as many other sources. The quantity and quality of integrations into other security tools separate a leading tool from the rest. Ultimately you need to integrate a SOAR with your existing security tooling and new tools and data sources. Without it, you cannot use the data to create automation or manual response procedures.

Google Cloud has acquired Siemplify, a leader within the SOAR market. It's an exciting addition for Google Cloud customers. As an infrastructure leader, ensure your security teams know the tool and how it fits with their security operations processes.

Information Security and Data Classification

An information security policy is a set of standards to describe how your organization keeps data and your workloads/systems safe from unauthorized access. In the Trust and Security section in Part 1, I detailed Google's layered defense-in-depth approach to infrastructure security, with Google taking care of the data centers:

- Hardware infrastructure

- Service deployment

- Storage services

- Identity

- Internet communication

- Operational and device security

This moves your information security focus onto having the appropriate controls in place to secure your workloads/systems and data in Google Cloud. Instead of implementing security controls for a Google Cloud data center, to better orient your focus, use existing guidance provided by ISO 27001 and NIST. Both frameworks focus on three principles or objectives, confidentiality, integrity, and availability (CIA) of your workloads/systems and data, in what is known as the CIA triangle, shown in Figure 27-8.

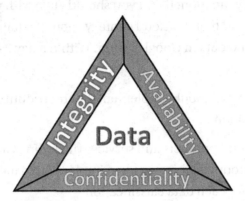

Figure 27-8. *The CIA triangle[3]*
Copyright National Institute of Standards and Technology (NIST)

NIST defines CIA as

"***Confidentiality*** *– preserving authorized restrictions on information access and disclosure, including means for protecting personal privacy and proprietary information*"

"***Integrity*** *— guarding against improper information modification or destruction and ensuring information non-repudiation and authenticity*"

"***Availability*** *– ensuring timely and reliable access to and use of information*"

(Executive Summary — NIST SP 1800-25 Documentation)

Let's go into a little more detail around how you can support the CIA of your workloads and data in a day 2 context.

Availability

Availability in day 2 operations, as I previously mentioned, is measured with service-level objectives (SLOs). Your workloads must be available for the data they hold to be accessible to your users.

---

[3]This image was created by the National Institute of Standards and Technology (NIST), and is used according to the terms described in the copyright notice https://www.nist.gov/oism/copyrights Source: https://www.nccoe.nist.gov/publication/1800-25/VolA/index.html

Confidentiality

For confidentiality, you need the appropriate controls to protect the data based on its sensitivity. I previously mentioned that you should align with your existing data classification standards and that the cloud strategy should detail how you will control and protect workloads and data in Google Cloud. Within a day 2 context, considerations include the following:

- How and when you should implement different controls based on the data's classification

- The Google Cloud products and services (including Google Cloud Marketplace products) that you must implement to meet the requirements for each data classification

Consider a simple table structure that shows the classification and definition and provides guidance on the Google Cloud products and services you should consider in order to protect the data. See Table 27-2 as an example.

Table 27-2. *Guidance on how data classification can be linked to Google Cloud products and service*

Data classification	Definition	Google Cloud products and services
Confidential	Contains data protected from disclosure by law such as personally identifiable information (PII); data that can impact the organization's reputation, safety, finances, or individual	Cloud Identity and Access Mgmt. Cloud Identity Aware Proxy Google Encryption at Rest Google Encryption in Transit Cloud Data Loss Prevention API Cloud Data Catalog Cloud Key Management Service Cloud HSM Cloud Operations Suite Cloud Security Command Center Cloud Armor VPC Service Controls Resource Labels Shielded VMs Assured Workloads

As you can see, there are many different Google Cloud products and services that can be put in place to mitigate the risk of data loss.

Other data confidentiality day 2 considerations include the following:

- Consistently applying labels

- Ability to assess data for correct classification

- Data retention and deletion periods

- Data sovereignty (Google Cloud regions)

Integrity

You should consider how a workload ensures the integrity of the data within it during the design stage. Doing so enables you to put data validation pipelines and checks in place, which can be auditable. That said, in day 2 operations, you can put controls in place to assist with data integrity.

There are proactive measures that you can put in place, such as restricting access to data and the ability to change the access permissions, both of which can help to reduce human errors.

If data integrity has been affected, you need to identify that as early as possible, the ripple effect will make a recovery harder otherwise. So what controls can you put in place to assist with early identification?

Enable the Google Cloud Audit logs. There are four different types which I described earlier. Ensure you enable any workload-specific logs. And parse them into a log aggregator to make it easier to view and alert based on events.

If the data's integrity has been affected, then recovery will be required. What Google Cloud products and services or third-party marketplace products you use for that depends on your workload.

For example, if the workload runs on Compute Engine, then you have the Backup and DR product, Cloud Snapshots, and other VM backup-as-a-service providers available via the marketplace. For Cloud SQL, you have automated backups and the ability to create on-demand backups. For containers running in GKE, you have Backup for GKE, which captures configuration and volume data.

The key consideration is understanding what Google Cloud products and services your workloads use. And that backup and recovery controls need to be implemented to meet the availability SLOs. Have well-defined and rehearsed recovery plans, along with automated tests to enable you to run them frequently to validate their completeness and measure the time taken to recover.

Patterns and Feedback Loops

As the infrastructure leaders, you are in a position to identify common patterns from both a best practice and an antipattern perspective. This could be as simple as a pattern to provide external access to a web-facing service or a pattern for granting users access to a Google Cloud project.

No matter what it is, you and your teams should be on the lookout for it. In doing so, you can automate the pattern by using infrastructure-as-code (IaC) and tooling. This helps to reduce the chance of human error and improves deployment velocity and provide the security teams with the ability to audit the pattern and provide their input during day 0 and day 1. This creates a continuous feedback loop of improvements.

The same approach should apply to the identification of antipatterns. These are patterns that lead to negative consequences or are ineffective. Identifying and remediation of antipatterns should therefore be a priority.

An example of an antipattern during Google Cloud adoption and migration would be moving workloads without having a well-defined, consistent approach to data classification and controlling data access. Another I often see is creating landing zones without security involvement in the design and development stages. Again look to identify these antipatterns that can be less obvious and ensure there is a feedback loop to remediate them.

Governance, Risk, and Compliance (GRC)

When discussing GRC, it's usually advisable to define it as often people have a different understanding of what GRC is. "Governance, risk and compliance (GRC) refers to a strategy for managing an organization's overall governance, enterprise risk management and compliance with regulations" (Lindros, 2017). With that in mind, let's consider the practical measures and controls you can implement. Let's start with risk first.

Risk management in Google Cloud

I will assume that your organization maintains a risk catalog or register. It's a place where organizational risks and IT risks are detailed. I will focus on IT risks, but given how reliant organizations are on IT, an IT risk is a risk to the organization these days.

Migrating your workloads to Google Cloud may address some IT risks. However, there will still be risks that you must manage. Adoption and migration to Google Cloud can also create new risks to manage. Start with assessing current risks and adjusting the controls to mitigate, retain, avoid, or share them. Understanding the shared responsibility/shared fate model allows you to reassess your existing risks more easily. Google Cloud may own some of those risks. And you'll find their compliance listed on the compliance reports manager public website.

How to Reassess Existing Risks

Ask these questions about each of your current risks:

- Has moving to Google Cloud increased or decreased the risk probability?

- Has moving to Google Cloud increased or decreased the impact?

- Do the controls to mitigate this risk need to change?

- Is there a cloud-native approach to control the risk?

- Can automated checks be put in place to verify this risk?

Perform a risk assessment to capture new risks resulting from migrating workloads to Google Cloud. And look at the probability and impact of that risk on a per workload basis. If you don't have a risk assessment framework or have one that is outdated, then consider using a framework such as the Cloud Security Alliance's (CSA) guidance around cloud threat modeling. In their approach, you define the threat, vulnerability, asset, and control.

Google Cloud provides additional data points upon which to observe a control. Previously in an on-prem environment, this capability likely didn't exist, resulting in centralized ownership and configuration of a control. Google refers to designing controls where you can leverage data in this manner as "confidence through control observability" (Google Cybersecurity Action Team). It unlocks the ability for the control owner to allow the wider teams to implement the control, and now a control owner can focus on observing the data to ensure the correct usage.

For example, you might put a technical control within some Infrastructure-as-Code that provisions a virtual private network (VPC). The control might specify a set of deny rules for inbound traffic that shrinks your attack vector. The admin activity audit logs capture API calls and other changes against resources or metadata. In this instance, you can monitor the logs to ensure that the new VPC deploys using the correct IaC and, as an additional check, the firewall rules apply.

Using data in this manner allows you to empower the wider teams to be self-sufficient. That increases the velocity you can adopt and migrate to Google Cloud.

Shift Left on Compliance

As I previously mentioned in the book, shifting left on security requires you to focus on security during the design phase. Shifting left on compliance is the same concept. Successfully shifting left is partly down to altering the team structure. You must empower a team with the ability to manage some aspects of GRC and by showing them what good looks like.

Shifting left on compliance is also down to creating feedback loops to ensure you capture remediations. And measures are put in place during the design and development stages to prevent future occurrences. And finally, it's down to implementing the appropriate automation and tooling, such as a Cloud Security Posture Management (CSPM) solution to simplify the process.

To be in or out of compliance, you need boundaries that help you measure where you are. These boundaries typically come from a benchmark or standard you adhere to. Typically these would be industry standards and regulations such as CIS Benchmarks, PCI DSS, NIST 800-53, ISO 27001, etc.

A CSPM tool helps to simplify the compliance process. CSPM is a new term coined by Gartner, who defines it accordingly "CSPM offerings continuously manage cloud risk through the prevention, detection, response, and prediction of where excessive cloud infrastructure risk resides based on common frameworks, regulatory requirements and enterprise policies" (Gartner, 2019).

Within Google Cloud, the Cloud Security Command Center Premium provides this capability, as do a host of other third-party vendors such as AquaSec and Palo Alto's Prisma Cloud. As the infrastructure leader, work with your security team. Understand how they plan to ensure that your workloads and data are secured and that compliance is maintained.

Moving Toward Continuous Compliance

To shift compliance left, you need to put controls in place to monitor your environments and automatically report noncompliant configurations. These are detection controls, such as the Cloud Security Command Center. You then need to remediate these misconfigurations. Again the Cloud Security Command Center can assist with that. Finally, you need to put preventative measures and controls in place that mean that misconfiguration won't happen again. A common preventative control would be only deploying infrastructure changes using Infrastructure-as-Code. This gives what Google Cloud knows as continuous compliance, forming a cyclical process as shown in Figure 27-9.

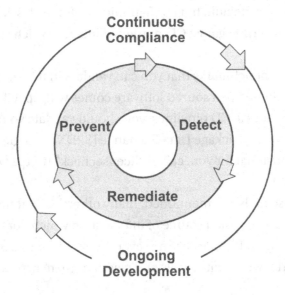

Figure 27-9. *The continuous compliance process*

An excellent example of implementing continuous compliance for Terraform-based IaC is using three open source tools. The first is tfsec by AquaSec. The second Terraform Validator is soon to be replaced by the third tool Terraform Vet. They are both by Google

Cloud. You can use all three to detect misconfiguration. They perform fast static code analysis against hundreds of rules. You can integrate them into a CI pipeline, which means you can know potential security risks before they get to production. This allows you to remediate the Terraform and put preventative measures in place.

AquaSec provides another useful open source tool called Kube-bench, which will scan your GKE clusters for compliance with the CIS Kubernetes benchmark, which the GKE CIS benchmark is a child of. Note that this is independent of the CIS team, so it aims to align to the CIS Kubernetes benchmark closely. Also, for GKE, Google handles certain elements of the control plane hardening, such as the master nodes, as per the shared responsibility model. So Kube-bench will mark those as a "fail" as it will be unable to inspect them. However, Kube-bench is still useful to assess your worker nodes' compliance with the CIS Kubernetes benchmark.

If you are using other CIS benchmarks, another tool to assist with continuous compliance is another Google open source tool. It's called localtoast, and it performs a local or remote scan of VMs or containers to verify their compliance with CIS benchmarks without being resource-intensive. Google uses this in their environments. An example would be if you use the CIS hardened images from the Google Cloud Marketplace. Hardened by default, but configuration drift is a classic day 2 operations challenge. Localtoast can run against CIS hardened images, which would highlight the drift.

And it's not just CIS benchmarks that you can validate in this manner. Think about license management. Some open source software comes with specific license terms and conditions. As part of your CI/CD pipelines, you should validate your usage against a source such as the Software Package Data Exchange (SPDX). Google has created an open source tool that does just that for you, called "licensecheck" (`https://github.com/google/licensecheck`).

In addition to those tools I've mentioned, many others are out there, so many, in fact, that it's useful to use a trusted source of information which does some due diligence on what is worth looking at. It can be a time saver. One such source is the Technology Radar by Thoughtworks, which rates tools and classifies them across Hold, Assess, Trial, and Adopt.

By combining tools like those I've just mentioned or others with similar capability with your CI pipeline, you can unlock the ability to deliver compliance as code.

Governance

IT governance is a set of rules and policies implemented through a standard framework like COBIT. COBIT is created by the ISACA and aims to provide practitioners with a framework that covers the end-to-end business and IT functional areas of responsibility. IT governance covers risk management, value delivery, performance measurement, and strategic alignment. It's the overlay that takes in the holistic view from across the IT estate.

Governance in a cloud context is much the same, except for the challenges of successfully implementing cloud governance increase. This is due to tens to hundreds or more people within your organization being empowered to make changes frequently and often.

What is the role of governance in the cloud?

"Cloud governance ensures that asset deployment, system integration, data security, and other aspects of cloud computing are properly planned, considered, and managed" (Imperva).

Practically speaking, what does this mean?

It essentially means overseeing all the moving parts I've covered in this book. Such as the following:

- Managing the identified risks of your workloads and data running on Google Cloud

- Having checks in place to validate the controls you've implemented to ensure the confidentiality, integrity, and availability of your data

- Understanding compliance standards your organization must adhere to and aligning your Google Cloud environment to new cloud-specific standards

- Ensuring you adhered to those compliance standards

- Measuring the value delivered by operating on Google Cloud and the performance gains

- Identifying metrics and collecting the data that helps you align with your organization's goals and objectives

Summary

Understand what options are available to help bring consistency to your day 2 operations. Work with business and technical application owners to define SLIs, SLOs, and SLAs. Define the scenarios that could lead to a workload needing to be recovered. Create a recovery plan that fits those scenarios and ensure you conduct regular tests. Identify the metrics to measure cloud costs against the business value. Put in place the practice of running cost optimization sprints once a quarter.

Change how security is perceived, and drive a culture that designs secure solutions by default. Shift-left on security by altering the team structure of where the security functions reside. Understand your responsibilities in Google Cloud vs. Google Clouds. Use an industry-known and publicly documented security framework. Discuss your data's confidentiality, integrity, and availability (CIA), and align Google Cloud products and services to mitigate risks. Identify patterns and automate to improve security posture and deployment velocity and reduce human error. Reassess your current and cloud risks and define the controls to mitigate them. Implement the practice of continuous compliance, and put the tools and controls in place to support it. Put in place a cloud governance framework.

CHAPTER 28

Other Key Day 2 Products and Services

In this chapter, I will cover some additional Google Cloud products and services that are useful to be aware of. Using them and guiding developers to use them will help improve your day 2 operations.

Google Cloud Marketplace

The Google Cloud Marketplace is an ever-growing repository of packaged software. You can simply click to deploy and pay for your software licenses (where applicable) through your Google Cloud monthly bill. This can save you from having to deploy a Google Cloud product or service, then install your software, and then purchase a license to use that software from the vendor or a reseller. At the time of writing, the Cloud Marketplace has over 5300 public applications for Google Cloud users to consume.

The marketplace isn't limited to virtual machines. You'll find container images, SaaS apps, industry-specific healthcare and financial services software, and over 200 datasets ready to be queried with BigQuery.

While adopting Google Cloud, I advise organizations to look at their existing third-party tools and products, firstly to rationalize if all of these products and tools are required once they are in Google Cloud but, secondly, to see if that vendor already has a Cloud Marketplace version available that can make it easier to procure, deploy, and manage.

In a day 2 operations context, you want to encourage teams to use the right tool for the job. And there is a good chance that the tool they need is on the Cloud Marketplace. Consistency through standardizing the tools used within your Google Cloud environment is also an important element of day 2 operations.

© Jeremy Lloyd 2023
J. Lloyd, *Infrastructure Leader's Guide to Google Cloud*, https://doi.org/10.1007/978-1-4842-8820-7_28

There is a delicate balance you'll need to strike. I often advise my customers that during the adoption/migration phase, let the teams use the tools they need. Then once into a more standard operation mode, reevaluate the tool's usage. Do you now have several application monitoring tools? Several security monitoring tools? Define your tooling requirements, and take in feedback from those teams actively using tools. Select a single tool for the job and remove the others. The sooner this is done for migrated workloads, the better. The longer the tools exist, the more people become familiar with them and their operating methods. Before long, processes get built to leverage the tool, and it becomes a project in itself to extract its use.

You can put governance in place to control who can make purchases from the marketplace. Based on the guidance I've just mentioned, I would avoid going down this route if possible. Use the marketplace's Request Procurement feature if you need to implement some governance. This feature allows Google Cloud users to request software from the Cloud Marketplace. And users with a Google Cloud billing account administrator role will be notified of the request and can approve it.

I previously mentioned how many useful open source tools are available to make your life easier. I also said that you should use a source that assesses open source tools for their usefulness, such as ThoughtWorks Technology Radar. I also recommend that once you have identified an open source tool of interest, you check if it's available from Cloud Marketplace.

Many software packages on the Cloud Marketplace don't charge an additional fee for their use. You only pay for the cost of running Google Cloud resources. However, some software does have an additional fee. You can quickly identify if this is the case, as the terms and conditions page will inform you. Your organization's Cloud Marketplace costs are line items within your Google Cloud monthly bill, which means you get a single statement for Google Cloud and Cloud Marketplace software costs.

This can greatly simplify the time and effort involved in the software procurement process, especially in organizations that require internal approval of a third-party vendor before you can use their software. Google has strict compliance requirements that all vendors offering software on the Cloud Marketplace must meet. You should work with procurement to ensure purchasing software from the marketplace also works with their processes.

Another helpful feature within the Cloud Marketplace is for software vendors who charge an additional fee. They can make available a discounted/custom offer specifically for your organization. Typically, this works well for large organizations with buying power or existing relationships with those vendors.

Private Catalog

In day 2 operations, automating common tasks and activities is an ongoing function, as is maintaining compliance with any organizational or regulatory standards. The challenge is getting your Google Cloud users to locate and use any solution patterns or software.

This is where Google Cloud's Private Catalog comes in. Private Catalog enables a central location for your Google Cloud users to find solutions designed to meet the organization's compliance standards and software from the Cloud Marketplace that has been preapproved for use.

So what exactly is a solution?

Private catalog supports four types of solutions at the time of writing:

- Link-based solution

- Terraform configuration

- Deployment Manager solution

- Cloud Marketplace solution

A link-based solution is just that. It's an entry in the private catalog that takes the user to a specific URL when clicked. It can provide the viewer with information on a service they offer that you can't deploy automatically. It might need you to sign up or complete an action outside of Google Cloud first.

The Terraform configuration solution enables you to publish any Terraform configuration you write. This could be simple code used to provision a VM in a specification compliant with specific standards. Or it could be code that deploys an entire environment with VPC, security controls, VMs, and more.

A Deployment Manager solution is an automated deployment using Google Cloud Deployment Manager.

A Cloud Marketplace solution is where you make available solutions currently on the Cloud Marketplace. This could be a preapproved list from vendors where you have existing agreements in place.

You can control solutions and software visibility at the organization, folder, and project levels.

Cloud Build

Throughout the book, a common theme is the creation of your Google Cloud infrastructure through Infrastructure-as-Code and storing it in source control. How you then deploy that code is where Continuous Integration (CI) and Continuous Deployment (CD) tools come in.

There are third-party tools like Jenkins, CircleCI, ArgoCD, and many others. From Google Cloud, we have Cloud Build, their serverless CI/CD tool. Cloud Build enables you to build and deploy images. The image contains your application binary, runtime stack, and base configuration. Images are either GCE images or docker images. Cloud Build also supports Hashicorp's Terraform declarative configuration language.

Cloud Build integrates with third-party source control providers such as GitHub, GitLab, and Bitbucket. These integrations enable you to build based on push and pull requests automatically. Add to this that Google's Identity and Access Management service allows you to federate with any identity provider that supports OpenID Connect, which both GitHub and GitLab support. This means keyless authentication, which reduces the burden of secret management for service account keys.

Cloud Build pipelines that the infrastructure teams look after will be related to your Google Cloud infrastructure, more specifically your cloud foundations and any landing zones. In a day 2 operations context, the common issue faced is someone makes a manual change through the GUI. And when the resource is part of a Cloud Build pipeline, it's now out of sync.

You can use the tools I mentioned to create a continuous compliance approach (tfsec, Terraform Validator, Terraform Vet). However, someone will always find a way to make a manual change. In these instances, use Terraform's capability to perform a refresh-only command to understand the drift. Then you can manually reconcile your state file.

Other day 2 Cloud Build issues related to failed builds, for reasons like a coding error or builds that make unsolicited/ undesired changes. In these instances, you can create triggers in Cloud Build, which mean approval is required before a build will start.

API Management

A common reference for modern software development principles is *Beyond the 12 Factors*, a book by Kevin Hoffman that lays out 15 factors. It's an evolution of the original

Twelve-Factor app by Heroku that I previously mentioned. However, one of these 15 factors missing in the original 12 is to be "API first." And it's fairly commonplace that when I speak to developers, they use that principle. However, it is uncommon to have proper Application Programming Interface (API) management in place.

API management exists to help organizations make available standardized services for internal or external consumption through an API. It provides visibility of those APIs by allowing you to select what APIs you expose and provide guidelines on how to consume them and even monetize them.

An API management platform allows you to put governance around this process. And it provides you with analytics on the metrics such as consumption trends, response times, who is consuming the API and from which countries, and generated revenue.

Google Cloud's answer to this is called Apigee. It comes in two flavors. A hosted SaaS version is called Apigee X and Apigee hybrid. The Apigee X runs in Google Cloud, and Google manages the underlying infrastructure. Apigee Hybrid enables you to deploy the runtime plane on-prem or in another cloud. On the other hand, the management plane runs in Google Cloud and is managed by Google.

From a day 2 perspective, educating your developers to use API management will improve the security, compatibility, and measurability of your organization's APIs. It will reduce the toil related to assisting the consumers of those accessible services. For example, developers can change the underlying services without affecting how people consume the API.

Being "API first" also helps with the decoupling of your services. This makes it easier to create microservices that you can update without taking the entire workload down.

Cloud IDS

An intrusion detection system (IDS) monitors your network and applications for malicious activity. The Cloud IDS in Google Cloud provides that functionality as a managed service, meaning no complex architecture decisions or high availability concerns. It's built using Palo Alto Network's industry-leading threat detection capabilities.

Cloud IDS is fast and simple to be deployed into your environment. It then detects exploits such as buffer overflows, remote code execution, command-and-control attacks, lateral movement, and more. Cloud IDS's alerts can be surfaced in Cloud Logging, Chronicle, and other third-party SIEM and SOAR solutions.

Managed Databases: Cloud SQL

At some point during your adoption and migration, you will have databases running on Google Cloud. So from a day 2 operational perspective, what will you need to do? Google Cloud has a fully managed relational database service for MySQL, PostgreSQL, and SQL Server, known as Cloud SQL.

Consistency

As with other Google Cloud managed services, Google is taking care of the reliability of the underlying infrastructure. This means your focus switches to maintenance, high availability, backup, and DR. Let's cover each.

Maintenance

As a managed service, Google needs to ensure it's running efficiently and kept secure with the latest updates. Mostly, these tasks happen in the background without any impact on you. However, certain updates can require brief service interruption. Google refers to these as maintenance.

Updates that can occur in a maintenance window are new features, database minor version upgrades and OS patches. You can set your desired maintenance windows and the order you'd like your instances to update. Updates can be self-served if you know a new feature is needed sooner or a fix to a bug you suffer from is in the latest version.

High Availability

For high availability of your Cloud SQL, the option is quite simple. You need to configure your instances to be regional instances. It gives you a synchronous replica of your primary instance within another zone in the same region.

Cloud SQL supports read replicas, cross-region read replicas, and external read replicas. Each solution offers you a replica of your primary instance. Read replica gives you that second instance in the same region as your primary. Cross-region read replica means your second instance will be in a different region to the primary. An external read replica means it's not part of Cloud SQL. So a good example would be a MySQL instance running inside a Compute Engine VM.

Read replicas can offset some analytics and reporting requirements your organization might have. Performing these against the read replica reduces the load on your primary instance.

Backup and Recovery

Cloud SQL has an automated incremental backup function. It also gives you the ability to create on-demand backups. By default, only seven backups are kept. You can configure this setting to a maximum of 365 backups. Transaction logs retention also defaults to seven. However, seven is the maximum setting.

Point-in-time recovery (PITR) is recovering an instance to a specific point in time. The process uses backups and transaction logs to perform a recovery operation. I'd advise you to recover to a new Cloud SQL instance as the operation overwrites all data on the target instance.

Observability and Optimization

Logging, monitoring, and performance tuning in Cloud SQL is a four-step cyclical process as shown in Figure 28-1. This process also includes optimization in the form of DB tuning.

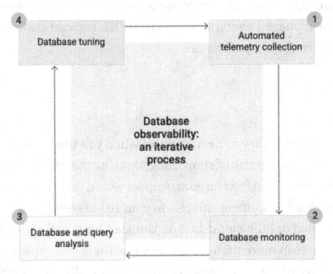

Figure 28-1. *Four-step database observability process[1]*
Copyright Google Cloud

---

[1]This image was created by Google Cloud, and is used according to the terms described in the Creative Common Attribution 4.0 License. Source: https://cloud.google.com/sql/docs/mysql/observability.

Step 1, automated telemetry collection, is simple as all Google Cloud products and services generate logs. It's as easy to ensure logging is enabled, and Cloud logging will collect the logs. Cloud Trace is also used to collect latency and query data.

Step 2 is where Cloud Monitoring comes in, a product that enables you to create dashboards based on your logs. The Cloud SQL overview page also provides key indicators for a quick review.

Step 3 is where Query Insights comes in. It gives you the ability to view, examine, and identify problematic queries. It also helps you trace the source of the problem.

Finally, step 4 is database tuning, which is optimizing the database based on your findings. Cloud SQL provides some recommendations for disk space and idle and over-provisioned instances.

Security

Access control in Cloud SQL is on two levels, instance-level and database-level. You must restrict instance-level access to the connection source (Compute Engine, Cloud Run, etc.).

Organization policies exist to secure your Cloud SQL further, such as preventing public IPs on Cloud SQL instances, restricting access to authorized networks only, and requiring customer-managed encryption keys (CMEK). You can also use Cloud SQL inside the VPC service control perimeters.

Support

A common question I get is do you need support when you use Google Cloud? It comes down to how big is the risk of something breaking that you cannot quickly fix with your internal teams? And how large an impact would that have in terms of brand reputation and revenue? Document this risk in your risk register. And when additional workloads are migrated or built cloud-first on Google Cloud, you should continually reassess the risk. I've seen more than a few times that there is a tipping point where the risk outweighs the cost of having a support contract. Typically, this is when a business-critical workload run in Google Cloud.

Google is aware of this and has recently given its support offering a shake-up with new pricing mechanisms. Google now offers four types of support: basic, standard, enhanced, and premium.

Rather than detailing and comparing each support offering against each other, I will guide you on the suitable use cases for each support offering. In doing that, I will cover the high-level features that differentiate each offering.

Basic support is essentially just billing support. If you have an issue with any element of the billing process, then you can log a ticket directly with Google.

Standard support is the first actual support offering to enable you to log technical support cases. You can log unlimited cases, and Google will respond within a 4-hour SLA. This service is available during local business hours only (8 a.m. to 5 p.m.). Cases can only be logged through the Google Cloud console with subsequent communication through email.

This support offering is helpful for organizations that host nothing in production or who's production workloads are noncritical. It's also for organizations planning to trial Google Cloud over a longer period and would like to ensure they can overcome any technical blockers. With the primary communication method being via email, it can take longer to progress toward a resolution.

Enhanced support also provides unlimited cases but with the ability to log P1 incidents with a 1-hour SLA. Enhanced support is available 24/7 for high and critical-impact issues.

Enhanced is the first support you should consider considering if you have critical workloads running in Google Cloud.

Premium support builds on the previous offerings, with P1 incidents receiving a 15 minutes' response SLA. Premium support also provides a named technical account manager (TAM) for 8 hours per week. The TAM will get to know your environment and guide and advise you on areas such as Google Cloud best practices and identify patterns in your organization's support cases that can highlight knowledge gaps or other blockers. You'll receive support for specific third-party products such as NetApp and Databricks. And there is an event management service to help prepare your architecture for peak trading events or help you run a disaster recovery test.

Premium support does cost considerably more than the previous offerings. As mentioned earlier, organizations should consider the cost of support against the risk of something breaking that they cannot quickly fix.

Google Cloud Partner Support – certain Google Cloud managed service provider (MSP) partners will offer support. Some of these will allow escalation to Google's own Premium support offering. This assures you that for incidents the partner can't fix, they can escalate to Google Premium for assistance.

What type of service is on offer will vary on a partner by partner basis, so ensure you know what you need and then ask plenty of questions of the Google Cloud partner. With partners, there is more chance you'll get to know the team supporting you. This allows them to build up additional knowledge of your environment.

Summary

Use the Google Cloud Marketplace for software purchases. Make patterns and preapproved software available to your Google Cloud users through the private catalog. Make use of Cloud Build or a third-party CI/CD tool, especially for provisioning your Infrastructure-as-Code. Guide developers on why API management is essential and how it can improve the security and consistency of your APIs. Understand what you are responsible for when using managed databases. And be aware there are still day 2 considerations to cover. Understand when you need a support contract in place, either direct with Google or via a Google Cloud partner.

PART VII

Productivity and Collaboration

In Part 7, I'll cover Google Cloud's supporting technologies that enable end users to access their workloads more easily and to be more productive using purposefully designed collaboration tools.

CHAPTER 29

BeyondCorp

This chapter focuses on Google's approach to the zero-trust networking concept.

For over three decades, organizations have needed to provide a way of remotely reaching internal resources hosted inside the data center. Back in the late 1990s, this led to the creation of the Point-to-Point Tunneling Protocol (PPTP). Then, the virtual private network (VPN) was created. VPNs started to gain popularity in the early 2000s. Organizations had begun implementing this type of infrastructure to connect offices to offices and offices to data centers. The technology also enabled end users to connect directly through the VPN to data centers. This meant IT could perform duties remotely, and end users could access internal resources without needing to be in the office.

Fast forward to 2009, the number of connected users wanting or needing remote access to resources to perform their jobs remotely hugely increased, unfortunately, so had the threats waiting to intercept the communication. And those threats had become more sophisticated than ever, from phishing attacks to infecting your computer and making it part of a botnet to Trojans that quietly and sometimes patiently wait to gain access to your credentials or backdoors into systems to steal your data. The VPN's limitations became more evident. Every device connected over VPN to your network essentially extended your network perimeter and offered a neat way around your primary defense systems, external-facing firewalls.

With Google's continued growth, it needed to empower its global workforce to access internal resources securely. It was in 2009 that Google released BeyondCorp as their implementation of the zero-trust network access (ZTNA) concept. In the zero-trust concept, you default to trust nothing and remove the weakness of VPNs' default trust of the device. Instead, you use a combination of access policies to verify that the user, the device, and the state meet the requirements to access internal resources.

And over the last 12 years, BeyondCorp has gone from a Google-only internal access method to a series of products available to us all. First made available in 2017 and known as BeyondCorp, then in 2020, it became BeyondCorp Remote Access with further improvements, and now it's known as BeyondCorp Enterprise.

© Jeremy Lloyd 2023
J. Lloyd, *Infrastructure Leader's Guide to Google Cloud*, https://doi.org/10.1007/978-1-4842-8820-7_29

BeyondCorp Enterprise is a suite of products with a per user per month license fee. There is a free set of baseline functionality available to Google Cloud users. This provides some security controls for users logging in and using the Google Cloud console. For the remainder of this chapter, I will focus on the paid-for version, BeyondCorp Enterprise.

What Is BeyondCorp Enterprise?

BeyondCorp Enterprise provides a way for you to grant your staff, contractors, and partners remote access to your internal resources and data in a controlled and secure manner. It doesn't matter where you host those resources. They can be on Google Cloud, another cloud provider, or Software-as-a-Service (SaaS) or hosted in your own data center.

As mentioned earlier, BeyondCorp Enterprise uses the zero-trust concept of trust nothing. Even when a device gets granted access, there is still little to no trust between that device and another user's device, meaning an attacker can't travel laterally through your estate looking for vulnerabilities and credentials.

The entry point into this solution is via the world's most popular web browser, Chrome. With 2.5 billion + users and counting, Chrome already has extensions to enable you to control the deployment and management of Chrome at no additional cost. Sometimes you'll see this referred to as Chrome Enterprise (more on this later), but it is the same freely available Chrome browser used and loved by many.

BeyondCorp Enterprise extends this solution with additional threat and data protection policy extensions, which helps with data loss prevention (DLP). "84% of IT leaders report DLP is more challenging when their workforce is working remotely" (Tessian, 2020). The BeyondCorp Chrome Enterprise DLP policies include the following:

Google lists BeyondCorp Enterprise data protection capabilities as follows:

- *Protection at file upload, download, and content paste*

- *Real-time alerts per protection rule*

- *Audit, warning, and blocking actions*

- *Support for different file formats, including documents, image file types, compress/archived files, and custom types*

- *Hundreds of built-in sensitive data detectors, as well as custom regex and lists*

- *Implementation of conditions such as URL filters and full content inspection*

Copyright Google Cloud

You can manage the policies at the device level and user level. User-level management enables you to grant users access to internal resources from unmanaged devices. At the time of writing, you can configure over 300 policies.

In addition to the Chrome Enterprise policy extensions, there is another extension called Endpoint Verification. This extension collects information that helps ascertain the state of the devices used to access internal resources. You can configure what Google calls context-aware access policies. They control access based on location, company-owned device, encryption status, and more. The data collected by Endpoint Verification gets used to ensure the device meets the policy requirements and approval gets granted or blocked if the device fails to meet the requirements.

Built on the Google Front End (GFE), the Identity Aware Proxy (IAP) is the central point of policy enforcement. Google extended GFE's functionality to provide authentication and authorization, self-service provisioning of workload access, and centralized logging.

From the management side of BeyondCorp Enterprise, numerous reports are available through the Google Workspace security center. It insights high-risk users to help further shape your policies and protect your internal resources.

Google has also provided a partnership program called the BeyondCorp Alliance. The vendors within the alliance share Google Cloud's vision for zero-trust. Their products and services extend the functionality of BeyondCorp Enterprise and enable organizations that already use these vendors to continue doing so.

Suppose your organization currently relies on VPNs to provide remote access to internal resources. In that case, you need to think about how access to those resources will change when those resources move to Google Cloud.

COVID-19 fundamentally changed the way that office workers have been working. You need a solution that prevents data loss while enabling users to work from home. And it must work regardless of whether they use personal or organization-issued devices.

Summary

BeyondCorp Enterprise provides a way for you to grant remote access to your internal resources and data in a controlled and secure manner.

Review your current risks associated with using VPNs. Review logs to understand if users are accessing internal resources from personal devices. If workloads are moving to Google Cloud or another cloud, think about how user access will change. Put a strategy together on how you will prevent data loss while also meeting your user's work from anywhere requirements.

CHAPTER 30

Other Google Services

The Google Cloud family has several offerings besides the hosting platform that are well worth understanding. In this chapter, I will cover them. For each of these technologies, think about who is responsible for your current products and implementation within your organization.

Google Workspace

The first is Google Workspace, Google's productivity and collaboration platform. You access the apps through a web browser, where all your work is online. That's right, no big downloads or lengthy installations. Google Workspace is compatible with all the major web browsers.

Sometimes you'll need to be productive when you don't have an Internet connection. For those situations, there is offline functionality, but note that it is only available when using the Chrome browser.

Google Workspace aims to make daily collaboration tasks easier for everyone, with many features and functionality that make real-time collaboration fast and effective. Google believes in turning your productivity apps into a competitive advantage for your organization, which with a remote or hybrid workforce is more important than ever. Google Workspace offers 99.9% availability SLA, giving you confidence that no matter where your users work, they can access the apps they need.

Google Workspace is used by global enterprises with hundreds of thousands of users to universities, schools, small businesses, and individuals. Google reports that it's used by three billion users globally.

You manage user accounts with the same administrative tools and APIs used for Google Cloud's Cloud Identity users. They can be considered the equivalent service.

© Jeremy Lloyd 2023
J. Lloyd, *Infrastructure Leader's Guide to Google Cloud*, https://doi.org/10.1007/978-1-4842-8820-7_30

There are several editions of Google Workspace to cater for different numbers of required accounts and types of organizations. You have as follows:

- Individual edition, single account only

- Frontline edition

- Nonprofit edition

- Business editions (Starter, Standard, and Plus) for up to 300 accounts

- Enterprise editions (Essentials, Standard, and Plus)

- Education editions (Fundamentals, Standard, Teaching and learning upgrade, and Plus)

As you'd expect, you get different functionality across the editions. For example, some editions won't have Google's Drive data loss prevention. Or you get different limits across each edition, for example, email storage or the number of participants per meeting.

Google Workspace provides a full suite of apps. There is a core set which is available for each version. They are as follows:

- Gmail, for email

- Drive, for storing and sharing files

- Docs, for writing documents

- Sheets, for creating spreadsheets

- Slides, for creating presentations

- Calendar, for creating and managing meetings

- Chat, for instant messaging

- Meet, for video conferencing

- Forms, for surveys

- Keep, for note-taking

- Sites, for websites

- Jamboard, for whiteboarding

Other apps that aren't part of the core offering are as follows:

- AppSheet, no-code

- Vault, data retention

- Cloud Search, organization wide Google Workspace search

- Classroom, creating learning spaces for students and teachers

Security and Management

Keeping your users and the data safe is a top priority of Google Workspace. Another priority is ensuring you can easily apply administrative controls through a user-friendly admin console. The admin console is where you can implement security policies, like the ability to disable offline data storage or block access to untrusted apps. It's also where you can manage your user's accounts. I'll cover identities in more detail in the following.

Endpoint management is a fully functional unified endpoint management offering. It enables simple and fast device enrollment and app deployment and works well in bring your own device scenarios. And it's included within the Google Workspace cost.

Alerts center provides real-time critical security-related notifications across accounts, devices, email, data, and your Google Workspace organization. You can create custom alerts based on logged events and integrate those alerts with a downstream tool like a Security Incident and Event Management (SIEM) tool.

Security center builds on the action center by integrating with it and offering security insights, trends, and recommendations for your Google Workspace, from insights on file sharing outside your domain to analyzing spam and malware. This feature is only available on the Enterprise, Standard, and Plus editions. However, note that the Standard edition only offers some of the security center features.

Vault

Vault enables your organization to retain data from Gmail, Drive, Groups, Chat, Meet, and Sites. The data is then available for users with Vault access to search and export, often used in situations where your organization is required to retain data for specific periods for regulatory and legal reasons. Business and Enterprise editions include Vault.

Work Insights

This gives you insights into the usage and adoption of Google Workspace within your organization. It gives you easy access to metrics like active users, collaboration trends on files shared, and apps being used (including legacy apps). It doesn't enable reporting on individual users. And to protect users' privacy, the aggregated data starts when you have ten or more users.

Google Workspace Marketplace

Google Workspace Marketplace is where you can find hundreds of third-party apps that work with Google Workspace, either paid or free apps that complement and enhance Google Workspace. From an administrator's perspective, you can control what users use by adding specific apps to an allowlist.

Adopting Google Workspace

Moving from your current productivity solution to Google Workspace requires an effective adoption strategy. The change represents the people, process, and technology paradigm again. People will be affected as Google Workspace will work differently from their current solution. So a comms and engagement plan is critical. Help users understand why you are making the change, followed by adequate training to get them productive on Google Workspace as quickly as possible.

Chrome Enterprise

Managing end-user devices is a complex area. You have the OS image engineering side where machine images need to be created and ongoing image maintenance as patches is released. Then you have the build process, requiring the deployment of the images to the devices. Then you have the logistics side of getting hardware to users and often having in-person or remote assistance available to support them for the first login or post login issues.

From a day 2 operations perspective, you have a monthly patching cycle for all current in-use devices, not to mention keeping antimalware software up-to-date and reporting in. Add in VPN clients and other lines of business applications you must deploy to the device. All of which you must keep up-to-date and operational. You end up with a sizable team dedicated to this purpose.

I recall a time years ago when I worked for a Microsoft partner. We were in a competitive bid situation for a new device rollout across a multinational organization with tens of thousands of users/devices. Our skills and credibility in device image engineering were exceptional. However, we lost the deal. What made us lose was that the competitor was able to build ten times the number of devices a day that we could. Yet our device build times were similar. So how did they do it? By running a 24/7 build team and scaling the team horizontally to meet the required velocity. It was then that I began thinking that the entire device build and maintenance process is destined for disruption.

Enter Chrome Enterprise. A modern approach designed to simplify the process and reduce the time and effort required to make a user productive no matter where they are, while also improving the security posture and end-user experience and reducing the total cost of ownership.

Chrome Enterprise spans three components: Chrome OS, Chrome Device, and Chrome Browser. Let's look at each of these components at a high level first before going into detail about how all three work together from a business perspective.

Chrome OS is an operating system designed for the cloud. It offers fast boot times while also being secure with multilayer OS architecture designed to protect the device's integrity. The device will verify the integrity on start-up and can auto-heal if required.

Chrome OS runs on Chromebooks, Chromebox, and Chromebase physical devices. Chrome OS aims for the consumer market. Where devices are essentially standalone, you must purchase the Chrome Enterprise Upgrade for each standalone device to enable enhanced enterprise capabilities and centrally administer the devices via the Google Admin console.

Chrome Enterprise Device

The device specification required by a user of business applications is often more than is needed by consumers. Google has the backing of all major OEMs (HP, Dell, Lenovo, Acer, Asus) to create devices with specifications suitable to run Chrome Enterprise. These devices are typically more cost-effective than similar devices running competitor operating systems.

Chrome Browser

It's hard to imagine that the Chrome browser needs any introduction, with a bold tagline of "the most secure browser in the world." And as I mentioned earlier, it has 2.5 billion + users, making it the world's most popular browser.

In the workplace, the browser offers optimal user experiences when used with Google Workspace. It has enterprise management controls that you centrally manage from a cloud console. It also has support for Active Directory's group policies.

A Powerful Combination

So Chrome Enterprise refers to the combination of Chrome OS and Chrome Browser running on a Chrome Enterprise device. This combination has numerous advantages such as the following:

Fast Deployment and Simple Cloud Management

Ship devices directly to your users, and they can be automatically enrolled into your domain and receive security policies, apps, and settings. It's a no-touch deployment process, a far cry from my earlier scenario. The cloud management controls give you access to functionality such as performing a remote wipe/disable on lost or stolen devices and many other controls and insights.

Access the Apps You Want from Anywhere

Chrome OS's encrypted cloud profiles enable you to share devices securely. They also mean you can sign in to any Chromebook to continue working where you left off.

Chrome OS and the browser can allow apps and their processes to run in isolation from each other. They refer to this as sandboxing, which is enabled by default. This dramatically reduces the blast radius of any malicious software.

Chrome OS has an app store called the Play Store, where your users can get preapproved business apps or other apps from third-party vendors.

Built-In Security

In the current era, the devices you use are the targets of a growing number of attacks, which are designed to get access to your data and phish for further credentials to gain access to more. The year-on-year increases reported by various sources are alarming. This is a growing problem area globally. And yet testament to Google's security-first mindset is that there have been no reported ransomware attacks on any organization using Chrome OS ever! Add to this that on Chrome OS, you don't need antivirus software. This is because the root file system is read-only on start-up. The verified boot I mentioned earlier can auto-heal if integrity gets breached.

Automated updates on Chrome OS are background tasks, and you don't notice them happening. There is a long-term support channel, which gives you updates every 6 months instead of 4 weeks, although security updates are every 2 weeks.

Cost-Effective and Eco-friendly

Chrome OS "starts fast and stays fast" says Google, and as a Chromebook user, I agree. This means you can repurpose devices that have become too slow for users to be productive. If you can keep users productive on hardware for longer, you are also reducing the carbon footprint of your IT assets.

Chrome OS Flex offers a simple way of being able to repurposing your old hardware with Chrome OS. You only need a USB stick and the Internet to download the required files.

Chrome OS is proven to be 46% more energy efficient than competitor operating systems when run on the same hardware in a study (*Determining End User Computing Device Scope 2 GHG Emissions With Accurate Use Phase Energy Consumption Measurement, 2020*).

Summary

Google Workspace offers an unrivalled collaboration experience across Docs, Slides, Sheets, and more. If you aren't already using it, try it.

Chrome Enterprise provides the browser, an OS, and the device to safely work online. Understand where your current security risks are with end-user devices and how Chrome Enterprise can solve them. Repurpose old hardware that became too slow after just a few years with Chrome OS Flex.

Final Words

The secret of getting ahead is getting started.

—Mark Twain

With every industry facing disruption from born-in-the-cloud organizations, business agility and having a bias for action are critical for long-term survival. And while migrating and modernizing your on-prem workloads to Google Cloud can seem like a daunting challenge, I hope this book arms you with the ability to lead that journey and guides you on how to prepare for it, undertake it, and successfully operate it afterward.

Finally, I love to hear cloud adoption stories from my readers. I'd also like to know your feedback on the book. So please do get in touch via the contact form on my website, `infrastructureleader.com`, or `jez@infrastructureleader.com`.

J. Lloyd, *Infrastructure Leader's Guide to Google Cloud*, https://doi.org/10.1007/978-1-4842-8820-7

References

Chapter 1. Introduction

Gartner. (2021, February 16). Gartner Forecasts Worldwide Low-Code Development Technologies Market to Grow 23% in 2021. www.gartner.com/en/newsroom/press-releases/2021-02-15-gartner-forecasts-worldwide-low-code-development-technologies-market-to-grow-23-percent-in-2021

Hatami, H., & Segel, L. H. (2021, September 8). *The future of leadership: Five priorities for CEOs.* McKinsey. www.mckinsey.com/business-functions/strategy-and-corporate-finance/our-insights/what-matters-most-five-priorities-for-ceos-in-the-next-normal

Chapter 2. About Google and Google Cloud

How Google Search works, Our mission. www.google.com/intl/en_uk/search/howsearchworks/mission/

Statista. (2022, March 1). • *Search engine market share worldwide.* Statista. www.statista.com/statistics/216573/worldwide-market-share-of-search-engines/

Privacy Resource Center, Google Cloud. https://cloud.google.com/privacy

Data deletion on Google Cloud Platform. (2018, September). https://cloud.google.com/security/deletion

Google Cloud. *Data Cloud.* Google Cloud. https://cloud.google.com/data-cloud

© Jeremy Lloyd 2023
J. Lloyd, *Infrastructure Leader's Guide to Google Cloud,* https://doi.org/10.1007/978-1-4842-8820-7

REFERENCES

Google Cloud. (2021). *Google Cloud at Google I/O '21.* Google IO. `https://io.google/2021/program/products/google-cloud/?lng=en`

The Global Internet Phenomena Report. (2020, May). `www.sandvine.com/covid-internet-spotlight-report`

Economic impact of Google's APAC network infrastructure. (2020, September 24). `www.analysysmason.com/consulting-redirect/reports/impact-of-google-network-APAC-2020/`

BroadbandNow Research. (2021, July 21). Google owns 63,605 Miles and 8.5% of submarine Cables Worldwide. `https://broadbandnow.com/report/google-content-providers-submarine-cable-ownership/`

Cockroach Labs, Cloud Report. (2021, January). `www.cockroachlabs.com/guides/2021-cloud-report/`

Google Cloud. (2021, November 30). *Shopify and Google Cloud team up for an epic BFCM weekend.* Google Cloud. `https://cloud.google.com/blog/topics/retail/shopify-and-google-cloud-team-up-for-an-epic-bfcm-weekend`

Google Infrastructure Design Overview. `https://cloud.google.com/security/infrastructure/design`

Transparency & Data Protection, Google Cloud. `https://cloud.google.com/security/transparency`

Data incident response process. (2018, September). `https://cloud.google.com/security/incident-response/`

Privileged Access Management in Google Cloud Platform. (2020, October). `https://services.google.com/fh/files/misc/privileged-access-management-gcp-wp.pdf`

Google Cloud leads in cloud data analytics and databases. (2020, November 30). Google Cloud. `https://cloud.google.com/blog/products/data-analytics/google-cloud-leads-in-cloud-data-analytics-and-databases`

The managed open source survey, Tidelift. (2020, June).
https://tidelift.com/subscription/2020-managed-open-source-survey

Open source by numbers at Google. (2020, August 5).
https://opensource.googleblog.com/2020/08/open-source-by-numbers-at-google.html

Google Open Source. https://opensource.google/

Sharma, P. (2020, December 17.). *Cloud Native Computing Foundation Receives Renewed $3 Million Cloud Credit Grant from Google Cloud.* Cloud Native Computing Foundation. www.cncf.io/announcements/2020/12/17/cloud-native-computing-foundation-receives-renewed-3-million-cloud-credit-grant-from-google-cloud/

Cloud Strategy | Gartner IT IOCS Conference. (2020). www.gartner.com/en/conferences/apac/infrastructure-operations-cloud-india/featured-topics/cloud

Oxford Languages. https://languages.oup.com/google-dictionary-en/

Using location to reduce our carbon computing footprint. (2021, May 18). www.blog.google/outreach-initiatives/sustainability/carbon-aware-computing-location/

IDC. (2021, March 8). IDC. www.idc.com/getdoc.jsp?containerId=prUS47513321

IDG. *IT Leaders Research Report.* IT Leaders Research Report. https://inthecloud.withgoogle.com/it-leaders-research-21/sustainability-dl-cd.html

Chapter 3. Future of IT

Gartner. (2020, September 14). Gartner Says By 2023, 65% of the World's Population Will Have Its Personal Data Covered Under Modern Privacy Regulations. www.gartner.com/en/newsroom/press-releases/2020-09-14-gartner-says-by-2023--65--of-the-world-s-population-w

Chapter 5. Business Case

Turner, E. (2020). *Be Less Zombie: How Great Companies Create Dynamic Innovation, Fearless Leadership and Passionate People*. Wiley.

Cost of a Data Breach Report 2021. (2021). IBM, www.ibm.com/security/data-breach

DORA, Google Cloud. www.devops-research.com/research.html

Uptime Institute 2021 Data Centre Industry Survey. Uptime Institute Resource Page - Uptime Institute. https://uptimeinstitute.com/resources/asset/2021-data-center-industry-survey

Chapter 6. The Cloud Strategy

Build a Business-Aligned IT Strategy. Info-Tech Research Group. www.infotech.com/research/ss/build-a-business-aligned-it-strategy

McKinsey & Company. (2020, October 5). *How COVID-19 has pushed companies over the technology tipping point—and transformed business forever*. www.mckinsey.com/business-functions/strategy-and-corporate-finance/our-insights/how-covid-19-has-pushed-companies-over-the-technology-tipping-point-and-transformed-business-forever

The Five Functions | NIST. (2018, April 12). National Institute of Standards and Technology. www.nist.gov/cyberframework/online-learning/five-functions

Chapter 7. Cloud Operating Model Strategy

Gartner. Definition of an Operating Model. www.gartner.com/en/information-technology/glossary/operating-model

Chapter 8. Migration Strategies

Watson, R. (2010, December 3rd). Migrating Applications to the Cloud: Rehost, Refactor, Revise, Rebuild, or Replace? www.gartner.com/en/documents/1485116/migrating-applications-to-the-cloud-rehost-refactor-revi

RAMP up your cloud adoption with new assessment and migration program. (2020, July 28). Google Cloud. https://cloud.google.com/blog/products/cloud-migration/google-cloud-ramp-program-simplifies-cloud-migration

Chapter 9. Modernization Strategies

Gartner. *Definition of Application Modernization Services.* Gartner. www.gartner.com/en/information-technology/glossary/application-modernization-services

Chapter 11. Cloud Adoption and Cultural Change

Logicworks Report - Challenges of Cloud Transformation. (2020). https://go.logicworks.net/hubfs/Logicworks%20Report%20-%20Challenges%20of%20Cloud%20Transformation.pdf

Our approach – How Google Search works. Google. www.google.com/intl/en_uk/search/howsearchworks/our-approach/

Sony. *Sony Group Portal.* Sony. www.sony.com/en/SonyInfo/CorporateInfo/vision/

Google Site Reliability Engineering. Google Site Reliability Engineering. https://sre.google/

Google - Site Reliability Engineering. https://sre.google/sre-book/preface/

The Google Cloud Adoption Framework. https://services.google.com/fh/files/misc/google_cloud_adoption_framework_whitepaper.pdf

Chapter 13. Skills

Google Cloud certification impact report. (2020). Google Cloud Whitepaper. https://services.google.com/fh/files/misc/2020_googlecloud_certification_impact_report.pdf

Google Cloud, Cloud Digital Leader. (2021). Google Cloud. https://cloud.google.com/certification/cloud-digital-leader

Chapter 14. Cloud Adoption Teams

Carucci, R. Why executives struggle to execute strategy. In *The Chief Strategy Officer Playbook.* Brightline Initiative / Thinkers 50.

Global Knowledge 2021 IT Skills and Salary Report. (2021). www.globalknowledge.com/us-en/content/salary-report/it-skills-and-salary-report/#gref

Chapter 15. Assess

CAST. *CAST Imaging.* CAST Software. www.castsoftware.com/products/imaging

Chapter 17. Migrate

Google Cloud, VM Migration Lifecycle. Migrate for Compute Engine. https://cloud.google.com/migrate/compute-engine/docs/5.0/concepts/lifecycle

Chapter 18. Optimize

Migration to Google Cloud: Optimizing your environment | Cloud Architecture Center. Google Cloud. https://cloud.google.com/architecture/migration-to-google-cloud-optimizing-your-environment

Chapter 20. Containers

Sonatype's 2021 State of the Software Supply Chain. Sonatype. www.sonatype.com/resources/state-of-the-software-supply-chain-2021

Kubernetes.io. https://kubernetes.io

Google Cloud. *Binary Authorization for Borg: how Google verifies code provenance and implements code identity | Documentation.* Google Cloud. https://cloud.google.com/docs/security/binary-authorization-for-borg

Chapter 23. Cloud Foundations and Landing Zones

Forsgren, N., Humble, J., & Kim, G. (2018). *Accelerate.* Trade Select.

Chapter 24. Compute

University Information Technology Services. (2021, September 21). Understand measure of supercomputer performance and storage system capacity. `https://kb.iu.edu/d/apeq`

Google Cloud. (2021, October 06). Planning for Bare Metal Solution. `https://cloud.google.com/bare-metal/docs/bms-planning`

Chapter 25. Containers and Serverless

Kubernetes and the challenges of continuous software delivery | Cloud Architecture Center. (2020, January 6). Google Cloud. `https://cloud.google.com/architecture/addressing-continuous-delivery-challenges-in-a-kubernetes-world#continuous_delivery`

Chapter 27. Additional Workload Architectural Considerations

Google Site Reliability Engineering. Google Site Reliability Engineering. `https://sre.google/`

FinOps Foundation. What is FinOps. `www.finops.org/introduction/what-is-finops/`

Backstage.io. (2020, October 22). backstage.io. `https://backstage.io/blog/2020/10/22/cost-insights-plugin#how-to-turn-dollars-into-sense`

Gartner. *Definition of Security Orchestration, Automation and Response (SOAR).* Gartner. `www.gartner.com/en/information-technology/glossary/security-orchestration-automation-response-soar`

Executive Summary — NIST SP 1800-25 documentation. (n.d.). NCCoE. www.nccoe.nist.gov/publication/1800-25/VolA/index.html

Lindros, K. (2017, July 11). *What is GRC and why do you need it?* CIO.com. www.cio.com/article/230326/what-is-grc-and-why-do-you-need-it.html

Google Cybersecurity Action Team. *GCAT Risk Governance of Digital Transformation in the Cloud_new logos_Ren.* Google. https://services.google.com/fh/files/misc/risk-governance-of-digital-transformation.pdf

Gartner. (2019, January 25). *Innovation Insight for Cloud Security Posture Management.* Gartner. www.gartner.com/en/documents/3899373

Imperva. Cloud Governance. www.imperva.com/learn/data-security/cloud-governance/

Chapter 29. BeyondCorp

Tessian. (2020). *The state of data loss prevention.* www.tessian.com/research/the-state-of-data-loss-prevention-2020/

Chapter 30. Other Google Services

Determining end user computing device Scope 2 GHG emissions with accurate use phase energy consumption measurement, 2020. (2020). www.sciencedirect.com/science/article/pii/S1877050920317506

Index

A

Access Transparency (AXT), 31
Active Assist, 286, 289
Agile methodologies, 8, 137
Agile-style approach, 120
Agile terminology, 137
Amazon Machine Images (AMIs), 280
Anthos, 221, 222, 226
    cluster management, 266
    clusters, 265
    container environments, 272
    day 2 operations, 265
    maintenance, 266
    resource/security management, 267
        binary authorization, 268, 269
        config, 267
    service-level monitoring
        capabilities, 271
    storage/networking
        dataplane V2, 270
        load balancers, 270
        volumes/persistent volumes, 271
App Engine, 31, 41, 227, 228, 287
Application Portfolio Management
    (APM), 173, 174
Application Programming Interface (API)
    management, 140, 214, 267,
    319, 324
AquaSec, 311, 312
Assess phase
    application owner, 169, 170
    assessment tools, 172
    automated discovery and
        assessment, 170, 171
    CAST Software, 172, 173
    CMDB, 169
    discovery and assessing, 169
    first movers, 178
    migration strategies, 176–178
    workload categorization, 173–176
Assured Open Source Software
    service, 217
Automation-first approach, 228
AutoML, 34
Autopilot mode, 214, 215, 222, 225
AWS/Azure skills, 143, 146
Azure Kubernetes Service (AKS), 213, 265

B

Backup, 26, 27, 30, 88, 250, 253, 289–291,
    301, 307, 308, 320, 321
Bare Metal Servers (BMS), 252, 253
BeyondCorp Alliance, 329
BeyondCorp Enterprise
    definition, 328
    DLP, 328, 329
    remote access, 330
    ZTNA, 328
BeyondProd, 209
BigQuery, 33, 34, 39, 229
BigTable, 33
Bringing your own license (BYOL), 189,
    251, 280, 282–284

© Jeremy Lloyd 2023
J. Lloyd, *Infrastructure Leader's Guide to Google Cloud*, https://doi.org/10.1007/978-1-4842-8820-7

Printed in the United States
by Baker & Taylor Publisher Services